Symbolic Gestures and the Generation of Global Social Control

Symbolic Gestures and the Generation of Global Social Control

The International Criminal Court

Dawn Rothe and Christopher W. Mullins

LEXINGTON BOOKS

A division of
ROWMAN & LITTLEFIELD PUBLISHERS, INC.
Lanham • Boulder • New York • Toronto • Plymouth, UK

LEXINGTON BOOKS

A division of Rowman & Littlefield Publishers, Inc.
A wholly owned subsidiary of The Rowman & Littlefield Publishing Group, Inc.
4501 Forbes Boulevard, Suite 200
Lanham, MD 20706

Estover Road
Plymouth PL6 7PY
United Kingdom

British Library Cataloguing in Publication Information Available

Library of Congress Cataloging-in-Publication Data

Rothe, Dawn, 1961–
Symbolic gestures and the generation of global social control : the International Criminal Court / Dawn Rothe and Christopher W. Mullins.
p. cm. — (Critical perspectives on crime and inequality)
Includes bibliographical references and index.
ISBN-13: 978-0-7391-1185-7 (cloth : alk. paper)
ISBN-10: 0-7391-1185-X (cloth : alk. paper)
ISBN-13: 978-0-7391-1186-4 (pbk. : alk. paper)
ISBN-10: 0-7391-1186-8 (pbk. : alk. paper)
1. International Criminal Court. 2. International criminal courts. I. Mullins, Christopher W., 1971– II. Title. III. Series.
KZ6311.R68 2006
345'.01—dc22 2006015988

Printed in the United States of America

The paper used in this publication meets the minimum requirements of American National Standard for Information Sciences—Permanence of Paper for Printed Library Materials, ANSI/NISO Z39.48–1992.

For Ron,
In appreciation of everything he has done.
D.L.R.

For Robin,
Without whom nothing is possible
C.W.M.

Contents

Foreword by Dave Kauzlarich ix

Preface: The Development of the International Criminal Court xiii

Acknowledgments xvii

I The International Criminal Court's Relevance to Criminology 1

II An Integrated Theory of State Crimes 9

III Developing an International Criminal Court 29

IV. The Rome Statute of the International Criminal Court 53

V The Contradictions of International Law 71

VI. The Illegal War on Iraq: The "Role" of the International Criminal Court
with Ronald C. Kramer 87

VII. Enhancing the Potential of the International Criminal Court 105

Appendix A. Contradictions of International Society 117

Appendix B. Significant International Contingencies 121

Appendix C Rome Statute of the International Criminal Court 125

Appendix D. Bilateral Immunity Agreements U.S. 98(2) as of December 2004 205

Appendix E. Integrated Theoretical Model 211

References 215

Index 227

About the Authors 229

Foreword

John Bolton showed up for his first day of work as U.S. Ambassador to the United Nations (U.N.) in early August 2005 and was booed. As he ignored those protests, as most politicians do, he hurriedly shook hands with a few people on the sidewalk and made his way to the front doors of the U.N. Secretariat building in New York City, which he once said could "lose ten floors and it wouldn't make a bit of difference" (Bolton 1994: 1). Bolton (1994: 1) is also on record as saying "There is no United Nations," which one would imagine could make his first work day highly confusing, as most people employed at an organization would presumably need it to exist. Bolton, a recess appointment by U.S. President George W. Bush, is clearly a controversial figure, as questions have been raised about: (a) his previous role as Under Secretary in the U.S. State Department and how he might have had a hand in fabricating the myth that Iraq had weapons of mass destruction prior to the 2003 U.S. invasion of that country, (b) repeated denouncements of international law and the United Nations, and (c) his abrasive demeanor, hot temper, and caustic management style. Most importantly for our purposes here, Bolton has also vociferously condemned the institution that is the singular focus of this book, the International Criminal Court (ICC).

It would be incorrect to assume that Dawn Rothe and Christopher Mullins do not also see major problems with the structure, process, and function of the ICC, but unlike Bolton, their careful description and analysis of the ICC is grounded in relevant scholarly literature on social control, crime causation, and international relations. Such work is badly needed because both in academic criminology and public policy discussions, few seem to be educated enough on these subjects matters to allow the type of inquiry that would lead to productive debate on what is probably the most significant development in international law and justice since Nuremberg. In this book, Rothe and Mullins advance our understanding of the ICC, the controversies surrounding it, and propose changes to the institution in order to maximize its potential for social control. There are three particularly insightful features of this book.

First, it is important to note that on a practical level, both the previous and current U.S. Presidential administrations have attempted to convince everyone under the sun that the ICC is too flawed, too vague, and too intrusive to be worth joining. This is reflected in Bolton's (2002: 1) radical view of the institution: "the ICC is an organization whose precepts go against fundamental American notions of sovereignty, checks and balances, and national independence. It is . . . harmful to the national interests of the United States, and harmful to our presence abroad." In addition to scrutinizing the historical and spatial evolution of international law and justice and how these have led to the ICC, Rothe and Mullins have produced a book that frames assertions such as Bolton's as an expected outgrowth of the nested ideological, pragmatic-political, and internal contradictions of international law and justice. This is most clearly illustrated in Rothe and Mullins's discussion of the awkward and oftentimes selfish political posturing of several states, especially the United States, before, during, and after the creation of the ICC.

Second, while the study of state crime and justice in criminology has grown over the last twenty years, the impact that such work has made on the epistemological framework of the field has unfortunately been marginal. While critical criminologists have made much headway in the empirical and theoretical understanding of crimes by governments and state agents, rarely is this literature mentioned in traditional criminology textbooks or even articles on subjects related to state crime in mainstream journals. For example, Hagan and Greer's (2002) article in *Criminology*, among the most prestigious journals in the field, examines the ebb and flow of international criminal justice as it pertains to war crimes and crime against humanity. The authors provide only one brief citation of critical criminological work on these subjects, ignoring the important work that Rothe and Mullins have thoroughly documented and expanded upon in Chapter I of this book. How the Hagan and Greer article was published in such a major journal without any attention to, to name a few, the work of Bill Chambliss (1989), Gregg Barak (1991), Ken Tunnell (1993), and Jeffrey Ian Ross (1995, 2000a, 2000b) can only be explained by author, editor, and reviewer unfamiliarity and/or indifference to the work of critical criminologists. My hope is that this book will fall into the hands of a broad spectrum of people in both the general public and the social scientific communities, and that this will help lead to the development of the kind of seriousness with which the study of state crime and justice deserves.

Third, Rothe and Mullins have expanded the theoretical understanding of state crime through the introduction of a new level of analysis to a well-known integrated theoretical model of state crime originally produced by Kramer and Michalowski (see Kramer, Michalowski, and Kauzlarich 2002). By convincingly advancing the idea that the international level of analysis must be an analytically distinct part of the overall understanding of the genesis, persistence, and control of state crime, the authors reveal how we can go about achieving a deeper level of understanding of crimes by states and state agents. A case study on the tragic events in the Democratic Republic of Congo reveals the significance of their position.

Crimes by states and those in positions of political power dwarf the harm caused by traditional street criminals. Genocide in Nazi Germany, for example, in the early 1940s resulted in over six million deaths; in Cambodia in the late 1970s, 1.7 million lives were illegally taken by state agents; recently in the Darfur region of Sudan, nearly a half a million people have died because of governmental and quasi-state agency actions. The list of atrocities could go on for many pages. Yet, despite the obvious need for many decades for a legitimate and sustained institution to address crimes as these and their victims, criminal justice institutions are overwhelmingly devoted to the detection, arrest, and punishment of street offenders. Of course this hasn't changed overnight with the arrival of the ICC, but it may very well be a good starting point. As Rothe and Mullins underscore several times, however, the institution is far from being a solution to the problem of state and political crime, particularly because of its restricted jurisdiction, narrow focus on individuals, and the limited amount of crimes which fall under its mandate. Institutions of social control are imperfect. Their very existence suggests that certain problems are just too difficult to fix through informal means. Sometimes these problems are difficult to even address in the first place, as nexuses of power, greed, inequality, nationalism, and indifference to the powerless congeal to form roadblocks to the creation of humanistic justice systems.

Despite all of the problems with the ICC, many of which are rooted in struggles over power, there is some reason to hope that over time, the ICC will evolve into a place where at least brutalities by those in political power will be known to those other than the victims, that the ICC can acknowledge its already profound limitations and work to remedy them, and that most of all, those without political power—the poor, the disenfranchised, racial and ethnic minorities, women, and anyone else finding themselves at the back of the line—will some day no longer be ignored. Fortunately, all of this does not rest entirely on the shoulders of John Bolton. True, the evolution of the ICC would certainly benefit from the absence of nationalist extremism, but there are two hundred other countries in the world, and they will have a say in the future of the ICC as well.

David Kauzlarich
Edwardsville, Illinois

Preface

The Development of the International Criminal Court

The creation of a permanent International Criminal Court, designed to investigate and prosecute the most serious violations of international law, marks a significant development for the international social order. In many ways, this event represents a key transition within the evolution of international law and interstate relations through the twentieth century. This era ushered the creation of multiple international institutions of social regulation and control (e.g., the League of Nations, the United Nations, and the World Court of Justice), international law (e.g., the Geneva Conventions and the Nuremberg Principles) and of economics (e.g., the International Monetary Fund and the World Bank). While these institutions often operate with highly divergent ideologies and processes, with distinct goals and direction, they all represent attempts to more formally regulate the way in which nation-states interact with one another. If the nation-state itself can be seen to represent the most significant element of social transformation and reorganization of the modern era, the evolution of these international institutions are the hallmarks of social organization processes central to what some scholars call, often for lack of a better term, the post-modern era. Central to the development of these institutions has been a contradiction between the ideological and legal image of fully sovereign nation-states and the real need for external regulation of those polities. This critical tension has played out strongly in the movement to create an International Court and to date remains the key strain in the implementation of the court itself and its mission.

The idea of an international court to adjudicate disputes over international law is not a new idea. Throughout the late nineteenth and twentieth century, the idea had been pursued and explored within the international arena. One of the founders and acting President of the International Committee of the Red Cross,

Gustave Moynier, was the first to formally propose an International Criminal Court in 1872 (Moynier 1872). The Franco-Prussian war resulted in mass atrocities committed by both sides, despite their obligations under the first Geneva Convention of 1864. Moynier, distraught at the violations of international treaties, proposed an ICC to try persons accused of war crimes. The proposed international court never received any support from international lawyers or state parties; it was left a one-man utopian desire (Harris 1954, 1982). The concept of an ICC was not revisited again until after WWI; the framers of the 1919 Treaty of Versailles revived the endeavor to establish an ICC to try the Kaiser and German war criminals (Cassese 2003). Regretfully, the call for an ICC was compromised: punishment for war crimes was to be handled by existing National Military Tribunals. The failure of the proposed court resulted in trials held in Lupzig, where 888 of the 901 persons accused of war crimes were acquitted, released, or not tried. The thirteen convicted all escaped serving any of their sentences (Bassiouni 1973).

In 1937, the League of Nations attempted to establish an ICC. Two International Conventions were concluded in Geneva on November 16: the Prevention and Repression of Terrorism and the Creation of an International Criminal Court (League of Nations Document Archived C.547.m.384. 1937). A Diplomatic Conference was held for the proposed Charters that included thirty-five nation/state delegates. The Charter for the creation of an ICC required the ratification of the Prevention and Repression of Terrorism Treaty. However, neither convention obtained sufficient numbers for ratification. Yet again, an ICC failed to come into existence (Bassiouni 1975).

WWII consumed the energies of states, postponing any collective interest in an ICC. However, as the war was coming to an end, attention refocused to a call for an international institution to try individuals for the most heinous crimes of war. The general concepts of international justice resonated throughout the world. Some had hopes that with the end of the League of Nations and the development of the United Nations, the world was a step closer to instituting a permanent criminal court (CICC 2003). However, the outcome was not an ICC, but International Military Tribunals instituted to address crimes against humanity.

This period of history proved to be fruitful in the development of customary and codified international law resulting in the Nuremberg Principles. However, the hope of a permanent ICC was again discouraged. Efforts to establish an ICC continued over the next several decades by institutional reformers and civil society actors (Hampson 2002); it was not until 1989 when the international society[1] seriously reconsidered the establishment of an ICC.

In 1989, Trinidad and Tobago approached the UN with a proposal for an ICC as a device to address drug trafficking and terrorism (Sadat 2002). An overwhelming number of nation-states appeared ready for the concept of an ICC. The following nine years proved to be challenging as the General Assembly of the UN, preparatory committees, and nongovernmental agencies worked on a proposal for an ICC: The Rome Statute.

Finally, in 1998, member states overwhelmingly voted in favor of the Rome Statute of the International Criminal Court (CICC 2003). On 1 July 2002 the International Criminal Court became a reality with more than 120 nation-states attending the convention of the Rome Statute. Currently, 139 nation-states have endorsed the Rome Statute and 97 states have become ratified members of the ICC. A century long struggle to establish an international system of justice has been achieved.

This book explores the developmental history, structure and functioning of the International Criminal Court. In Chapter I we explore the criminological relevance of the ICC and state crime. Drawing heavily upon the white-collar crime literature, particularly work focused on organizational crimes such as state-corporate and state crime, we examine the epistemology and etiology of the sorts of crimes the ICC was designed to prevent and prosecute.

Chapter II provides an integrated theory of state crime that can explore the etiological roots to crimes against humanity, genocide, and war crimes that are covered by the Rome Statute. We then utilize this model to analysis a current cases under ICC jurisdiction, the Democratic of Congo.

In Chapter III, we investigate the historical development of international law and of the court itself. We place the drive to create the court firmly within its historical context, focusing on how historical and political forces throughout the twentieth century lead to a number of "fits and starts" along the path to the eventual creation of the ICC.

Chapter IV presents a detailed look at the historical and political development of the Rome Statute itself. We explore the issues and dynamics at play within the Rome Statute Prepatory Commission meetings, the ideological conflicts which not only shaped the final version of the court, but which almost derailed the formative process at several junctures. We then provide an overview of the institutional structure and intended functioning of the International Criminal Court. In many ways, the development of the court is an ongoing process. This includes the role of the Presidency, Prosecutor, Judicial Chambers, and Registrar within the system of the ICC. This chapter also examines the crimes covered under the purview of the ICC and its jurisdictional scope.

In Chapter V we discuss some of the key current controversies surrounding the implementation of the Court. We examine contentious articles of the statute, current political struggles over impunity agreements and survey the debates over jurisdictional scope. This chapter also entails a section exploring the United States' position and proceedings towards the ICC.

Chapter VI, co-authored by Ronald Kramer, raises a series of hypothetical questions regarding the 2003 invasion of Iraq by U.S.-led coalition of nations. Drawing upon extant international law which ICC prosecutors have at their disposal, Kramer explores where and how the coalition's actions violated international law; then we discuss what role a more empowered ICC could have played in the process leading up to the war. This section uses a current example to explore the actual powers and provisions of the court itself and how elements within its charter fundamentally limit its effectiveness in carrying out the mission at its core.

Chapter VII presents a sustained and detailed critique of the extant court based upon the theoretical discussions of Chapter I and II. We examine where the court falls short of being able to strongly achieve its stated objectives and, based upon criminological theories and understandings, what can be done to better allow the court do its job. We conclude this volume by exploring how changes in international social organization presents new problems and possibilities for global social control and explore the role that can be played by the International Criminal Court in the future based on proposed suggestions and potential policies.

Notes

1. The term *international society* is indeed, an imagined society, an ideology, to promote a unity at the international level and is often associated with international organizations representing civil actors as well as political institutions. We use the term international society to represent a collection of state and civil actors, active in the international political arena and in positions of power to impose or create international institutions, international policies or international laws that affect the existing international political realm in its historical contexts

Acknowledgments

We would both like to thank those who came before us in the study of state crime. We have done our best to build upon and expand your work. The scholarship of Ron Kramer, Ray Michalowski, David Friedrichs, Gregg Barak, David Kauzlarich, Rick Matthews, and Jeffrey Ian Ross has all been central to our work here and elsewhere. They are also all wonderfully supportive colleagues and have encouraged us along the way. We are grateful for you, your work, and your support. We also thank Jeffrey Ian Ross specifically for his insightful comments, suggestions, and review of our manuscript. We would also both like to specifically thank David Kauzlarich for our separate introductions to the study of state crime and for insightful comments on an earlier draft of this volume.

Thanks also from Dawn to her family, Christopher, Nathan, and Hahnna, for their love and support. I also wish to thank my co-author, Christopher W. for his friendship and support over the years. Without that I may not be where I am today. I also wish to acknowledge and thank a very special person for being my inspiration, social support, and friend. I am grateful for the moments you have been a part of my life and the memories of these times will always be a part of me.

We both owe a debt of gratitude to Karen Jobe of Southwestern Illinois College. Karen, your support and encouragement of both of us got us to where we are today. Thanks.

As always, Christopher is grateful for the love and support he receives from his family: Robin, Jerry, and Arwen. You are the best and are why I do what I do. Yes, Jerry, Chapter V is done. I also owe thanks to my mother and brother for encouraging me toward academia well before I even knew what it was. I also am grateful to my co-author for our friendship and scholastic simpatico. Portions of this work were supported by a grant from the College of Social and Behavioral Science, University of Northern Iowa.

Chapter I

The International Criminal Court's Relevance to Criminology

While the International Criminal Court has been touted as the most fundamental development in international society to date, there has been relatively little criminological research examining the potential influence of the ICC. Criminologists should increasingly focus upon transnational and non-conventional forms of crime, international institutions of control, and the challenges in addressing such crime. Of course all of these matters have generated a huge volume of commentary, but the number of criminologists who have contributed to this discourse have been few and far between. It is one of our premises that this neither has to be the case, nor should it be (see also Rothe and Friedrichs 2005).

The creation and empowerment of the court significantly changes the landscape of international criminality. As criminologists, we are most interested in how the ICC can be brought to bear to control these actions which threaten humanity's ability to live in peace, without the threat of victimization. As of now, the court has a limited jurisdiction. It covers only: genocide, crimes against humanity, and war crimes. In this chapter we will discuss the nature of state crimes, examining what contemporary criminological theory and research suggests about the etiology of these phenomena. We will also explore the efficacy of potential control modalities, especially the court.

The crimes currently prosecutable by the International Criminal Court all fall under the rubric of what criminologists refer to as state crime: internationally defined unlawful actions committed by nation-states, typically to advance the social, economic, ideological, or political interests of the state or those in control of the state. Currently, a decade and a half of critical criminological scholarship has been devoted to the definition, exploration, and theorization of crimes by the state; to fully understand the potential power of the court to control these most egregious of acts we need to contextualize these crimes within the framework of state criminology and bring current theorizations to bear.

State Crime and States as Criminals

Since the early 1990s, criminologists have been developing a criminology of the nation-state. State crime is typically defined as "harmful activities carried out by the state or on behalf of some state agency" (Friedrichs 1996a: 122). From its inception, the growth and development of state crime studies have been faced with a key conceptual problem: how can the state be a criminal actor when legally it is the state itself that defines criminal behavior? Barak (1991: 8) points out that "the study of state criminality is problematic because the concept itself is controversial, in part because of a debate over whether one should define crime in terms other than law codes of individual nations. Some argue that if a state obeys its own laws, it should be judged by no higher criterion."

Sharkansky (1995) presents such a critique, arguing that while states may commit many undesirable behaviors one can not call them criminal unless they expressly violate their own laws. Labeling a state criminal on other grounds violates key precepts of national sovereignty and a nation's right to regulate itself. However, this critique sees even well-recognized instances of state criminality, like the Holocaust, as "nasty" behaviors but not criminal. In general, the critical critique of using legal codes as the base definition of crime is well discussed. Alternative formulations have been advanced, ranging from international legal codes to basic human rights precepts to the perceptions of the state's citizens (Spitzer 1980; Barak 1991; Chambliss and Zatz 1993; Tunnell 1993; Ross 1995; Friedrichs 1996; Kauzlarich and Kramer 1998; Ross et al. 1999; Green and Ward 2000). We follow a more legalistic approach by drawing upon existing international law in the definition of an act as criminal similarly to the recent definition proposed by Kramer and Michalowski (2005) wherein state crime is defined as any action violating public international law, international criminal law, or domestic law when these actions are committed by individuals acting in official or covert capacity as agents of the state pursuant to expressed or implied orders of the state, or resulting from state failure to exercise due diligence over the actions of its agents.

Their definition recognizes that offenders "under international or domestic law can be states qua states and/or officials using state power in pursuit of state goals" (2005: 9). Before we attempt to further delineate this definition, it is essential that we first define what we consider to be a state.

We suggest that the state is the institutions, organizations, and/or agencies composed of actors representing and entrusted with the functions of the political apparatus governing the corresponding population via the legitimate and symbolic use of power, contained within a historically and culturally defined milieu and bound territory. This allows us to think of the state as both composed of individuals and as an entity that has been reified within the existing territory and culture. Consequentially, state crime can be defined as: "Any action that violates international criminal law, humanitarian law, customary law (including contractual agreements), and states' own domestic law when these actions are committed by individual actors acting on behalf of, or in the name of, the state or of their own individual economical, political, and ideological interests" (Kramer and Michalowski 2005: 448).

We also see three distinct subcategories of state crimes: *political crimes,* those crimes committed by individuals who hold state offices or have access to state resources, done in the interests of the individual or a non-state organization the individual belongs to (e.g., a political party); *state crimes,* crimes committed by a sovereign polity to advance its interests; and *state-corporate crimes,* those criminal acts which involve collusion between nation-states and private corporations. While these phenomena all possess many commonalities in motivation, enactment, and control, we will discuss each separately.

Political Crimes

White collar crime scholarship in general has differentiated between occupational crimes, illegal acts committed during the course of one's daily job activities for the purposes of the attainment of personal goals and organizational crimes, those illegal acts committed during the course one of one's daily job activities for the purposes of corporate goal attainment (see Friedrichs 2004). Similarly, state crime research distinguishes between political crimes, those illegal activities committed by state actors for the fulfillment of personal goals or those of non-polity organizations work within, and other state crimes (see Friedrichs 2004; Ross 2003). Political crimes, such as corruption and election fraud, are typically done by state actors who use their access to state resources for the accomplishment of the criminal act. Yet, motivational drives and criminal outcomes are focused on personal enrichment and/or direct benefit to non-state groups, such as political parties. As with occupational crime, we see the key trait of political crimes being individuals taking advantage of their occupational positions of trust (Sutherland 1939) to enhance their own social status and positions.

Archetypical cases of this type of political crime include Boss Tweed's corruption of Tammany Hall, the Teapot Dome Scandal of the Harding Administration, and the Watergate break-ins ordered by the Nixon White House. Such scandals and abuses of power are nearly omnipresent in modern nation states (see Ross's 2000 volume for a veritable laundry list of criminal corruption in modern democratic nation states). Currently, this form of criminal behavior is not under the jurisdiction of the International Criminal Court, nor is it under the jurisdiction of international legal paradigms unless the activities extend into transnational social space or reach the extent of a crime against humanity.

There are other types of political crimes as well—those crimes whose primary direction and motive is a political statement. These are actions which violate established legal codes, be they national or international, whose primary motivation and the direction is an attempt to influence a political process or entity. Thus, one can commit a political crime without access to mechanisms of the state. These crimes can include non-violent but illegal protests, treason, and terrorism. It is the later crime that we now turn to, as the ICC could have a specific relevance to its prosecution and control.

Terrorism

While currently not specifically under the jurisdiction of the court, terrorism in its standard form can be jointly a political crime and a crime against humanity. While we recognize the complexities in addressing the multiple forms of terrorist tactics such as the religious, ideological, and economical, and the definitional quagmire and contradictions, we explore one component of terrorism: political crime or terrorist tactics that can be considered widespread and systematic. Consequentially, following Schmid (1983) and Ross (2003), we define other forms of terrorism as a political crime. The strongest rationale for doing so is the political nature of many terrorist acts: the core motivation behind the phenomena is a political statement and the desire to obtain a political outcome. Due to its violent nature, and the fact that terrorist actions often direct that violence at civilian populations, such crimes fall under the established rubric of crimes against humanity. This places them under the purview of the ICC.

The strongest argument for bringing terrorism under the court's jurisdiction is the ability of the court to prosecute such crimes apolitically. As the world has seen, the application of terrorism as a label is highly subjective and overtly political. Many nation-states pursue counter-terrorism policies which are overtly militaristic and often outside the bounds of any establishment of law and court processes. Clearly, the United States' so-called "war on terror" is a chief example. In selecting military over legal recourse in response to the attacks on 11 September 2001, the U.S. has not only lost the good faith of much of the international arena but has mired itself in numerous legal and military quagmires of which no ability to extract itself is foreseen. Moreover, the U.S. response has been defined as illegal under international law (UN 2004). The U.S. is not the only nation to take this strategy. Russia has chosen a military over legal model in its dealing with Chechnyan separatists; Israel has opted to do the same in its dealings with Palestine. Due to the complexities and contradictions of what terrorist tactics are or who are the terrorists, the responses of Russia and Israel have also been classified as terrorism (Rothe 2005). By maintaining a military-focused definition and policy approach, the unrest and distrust which produced the terroristic impulse to begin with are only exacerbated. Indeed, the origins, causes, consequences, and most efficacious way to combat terrorism are widely debated. Yet, there has never been a successful military-based solution to a conflict that has produced terrorism as a mode of engagement.

By conceptualizing, and trying, terrorist incidents as crimes against humanity, the ICC could provide an apolitical location bring charges and determine guilt.

This is not a new concept. In 1937, the League of Nations held two International Conventions to pass a Charter for terrorism as an illegal act and for an international criminal court to prosecute those committing terrorist acts: the Prevention and Repression of Terrorism and the Creation of an International Criminal Court (League of Nations Document Archived C.547.m.384. 1937). The Diplomatic Conference was concluded in August 1937 for the proposed Charters with thirty-five nation/state delegates. However, neither convention obtained sufficient numbers for ratification; subsequently terrorism did not fall under the rubric of international criminal law nor did an ICC come into existence (Bassiouni 1975). However, the potential today of bringing terrorism under the purview of the Court as an apolitical outlet remains a viable solution. The Court would not seek a solution to the perceived grievances which stimulated terror cells and activities, but would rather act as a site for the victims of terrorism to obtain restitution for their injuries. By its very nature, terrorism draws uninvolved innocents into a broader political struggle and dispute. It is this which may qualify it as a crime against humanity.

State Crimes

State crime has been approached in a number of fashions by a number of disciplines (i.e., criminology, history, political science, sociology), but the strongest body of work has been done in critical criminology. State crime studies were energized by Chambliss's (1989) seminal presidential speech to the American Society of Criminology in which he introduced the concept of state-organized crime. State crimes, according to Chambliss (1989: 184) are those that are "acts defined by law as criminal and committed by state officials in pursuit of their jobs as representatives of the state." Chambliss has conceptualized state crime clearly as a form of organizational crime (as opposed to occupational crime) and those writing on the topic since have followed his lead. While the concept of state crime had been addressed by other criminologists (Kramer 1982; Turk 1982; and Michalowski and Kramer 1987) one can argue that Chambliss's (1989) American Society of Criminology Presidential address provided the more direct and immediate inspiration for more systematic attention to crimes of the state on the part of a number of criminologists (Friedrichs 1992; Kramer 1994, 1995a, 1995b; Ross 1995). For example, Kramer and Michalowski (1990) quickly followed with the definition of state-facilitated crime, those activities of the state which fail to constrain criminal and dangerous behaviors. Chambliss (1995: 9) subsequently again called for resolving the key question at the foundation of the discipline, the definition of crime, so that the discipline could remain viable and vital. He stated: "State organized crimes, environmental crimes, crimes against humanity, human rights crimes, and the violations of international treaties increasingly must take center state in criminology. . . . Criminologists must define crime as behavior that violates international agreements and principles established in the courts and treaties of international bodies" (Chambliss 1995: 9).

Green and Ward (2000, 2004) have objected to general critical criminology definitions of state crime and opted for a deviance-based definition that draws upon the work of Howard Becker (1963) and other labeling theorists. Green and Ward assert that state crimes are only offenses when the action is labeled as such by a social audience. Other definitions, they claim, lack legitimacy. Moreover, their latest work (2004) examined state crime in relation to corruption, state-corporate crime, natural disaster, police crime, organize crime, state terror and terrorism, torture, war crimes, and genocide all under the rubric of International Human Rights Law (IHL) and the labeling of such by some social audience. This approach is far too vague concerning what constitutes a social audience and which audiences may legitimately label behavior a crime. Moreover, IHL draws from existing customary law and is incorporated in many Treaties. Other components of IHL are based on principles and values yet to be obtained. Moreover, we contend that in general, most critical criminologists studying state crime agree that using international law (customary, principles, or codified treaties) do constitute a basic foundation from which we can define state crime (see also Rothe and Friedrichs 2005).

State-Corporate Crimes

Building upon the growing interests in political and state crimes, Ronald Kramer (1990a, 1990b, and 1990c) made several presentations of articles bringing the concept of state/corporate crime to the attention of criminologists. The earliest definition of state/corporate crime given by Kramer (1990a: 1) was:

> State-corporate crime is . . . illegal or socially injurious social action that is the collective product of the interaction between a . . . corporation and a state agency . . [they] involve the active participation of two or more organizations, at least one of which is private and one of which is public. They are the harmful result of an inter-organizational relationship between business and government.

That year, Michalowski and Kramer (1990: 4) revised Kramer's earlier definition, and set forth the following, widely cited definition of state-corporate crime: State-corporate crimes are illegal or socially injurious actions that occur when one or more institutions or political governance pursue a goal in direct cooperation with one or more institutions of economic production and distribution.

State-corporate crime increasingly came to be seen as taking two forms, although these forms often interacted with each other. Accordingly, a distinction emerged between state-facilitated and state-initiated crimes (Kramer 1992;

Kauzlarich and Kramer 1993; and Michalowski 1993). These earlier works proposed and explored a "framework for examining how corporations and governments intersect to produce social harm" (Kramer et al. 2002: 263). Such intersections can work in a myriad fashions. States can create laws which facilitate corporate wrong doing and crimes (e.g., the infamous Savings and Loan debacle within the United States), regulatory and advisement agencies can simply fail to do their appointed tasks and all corporations to pursue criminal wrong doing unabated (e.g., OSHA's failure to provide remedy to safety violations at an Imperial Chicken plant in Hamlet, North Carolina [Aulette and Michaslowski 1993], the FAA's failures to ground ValuJet [Matthews and Kauzlarich 2000], and NHTSA's failure to investigate tire failures and roll over events on Ford Explorers [Mullins 2005]). States and state actors can also directly collude and conspire with private corporations to violate laws (e.g., Halliburton's behaviors in Iraq [Rothe 2005a, 2006]).

On the surface, these cases and types of crime would seem to have little to do with an international court, as they are domestically-based violations. Yet, with the increasingly international nature of corporate operation, capital accumulation and dispersement, these types of crimes will take on an increasingly international flavor and situation (Friedrichs and Friedrichs 2002; Rothe, Muzzatti, and Mullins 2005). Recently, agreements have been framed by the UN which compel transnational corporation to obey Human Rights Laws. For example the 2003 Norms on the Responsibilities of Transnational Corporations and Other Business Enterprises with regard to Human Rights agreement expressly brings the behavior of corporations operating in multiple nations under the rubric of human rights laws. Drawing heavily upon the UN Charter, especially Articles 1, 2, 55, and 56, this agreement acknowledges that globally-active for profit corporations are major players in the international arena. Traditionally, it has been the internationally held expectation that nation-states are the key players responsible for the maintenance and enforcement of human rights standards. Yet, due to the increasing power and influence of these corporate entities, it is their obligation as the core of a key social institution—e.g., the international society's economy, to abide by existing human rights law. If they are either active or complicit in such actions, then they are prosecutable by the ICC. It should be made clear, that while both historical legal actions, and the majority of our analyses here focus on nation-states as they key social actors—be they criminal actors or control actors, there is nothing within the Rome Statute that limits the ICC's jurisdiction to only state actors. In fact, due to the court's focus on the prosecution of individuals, it does not matter what social location or motivation drives an individual to engage in crimes against humanity. Corporate actors, state agents, and even private citizens unconnected to a transnational or national entity are currently under the court's jurisdiction as long as the action in question occurs within a signatory state that has ratified the Rome Statute or they are nationals of signatory states. This means that representatives of transnationals who operate within signatory states must abide by international human rights law or face prosecution.

Chapter II

An Integrated Theory of State Crimes

Traditional criminological inquiry into the epistemological and etiological factors of crime and crime control has, for the most part, produced theories addressing one specific level of analysis. While some scholars have ventured into integrating traditional theories, they have done so by integrating theories addressing the same level of analysis. While this may be an acceptable form of integration for some, we believe that an analysis of phenomena that has such complexities as time-space, history, culture, politics, ideology, and economics must include an integrated model that addresses all levels of analysis: the structural to the individual(s) involved in crime or crime control. We begin this chapter by presenting an integrated model of state crimes. We then explore the model through analysis of a case which the ICC prosecutorial arm has begun investigations: war crimes and crimes against humanity within the Democratic Republic of the Congo. From there we will examine current theorizations of existing and potential social controls of state crimes, then turn these theories expressly upon the Court itself to examine what it brings to the table for the control of state crime.

The Dialectic of Structure and Agency

While this volume is not the place to fully lay out or resolve the key theoretical tension within social science since its inception, we cannot enter into a theoretical examination without acknowledging the tensions between social forces on the macro level guiding the behavior of states and individual level agency. For generations, scholars have wrestled with the contradictions inherent in attempts to uncover the nature of the influence of social structure on individual human action and vice versa. Structure clearly frames action and thought, channeling human behavior toward certain outcomes and away from others; it defines possibilities and molds goal structures. Social actors respond to stimuli within their environments, yet exercise individual choice in decision-making processes based on any number of variables. Consequentially we define agency as bounded volunteerism or bounded free-will. We see a clear dialect where individuals respond to structural parameters which can influence what those parameters are by either reinforcing them, challenging, or constructing them. Further, for our intents here, we must also consider the structure/agency interactions as they apply within and to complex organizations.

As criminologists studying international law and social control mechanisms, we clearly place a strong emphasis on macro-level behavioral influences. Culture and structure form the cognitive landscape on which individual decisions are made. Global and historical forces come to bear upon organizations and establish environments in which decisions are made and that organizations must respond to. Any given incident of state crime is a product of a myriad of social forces which come together in the production of the event in question. Thus, attention must be given to specific time-space. Global political and economic conditions make state crimes more or less likely, provide tensions and contradictions for nation-states to navigate, and present problems for state actors to resolve—either criminally or legally. Contextualization of such acts is essential to understand both the idiosyncrasies of an individual event as well as the patterns which emerge in the phenomena as a whole.

Yet, in our focus on the broadest of socio-historical forces, we do not ignore the influence of individual decision makers within these events. Of course all acts require that a singular social actor make a decision and produce an act. In any state crime, orders to carry out the activities must be developed, agreed upon, and enacted. Within a bureaucracy as complex as a polity, this involves not one, but a multitude of social actors in a number of organizational positions. While individual agency is indeed modified or even extremely constrained by the social conditions present within any complex organization, no bureaucratic actor is a mere automaton. Individuals carry with them pre-established cultural and ideological visions. Such lens influence how they evaluate information, create policy objectives and direct organization activities to the realization of those policies. More essentially, at the top levels of power, agency can often be fully revealed and active. While indeed processes like groupthink can come into play, original decisions, directives, and directions must be established through some form of agentic decision making process.

Looking ahead to the case of state crime in the war on Iraq can make this point the clearest. Would the U.S. have invaded Iraq were George W. Bush not President at the time? If Rumsfeld and Wolfowitz did not control the Pentagon, would the same forces have been brought to bear on intelligence analysis? Would Cabinet and Joint Chiefs of Staff meetings have come to different operational directives without the influences of Bush, Cheney, and Rumsfeld? Of course, all of these questions are hypothetical and unanswerable, but they do illustrate the influence of a single person or small group of decision makers on the behavior of nation-states. Moreover, these questions demonstrate the weaknesses of pure linear analysis and call for sensitivity and attention to specific time-space within any theoretical analysis. It is with this broad framework in mind that we turn to an integrated theoretical model of state crime that will not only help us explain the criminal behavior of states, but will also allow us to examine the International Criminal Court's ability to effectively control such behaviors as an institution of social control.

An Integrated Model of State Crime

While many mainstream and critically-orientated theories of crime and criminality have relevance to the study and prevention of state crime, standing alone each presents short comings in the ability to adequately explain offending by sovereign nation states. Kauzlarich and Kramer (1998), building upon earlier work by Kramer and Michalowski (1990), present an integrated model of state offending that explores motivation, opportunities, and controls at three levels of analysis: the interactional, organizational, and the cultural-structural level. Moreover, their model integrates components of several criminological theories that fall short by themselves in addressing state crime. For example, Kauzlarich and Kramer utilize anomie and strain, rational choice, differential association, routine activities, political economy, and organizational models.

At the social-psychological level of analysis, Kauzlarich and Kramer recognize the utility of differential association wherein a person in a particular environment may engage in a criminal act if the weight of the favorable definition of an act exceeds the unfavorable definition. They also incorporate sociological models of socialization (see Appendix A under motivation). At the social-psychological or interactional level, Kauzlarich and Kramer discuss how motivation is affected by one's socialization within that environment, the social meaning given to their behavior, an individual's goals, and issues of personality such as personal morality and obedience to authority. Borrowing from Sykes and Matza, they include techniques of neutralization as a variable of control.

At the organizational level, Kauzlarich and Kramer draw heavily from organizational theorists who argue that "there is built into the very structure of organizations an inherent inducement for the organization itself to engage in crime" (Gross quoted in Kauzlarich and Kramer 1998: 145). They, along with organizational theorists, argue that organizations are strongly goal-oriented[1] and concerned with performance while governing norms may be weak or absent (anomie). Moreover, these goals may be blocked internally or externally causing strain (e.g., standard operating procedures or codes of conduct). As Kauzlarich and Kramer argue, organizational crime depends on two other factors—availability of illegal means and the social control environment that fosters organizational crime (146). Organizational opportunities are said to include instrumental rationality, role specialization, and task segregation while controls include a culture of compliance, reward structure, safety and quality control procedures, and effective communication processes.

At the structural or institutional level of analysis, the major social institutions and social structure are included, particularly the political and economic institutions and their interrelationship merit special attention in any effort to explain organizational crime. They suggest the primary assumption of that perspective is that the very structure of corporate capitalism provides the impetus toward organizational crime (146), thus becoming crimes of capital (Michalowski 1985). They further propose that the political economy perspective stresses the shaping and/or constraining influences of the broader historical structure of a society as a factor on organizational behavior. This includes factors such as the culture of competition, economic pressure, and performance emphasis under the catalyst of motivation. Also needed is the availability of legal and illegal means, blocked goals, and access to resources that are included under opportunities. Controls at the structural level are said to include international reactions, political pressure, legal sanctions, media scrutiny, and public opinion.

While we find this to be one of the most useful models in existence due to its integrated and multi-level nature analysis, we believe it fails to adequately delineate the concepts of opportunity and controls. Controls that are assumed to be non-existent or non-functional are conceptualized under the rubric of opportunity. Yet, controls and opportunity exist (and vary) independently of each other. Additionally, constraints and controls are intertwined while they potentially represent two separate fundamental catalysts.

Phenomenologically, a constraint differs from a control in that it is an inhibitor or barrier that occurs *at the onset* of an illegal action. This constraint can act as a complete blockage to the act, or it can act as a restraint, thereby inhibiting or causing the actor(s) to find alternative means to crime enactment. For the purposes of state crime, this could take the form of a propaganda campaign, a reduction in the scope of the act itself, more intense development of neutralizations, to name a few outcomes. We view a control as a *complete* blockage to an act or a criminal penalization is ideally inevitable after the fact. This means that conceived criminal action will not occur and, if it does, ideally there will be legal repercussions. This could lead to additional organizational strain, and the seeking out of other illegitimate means. A control is a perceived blockage due to existing and after the fact controls such as laws, regulations, and belief in sanctions or punitive measures, outweighed costs to benefits. These two concepts are separate conditions that do more than affect opportunity. They work independently of opportunity and can thus be conceptualized separately.

We also find that this model needs to be expanded to further incorporate the increasingly international nature of state and state-corporate criminality. Traditionally, the nation-state has been the preferred unit of analysis within sociology (see Mills 1959). Macro-level sociological theory developed in opposition to other social sciences (e.g., psychological models over-emphasizing the individual out of social context, while economics and political science models removed singular social institutions from their structural context). In that intellectual milieu, a focus on a single society's social structure arose, rightly so, to provide a holistic perspective which would allow scholars to understand institutional interrelationships and social forces at work. However, it is clear that singular societies are not atomistically separated from each other. Institutional arrangements and forces do not cease their influence at the arbitrary political boundaries currently drawn upon our maps. We do not propose an invalidation of this level of analysis; historical contingencies have created unique social arrangements that approximate geo-political units. There are social forces, arrangements, and interactions which operate outside of this arena.

As criminologists expand to areas of specialization which include the international level such as state crime, crimes of globalization, and international controls, the given macro level or cultural structural level is not sufficient to address the culture, economic, political, and historical environment of both, the international realm and the nation-state. It can be argued that the current levels of measurement are fluid to address the surrounding environment regardless of it being at the state or international level. We will argue that this cannot be the case as the aforementioned affirms: the conceptualization of different levels of analysis should be consistent and objective. The macro level must be separated into two distinct realms of analysis. The culture of a state—its economic, political, cultural, and historical environment—is distinct from and often in contradiction to the international level. This in and of itself illustrates an essential need to conceptualize a new level of analysis. Beyond this, as the process of globalization continues, imperialistic agendas resurface, and transnational corporations become the norm in global economic relations, examining the macro at both the state and the international level is crucial. This cannot be done within the same level of analysis (macro) as the distinct environments proffer divergent forces, information, culture, laws, history, relations, and ethos. Instead, it becomes necessary to speak of the organization (transnational corporation) at the meso level, the state as the domestic environment of that organization and/or the state itself, and then the level examining the realm for the international ethos, culture, history, politics, law, and economics.

The process of integration also includes utilizing different theoretical perspectives or frames within the overall frame. Not only do we recognize four levels of analysis, each with specific catalysts such as motivation, opportunity, constraints, and controls, we recognize the theoretical history within the integrated model. For example, Kauzlarich and Kramer's (1998) model utilizes anomie, rational choice, differential association, routine activities, political economy, and organizational models. We also believe these are necessary integrations to address all of the levels of analysis.

Broadly, state crime scholars identify both external and internal controls on the behavior of states (see Ross 1995, 2000). External controls are those that lie outside of the specific state apparatus and are imposed on the state itself. Internal controls are those that arise within the state and are directed against itself such as previously discussed domestic laws and self-regulation. These controls can be tangible (i.e., the firing of an agent) or symbolic (i.e., an official statement of denial or a promise to investigate). Internal controls are broadly conceived of as restrictions placed on state agencies by themselves or other state agencies. The United Kingdom's establishment of a Royal Commission on Police Procedure and a Police Complaints Board in response to police brutality (Ross 2000b), the passing of the Parliament of Canada Act and the Canadian Security Intelligence Service Act (Corrado and Davis 2000), the Zorea, Blatman, and Karp Commissions in Israel (Miller 2000) and campaign finance reform laws in Japan (Potter 2000), are all examples of such internal controls. All of these internal control mechanisms were established in the wake of publicity generated by various criminal state practices—most of which involved the abuse of power by state-run intelligence agencies against their own citizens.

Internal controls are those created by the state itself to govern itself. Generally, they are attempts to assuage public criticism over state actions. While the above examples all produced results, they are often limited to specific types of offenses that have already occurred (i.e., the Israel and U.K. investigative commissions) or often get quickly circumvented by new procedures or new depths of secrecy (i.e., the FOI acts in Japan's campaign finance laws), or are left underfunded or understaffed (i.e., OSHA and the EPA). Further, for our purposes here, internal controls have little relevance to the ICC except insofar as their consistent failures have created an overwhelming need for the court to exist.

External controls lie outside the apparatus of the state itself. To be effective, such controls actually have to exert some form of pressure and or ability to penalize after the fact (political, economic, legal, or military) on the state. External controls can be localized either within states' own domestic territory or external to it. Suggested external controls *within* the state have included (1) media organizations, (2) interest groups, and (3) domestic non-governmental organizations (NGOs). We view these external agencies as constraints versus controls. Such pressures raise inherent contradictions within modern democracies that are supposedly citizen-driven, but operate in a more elite-orientated fashion. When media or other agencies specifically address these contradictions in a public sphere, the state has to respond. Responses are typically symbolic, and often involve the erection of new veils of secrecy.

External controls located outside of the state would include the United Nations (UN), the World Court (WC), the International Criminal Court (ICC) and, potentially, other nation-states. As internationally-sanctioned bodies, these organizations hold the power to apply sanctions to states which violate either international law or are overly abusive of their own citizens. However, save for other nation-states, the ability to back up sanctions with coercive force is limited to members who are willing to volunteer the necessary force to act in the organization's name. It is for this reason that U.S. violations of international law regarding nuclear weapons have gone unsanctioned (Kauzlarich and Kramer

1998). Also, economic organizations such as the World Bank (WB), the International Monetary Fund (IMF) and the World Trade Organization (WTO) represent potential controls on criminal states through the manipulation of financial assets, trade agreements, and trade sanctions. While the former set of organizations would be more broadly seen as having legitimacy to sanction and control criminal states, it is most likely the later that hold real coercive power over the behavior of sovereign states. It is also more likely that such organizations would not use this coercive financial authority against some of the very modern industrial democracies that need it.

Theorizations of such relationships all ready exist within Black's models (1976, 1998) of relational distance's influence upon social control actions. Essentially a theory of third party intervention, Black's "pure sociology" suggests "the likelihood that a settlement agent will intervene in a conflict varies with the degree of intimacy, or relational distance, between the parties in conflict" (1998: 15). This relationship is not directly linear, but curvilinear in that "this likelihood seemingly increases with the relationship distance between the parties until they are complete strangers . . . at which point the likelihood of intervention declines." From this basic set of postulates, Black derives a continuum of settlement behavior based on a triangulation of the relationship between the principles of a dispute and the settlement agent. The general pattern is "[t]he authoritativeness of settlement behavior is a direct function of the relationship distance between the settlement agent and the principles" (Black 1998: 16) with friendly pacification being the norm when there is little distance and repressive pacification when there is extreme distance. Again, we also recognize that economics and ideological interests can also serve as catalysts for the relational distance or for response as much as geographic placement.

For our purposes, a highly important aspect of this behavioral dynamic is Black's (1998: 17) contention that "[s]ettlement behavior is more likely to occur when a third party is higher than the principles in social status . . . authoritativeness of settlement behavior is a direct function of the relative status of the third party" especially in relation to the status of the principles. The U.S.'s continued violation of international law and UN resolutions regarding nuclear weapons and the lack of sanctions exhibits this basic principle. On the international stage, the UN is not necessarily higher in social status than the U.S. and does not have the ability to use coercive force to enforce the sanctions. Again this depends on how we define social status; however, in terms of realism of relational powers, clearly the U.S. holds relatively equal if not more international weight and social status that the UN. The ICC could rectify that imbalance.

In addition to the issues that Black addresses, relational distance include differences in geographic location, broad cultural affiliation distances (essentially western vs. oriental—see Said 1979), economic power, and military might. All else being equal, closer geographic proximity will work in the same fashion as a close relational distance. Similarly, a western-based culture will be seen as socially closer than an oriental-based culture to another western society. However, a universal, transnational court empowered to enforce international law should work to reduce such distances by legitimating—by its existence and actions—a singular set of legal codes and standards.

Additionally, a nation's position in the global market will have a strong effect in determining how "close" it is to other nations; this relationship can be conceptualized by the number of economic interconnections, especially involving the moving of consumer goods and services between nations. If a nation is highly economically interconnected to another nation but the relationship is one of dependency, this will create some social closeness but not as much as if the connection were based on an equal exchange. For example, the U.S. and Japan are tightly interlocked by trade relationships and social distance between the two nations is rather low. U.S. multinational corporations have established major centers of manufacturing within the developing world, i.e., Nike in South Asia. While this does create a connection between various parts of the world, it is not a tight relationship because the U.S. corporations hold the power in terms of their ability to pull out and move to another developing nation almost at will. Black's postulates would predict that South Asia policy would be directed towards stabilizing the region for the benefit of U.S. corporations—whose social distance with the U.S. government is minimal—and not for the South Asian people or states, who have a higher level of relational distance. Military might can be conceptualized in a rather self-evident fashion, based on the size and strength of the armed forces a nation supports. It can also be conceptualized in terms of a nation's ability to marshal allies to assist in a military action whether symbolic—i.e., Japan's contribution of ships to the anti-Taliban military action in Afghanistan—or tangible—i.e., Pakistan's allowing the use of its territory as staging areas in the same action.

Exploring the issue of the ability of quasi-governmental bodies to act as control agents is important, even if these agencies have had an historically poor record of enacting control. The UN, the World Court, and the new ICC are uniquely positioned to act as global dispute resolution agents. However, in light of the actual power wielded by these agencies, the social distance between them and the major industrialized democracies is rather large. While possessing a clear mandate, these organizations have no real authority or ability to use coercive force. Where these agencies have been successful in taking the role of dispute resolvers, western industrialized powers provided their armies as enforcement mechanisms—and only tend to do so when they have a distinct self-interest in the outcome. The UN peacekeeping mission, and the Serbian war crimes trials at the WC, is case in point. Little real social control was enacted during the Bosnian phase of Serbian-led genocide. However, when this pogrom was extended to Kosovo, and it became clear that Serbian aggression was not going to be limited to its immediate neighbors and could destabilize the entire region, the UN and the U.S. stepped in using military power to enforce compliance with UN resolutions. Moderately distant from the rest of Europe and the world, the early genocide went unsanctioned until it endangered south central

European stability. Geographic proximity eventually compelled action. Similar genocides in Rwanda generated no military responses, only UN "talk" (per Cohen 1985) due to the country's social, economic, and geographical distance from the industrialized west.

At the international level, existing relations based on specific conditions create broad social forces that can act as constraints against a state's intended policy. This can include NGOs, other nation-states, and inter-governmental organizations such as the UN. Moreover, there are the broader global economic forces that can produce or constrain competition and goal attainment. The larger international culture or ethos can also produce an environment wherein a set of objectives can be replaced with covert or overt activities by a state. Presently, controls at the international level can occur by means of economic of political sanctions or threat of military actions; at the same time, these mechanisms often fail to act as controls for other nation-states due to lack of consistent application. For example the UN Security Council can (and has) sanction states endlessly, but without formal mechanisms to enforce those sanctions, there is nothing to compel compliance, thus providing further opportunity for state crimogenic behaviors.

Alternatively, international law may hold more power. As street crime research has shown, social location and position strongly influences deterrence (Paternoster and Piquero, 1995; Paternoster and Simpson, 1992; Piquero and Paternoster, 1998; Sherman and Berk, 1984; Stafford and Warr, 1993). Those actors most likely to be involved in state crime would seem to be those who are most influenceable by law. This observation forms the foundation of our arguments here focused on the ability of the ICC to eliminate impunity and engender a deterrent value of certain international laws. However, for the most egregious of crimes, those which the ICC has been designed to prosecute, such controls have historically done little to deter; typically, they come into play long after the criminal actions are over and the viability and integrity of the state which has committed them has been compromised.

At the macro, or institutional level, broad social forces of competition and goal attainment intersect with the lack of effective controls to produce an environment where states are, once the micro and meso level elements align, able to ignore domestic legal codes as they see fit in the process of enacting their policy objectives. Moreover, any constraints, such as media, general population opinion, and/or internal state obstacles, can often be ignored or manipulated via hegemonic discourse, symbolic political gestures, or altering policy to immediately appease while continuing in a covert direction. Drawing upon anomie theories (e.g., Merton 1938; Messner and Rosenfeld, 2005), broader forces of cultural goals of success and competition when met with blocked goal attainment processes push political organizations—and actors within them—toward the violation of law in the accomplishment of their objectives. Being a nation-state strongly enhances the ability to create and capitalize upon criminal opportunity. Even the poorest states have tremendous amounts of human and financial capital to draw upon for crime commission. Illegal means are often available; the desirability of drawing upon these means will be even more tempting when legal means of accomplishing the goals are absent, blocked, or constrained. While this is not to say that legitimate means may also be present, however, due to the concept of instrumental rationality, it is often the "by any means necessary" and the least costly in terms of consequences, thus resulting in the choice of illegitimate over legitimate means.

An unexplored, though significant, aspect of social structure at the macro level which needs attention is the conceptualization of institutional order and institutional disruption. A recurrently popular approach within criminology over the generations, the idea of social (dis)organization as intimately linked with crime patterns is well established. Most strongly articulated by the Chicago school, though drawing upon Durkheim's original work with the notion of anomie, and later revitalized by the work such as that of Bursik and Grasmick (1993), Sampson et al. (1997), and Baumer et al. (2003) as well as the direction taken by Gary Lafree (2002, 2005) in recent years. Essentially, when strong, functioning social institutions are not present, this creates both motivation and opportunity for organized criminal activity. As we will see in both case discussions later in the chapter, this element of anomie-as-disorder is critical to understanding the crimes the court is currently investigating for prosecution. Weak institutions produce a vacuum of formal and informal social control. A nation unable to adequately police or subdue a paramilitary force in its hinterlands creates a gap of institutional control that simultaneously provides motivation and opportunity for the arisal of organized criminal activity.

Criminology's (and history's) literature is full of such organizations: modern urban street gangs, organized crime networks, and paramilitary militias are just a few. Informal controls, such as modalities of socialization, behavioral controls operating within other institutions such as the family, education, or religion, are distinctly weakened in these environments. This allows for more easeful transmission of subcultural values allowing and encouraging criminality, as well as other beliefs which can feed into criminogenic forces (e.g., racism aiding genocidal events). On the other hand, Durkheim and others such as Colvin and Cullin (2004) have recognized that overregulation can also create crimogenic environments at the state level. For example, history has shown that overregulated nation-states have resulted in terrible atrocities such as the Soviet Gulag system. However, the current cases under investigation at the ICC demonstrate the effects of lax regulations and a state in social, political, and economic disorganization.

Control at the macro level emerges from a number of loci. While domestic legal codes are key, public scrutiny also is seen as playing pivotal roles. Clearly law can serve to control actions, but, due to the unique position of a state vis-à-vis its own domestic law and the problematic ways in which it is enforced, law may not hold the same deterrent power over a political body as it does over citizen actors. Moreover, public forces embodied in the media, opinion, and activism can potentially operate as constraints on state criminality at this level.

At the meso, or organizational level, elements of organizational culture and goals structure decision-making environments which can lead either toward or away from criminal activity within a polity. Drawing upon broader theories of organizational behavior and corporate offending, it is highlighted that certain states may develop bureaucratic environment where goal attainment is pushed to an "any means necessary" degree. Certain organizations further reinforce instrumental rationality within decision making processes (see Perrow 1986; Weber 1946) that can enhance the perceived value of criminal behaviors and reduce the perceived harm of the same act. Cultures can develop within organizations or subunits that can motivate criminal endeavors; further, managerial influences can push for illegal solutions to goal accomplishment. Another factor within complex organizations is the ability of those in charge of staffing positions to fill those roles with individuals who tend to think and act like the managers themselves.

The very nature of complex organizations provides a host of opportunity producing elements. Any given governmental agency (or corporate unit) will have resources (human and otherwise) that can be directed toward a criminal action. Bureaucracies can maintain levels of secrecy on how their resources are utilized; external actors need not know what was done within the organization or by whom. Information may also be hidden from other organizational actors, including those who are actually carrying out elements of the criminal activity. Due to internal organizational structures of information control, the ability of external agencies (be they public media or law enforcement) to obtain information on the nature and dynamics of these decision-making events heighten criminal tendencies within some states. Simply, the ability to avoid detection is a strong motivator and facilitator.

At the micro, or interactional level, this model combines aspects of associational and social learning theories (e.g., Akers 1977; Sutherland 1939) as well as core elements of symbolic interactionism (e.g., perceptual aspects and definition of the situation). These factors are relevant in understanding state crimes at all levels of power within the polity—from the decision makers, to those who organize the act's implementation, to those who actually carry out the actions. Individual level motivations can be personal, but these individualized outlooks and motivations are highly malleable within the organizational culture and context that encapsulates the social actors. Again, cultural elements discussed above come to bear—both in the broader socio-cultural sense (singular actors motivated for personal success and advancement) but also organizational cultures which the individual has been socialized into. Certain organizations may inculcate employees into broader ideological beliefs that facilitate violating laws for the sake of the institution; day-to-day interactions with coworkers provide ample opportunity for the transmission not only of criminogenic value systems but also of neutralizations to excuse such behaviors.

To explore the analytical power of this theory, as well as to illustrate the potential abilities of the ICC in acting as a constraint and/or control of War Crimes and Crimes Against Humanity, we now turn to the examination of one of the cases currently under investigation by the court's prosecutor: the situation in the Democratic Republic of Congo.

Democratic Republic of Congo

The Democratic Republic of Congo (DRC) has devolved into uncontrolled genocidal warfare between ethnically-based factions within an unresolved civil war. Unlike some other examples of this phenomenon within Africa, the DRC's conditions have remained unstable due to international involvement on behalf of its neighbors (e.g., Uganda and Rwanda), transnational corporations (e.g., AngloGold Ashanti), and those corporations' Western trading partners (Metalor technologies and the nation of Switzerland). Central within the conflict (and the war crimes and crimes against humanity perpetrated within the conflict) is the control of rich mineral fields of the nation. It is the sustained conflict over, and the nature of international involvement in, the purchase of these resources, that makes the DRC's circumstances an example of transnational state corporation crime instead of state crime. The case also provides illustration of how the ICC will need to not only deal with the crimes that emerge in these processes, but will also have to embrace its jurisdictional powers over western nations and extend its purview over transnational corporate actors. Moreover, this case illuminates the need for international organizations such as the UN to deal with a disintegrating state.

Civil and political unrest in the DRC stems from the collapse of its political system and an ongoing civil war. In 1996, Uganda and Rwanda invaded the Congo and deposed sitting president Mobutu Sese Seko, installing Laurent Kabila in his stead. Two years later, Kabila attempted to expel Rwandan forces triggering what is often referred to as Africa's First World War. Uganda, Rwanda, and Burundi poured troops into northeastern Congo, while Zimbabwe, Angola, and Nambia came to the aid of Kabila's government. When the Lusaka peace agreement was signed in 1999, over 3.5 million people had died. The UN entered into peacekeeping operations that year. Numerous militia groups have historically and contemporaneously operated through out the DRC. For the sake of space and analytical focus, we direct our attention here to one specific region: the mineral rich northeast. Our focus does not suggest that this is the only location of war crimes and crimes against humanity, or even this is the locality of greatest intensity. We focus here because: (1) existing Human Rights Watch (2003, 2005), Amnesty International (2003), and United Nations (see especially United Nations Security Council, 2003) investigations provide rich sources of information on specificities of conflicts in this region; and (2) the role of other nations and transnational corporations of expressly clear in examining specific slaughters and militia-perpetuated violence.

When Uganda and Rwanda decamped from Congo in 2003 and 2002, respectively, they left behind factional militias which continued the conflicts. Uganda supported the Front des Nationalistes et Integrationnistes (FNI), a Lendu-based ethnic armed force; Rwanda supported the Union des Patriotes Congolais (UPC), a Hema group. These ethnic groups have a history of conflict over land rights; with Ugandan occupation of the region, the tensions flared and Rwanda and Uganda poured arms into the struggle, using the ethnic warfare as a proxy for their own conflicted control of the region. The Lendu and Hema have continued to struggle over control of the rich gold fields, especially those in the Mongbwalu and Durba areas (both of which share a border with Uganda). Fighting has been intense, with war crimes and massive human rights violations committed frequently by all parties (Human Rights Watch, 2003, 2005; Amnesty International, 2003; UN SC, 2003).

In addition to internecine factionalism, Uganda and Rwanda at time occupied portions of the DRC and aided ethnic factions and militias in the region. The motivation for international involvement was clearly the presence of rich mineral fields and associated trade routes in the northern portion of the country (Human Rights Watch, 2003, 2005; Amnesty International, 2003). The major reason this region has been so heavily contested during this period are the mineral deposits, which represent a major source for profit in an overall, destabilized African economic system. During the Second Congolese war (begun in 1998), Uganda occupied gold rich lands in the north, establishing control over the Gorumbwa, Dubra, and Agbarabo mines. According to Human Rights Watch (2005), almost a ton of gold was extracted during a four-year period (1998-2002) worth approximately nine million U.S.D.

Without the resources to engage in industrial mining practices, they forced miners to engage in artisan labor practices, which are very dangerous and reckless. Ugandan soldiers frequently beat and extorted the local miners by requiring monetary payment to enter the mines and taking a percentage of the ore which they mined. Specifically at the Gorumbwa mine, these practices led to the collapse and loss of the mine itself in late 1999 (Human Rights Watch 2003, 2005). Not only was the treatment of miners and the local communities a violations human rights laws, their destruction of the mines and surrounding infrastructure constitute war crimes—specifically violations of the provisions of Geneva conventions which insist that occupying powers protect non-military assets of the occupied territory.

With the withdrawal of Ugandan troops in 2003, the fight for control of the mines was taken up by local militia groups. The central Congolese government asserted no control over the region; Rwanda and Uganda continued to struggle for dominance in the region each by providing material support and military advisors to the local, ethnic-based militia groups. These militias drew heavily on base tactics of terror, genocide, torture, arbitrary detainment, and constant extortion in their attempts to gain and maintain control over a community. Between 8 and 18 November 2002, the UPC, a Hema group supported by Rwanda, attacked

Mongbwalu, slaughtering and raping ethnic Lendu. December 2002, into January of 2003, saw the UPC repeated these acts in Kilo, Kobu, Lipri, Bambu and Mbijo. Human Rights Watch estimates the death total at over two thousand, with over one-hundred-forty thousand peoples displaced. With the population subdued, the UPC began forced mining practices similar to those carried out by the Ugandan troops. The gold was destined for Rwanda; in exchange, the UPC received arms to continue their conflicts (Human Rights Watch 2003, 2005; Amnesty International 2003).

In March of 2003, the Ugandan army switched allegiances. It ceased its support of the UPC and cobbled together a coalition of Lendu militias, the FNI and FAPC. In early March, the combined forces took control of Bunia, then drove north to Kilo. Arriving on 10 March, the Lendu groups enacted a revenge slaughter, which stopped only when their Ugandan allies arrived and began firing into Lendu groups to stop the killing. In May, Uganda troops proper left the Congo, with their militia allies firmly in control of the gold-rich north. A UPC counter strike in 2003 returned control of the Mongbwalu to the Hema for approximately forty-eight hours; the Lendu response was not just to retake the town, but to continue its genocidal retributions against the Hema from July through September of that year. Without Ugandan forces on the ground to stop them, the Lendu slaughtered men, women, and children. They killed wounded as they lay in hospital beds.

As with the Ugandans and the UPC before them, the FNI and FAPC took control of the mines, maintained the forced artisanal labor situation, levied random taxes, and maintained a general policy of ruling through the use of extortion, terror, and force (Human Rights Watch 2003, 2005; Amnesty International 2003).

Due to the highly valued mineral wealth found especially in the northeastern portion of the nation, both transnational corporations and Switzerland were either directly involved or duly complicit with the violences in northern Congo (Human Rights Watch 2005; UN SC 2003). Gold, silver, diamonds, coltan, and other precious minerals constitute the major exploitable natural resources of the area. With the political and economic chaos instigated by the civil war of 1998, and the continued unrest since, these mineral resources are effectively controlled by militia groups. While the sitting government can, and has, issued contracts and deeds for mineral extraction, such official permissions are meaningless in the hinterlands. To actually take advantage of these economic agreements, companies must also negotiate with the on-the-ground powers or establish relationships with neighboring nations to purchase raw materials illegally taken over the border and then shipped into major global markets (Human Rights Watch 2005; UN SC 2003). Involvement in this sort of trade can violate human rights laws when the nature of mining operations fail to follow existing international guidelines. This is precisely the situation which has widely existed in the northeastern region of DRC. The UN Panel of experts (UN SC 2003) named over one hundred corporations with problematic or suspect dealings within the DRC during the chaos of the past eight years (see the UN SC 2003 report for a full accounting of those involved). While the majority of these were African-based companies (most based in neighboring nations), major transnationals, like DeBeers, were also named. Belgium, Canada, Germany, Israel, the Netherlands, Switzerland, the United Kingdom, and the United States all have multiple companies on the list.

After the June 2003 establishment of a DRC transitional government, transnational corporations almost immediately began seeking the state's license to pursue gold extraction in the north. AngloGold Ashanti Ltd. (AGA) has been given sole mineral extraction rights in the Ituri region (Human Rights Watch 2003, 2005). Yet, as both the government and AngloGold Ashanti acknowledge, since the mines are in militia-controlled regions, these allowances mean nothing on the ground. In order to activate the governmental contract and to begin gold extraction, AGA had to enter into negotiations with the individuals who controlled actual access to the mines (Human Rights Watch 2005). Specifically, they had to deal with the FNI and its leader Floribert Njabu. In an interview with Human Rights Watch, Njabu was perfectly clear about the nature of mineral concessions and the way in which any economic activities would work in his (or any other) militia controlled area: "I am the one who gave Ashanti permission to come to Mongbwalu. I am the boss of Mongbwalu. If I want to chase them away I will. . . . The contract for Ashanti is with the government but we [the FNI] control Mongbwalu so they need to come see me if they want to work there" (quoted in Human Rights Watch 2005: 62).

When such militia groups are involved in war crimes, forced labor, and other crimes against humanity, this makes the transnational corporation both complicit and responsible itself for these crimes. In general, these actions may potentially violate specific UN Security Council or General Assembly resolutions, such as arms and other trade embargoes. Specifically, such actions also violate the Norms on the Responsibilities of Transnational Corporations and Other Business Enterprises with Regard to Human Rights. Engaging in, supporting, or taking advantage of the forced and otherwise exploitive labor practices identified with the DRC constituted a Crime Against Humanity. This opens up a new realm of jurisdiction for the ICC—the behavior of transnational corporations. Metalor Technologies, a leading Swiss refinery, is responsible for purchasing Congolise gold from Ugandan sources (Human Rights Watch 2005). While claiming to follow all Swiss and international laws, Metalor's due diligence is problematic. Quite simply, and despite claims otherwise, they knew the gold is coming from Uganda. It is also well known that there is essentially no indigenous Ugandan gold production and Uganda does not import gold from other nations. This leaves one likely source of the metal: northeastern Congo. Metalor's purchases were facilitated by the Swiss freeport system. Freeports provide a place for the importation of goods which are legally outside the realm of governmental control. No duties or tariffs are applied to goods brought in through these zones and thus no governmental record keeping or oversight occurs. A company like Metalor can buy gold within the freeport zone with no official taxation or, more importantly, with no tracing of its origins.

While aware of the military and humanitarian crisis in the region, and fully cognizant of the illegal gold trade across the DRC-Uganda border, the Swiss government has shown no interest in altering import laws to shut down the market. This is not the first time that the Swiss financial system has been implicated in facilitating criminal action, or even the first time it has been linked to Crimes Against Humanity (e.g., the now infamous use of the system to hide Nazi gold and other wealth extracted from nations conquered in World War II).

This case is complex, with numerous state and non-state actors involved at a number of levels. To sort out the variety of influences and social forces at work, we now return to our integrated theoretical model.

Theoretical Analysis

Our integrated theoretical model highlights not only causal processes at work within the case explored above, and directs us toward an understanding of how the International Criminal Court can act as an agent of social control of individual and organizational actors. The core of this case is the dissolution of legitimate institutions within a civil war. Out of this social chaos, pre-colonial (and colonially enhanced) ethnic tensions undergird broader economic and political competitions between groups combine to give rise to active paramilitary groups struggling for supremacy in an essentially uncontrolled, and often uncontrollable, environment. To date, these situations have been underanalyzed sociologically and criminologically. However, these anomic conditions are prime producers of war crimes and crimes against humanity. While more mainstream criminologies have tended to ignore these phenomena, the literature we explored at the start of the chapter has taken upon itself to place these crimes—arguably some of the most severe in the world—firmly within the purview of our field.

At the macro level, the connection between the vacuum created by the withdrawal of European colonial power structures and current disorder is stark. Economically and politically, post-colonial nations are often faced with having to build from scratch major social institutions. This is often made problematic in that the nation will attempt to adopt a set of political institutions similar to former colonial powers, often without a historical-cultural tradition of such forms of governance and little citizen experience with participation. The last half of the twentieth century showed a strong tendency for such states to become corrupted by the nation's elites. Further, these nations' boundaries and constituent populations are by no means organic in the sense of bringing together a geographic region or population with a sense of shared identity. The political boundaries were established during colonial domination; during this historical period cultural, ethnic, and other differences were submerged by the controlling foreign power. Most of the nations which achieved post-colonial stability did so under a one party system which likewise subordinated varying group interests to a monolithic power system. The internecine conflicts plaguing these areas are the result of the fracturing of a centralized government and the people's realignment along pre-existing ethnic lines. Deeply historical differences and conflict re-emerge, some of which where heightened under the colonial or one-party state periods (e.g., the Hema-Lendu tensions in DRC).

As discussed, hinterland areas are often uncontrolled (and uncontrollable) by a weak centralized state. Militias arise within these regions to become the de facto political organization mechanism. When a militia is supportive of a standing government or of a regular military force, the legitimate authorities have little incentive to control their actions. States which draw upon militia allies are in a precarious situation at best to begin with. With few resources and a nation in general embroiled in social, political, and economic chaos, militias allow a sitting government to extend some measure of token control over additional territory. Further, due to the self-supporting nature of militia groups—be it a support based upon civilian exploitation and often blatant thuggery—they do not have to spend scare resources on them. Of course, this assumes that the legitimate authorities could challenge militias if they wanted to; this may not be the case.

Economic chaos exacerbates these situations. Just as many post-colonial nations have to construct a viable political structure, they are also faced with a highly disorganized economy. Colonial domination destroys indigenous economic systems and life ways. As the populace's labor is expropriated into an export economy beneficial to the dominant state, traditional industries are lost. Throughout Africa, colonial nations kept infrastructure construction and maintenance at a bare minimum, which kept profitability high. With the withdrawal of European powers, native populations found themselves in control of a disorganized economy, depleted of natural resources and lacking in the capital necessary to enter into viable competition within the post-World War II global economy. While monies for development have been historically available from such organizations as the World Bank and the International Monetary Fund, these resources come with numerous strings attached. Nations who have accepted such assistance find themselves having to organize their economic along the desires of their western creditors. Such arrangements have also shown the marked tendency to prove beneficial to social and economic elites, while leaving the broader populace to deal with the side effects and consequences (see Friedrichs and Friedrichs 2002; Rothe, Muzzatti, and Mullins 2005).

As seen in the discussion of the DRC, a poorly organized economic system, combined with an ineffective central polity, led to years of warfare focused on the control of mineral fields. Both neighboring nations and transnational corporations sought to exploit the chaos for their own economic gain, with the local populace facing violence, disorder, and forced labor. Criminologists working in first world, urban locations have long noted the criminogenic nature of disorganized economic situations; the amplified nature of these forces within post-colonial nations produces a similarly amplified criminogenic push.

Most of the factors discussed in the social control literature are inadequate to prevent or control these sorts of crimes. Without a strong, viable government, existing laws are inapplicable in militia-controlled regions. Domestic media provided a lot of attention to the issues, but as a form of propaganda to incite more violence and destruction—not to create a public outcry against it. International media sources drew global attention to these issues—though some media sources offered more attention then others. Yet, little pressure was brought to bear on social control institutions to do any thing. In both cases, the UN Security Council passed resolutions calling for the end of the activities, though only small peacekeeping forces were sent to the regions.

At the organizational level, widespread use of strategies producing crimes against humanity are the result of both the general paramilitary structures of militias and the strong ethnic biases which form the core of membership identities within these groups. A dangerous combination to say the least. As loosely-organized groups which are strongly controlled by their leaders, the potential for criminal cultures to develop is high. The ability to transmit and reinforce criminal values throughout a militia is strong. For transnational corporations, profitability is often the core drive of their actions in global systems. Politically and economically disorganized nations provide fertile grounds for asset enhancement. Already driven by cultures of corporate accumulation, the organizational structures allow subunits to operate without a more general knowledge (on behalf of the public and potential other units within the corporation) of their actions. International trade agreements which established freeports and other locales for the uncontrolled transfer of resources, further facilitate the possibility and profitability of these endeavors.

At the micro level, personal gain and empowerment is clearly a strong motivation for those in power. Military (regular and irregular) leaders stand to personally profit politically and economically from their positions. With no formal social control mechanisms to dissuade them, they can easily become the embodiment of law and order in the lands their militias control. Under the ad hoc system of trying war crimes and crimes against humanity, such individuals faced prosecution only if they lost power and the international community saw fit to establish inquiries and tribunals. This is where an active and empowered International Criminal Court can offer itself as a strong deterrent. There is not an issue of "will there be a tribunal?" If the court establishes itself as an active and consistent pursuer of cases, petty tyrants lose impunity. Such deterrent processes will be even strong if the Security Council acts upon its powers to levy economic sanctions, thereby putting pressure on central governments to bring their own hinterlands under control.

In terms of individuals joining militias, our integrated model points toward community disorder providing micro-level motivations. Young men who find themselves without other social and economic opportunities will gravitate to joining the only real social organization present in their social environment. The criminological literature on street gangs has long established the draw of gangs in the absence of other empowered social institutions. Militias are merely another form of this phenomenon. With few viable institutional paths to success and survival, and no external social controls, militias become the only stable and empowered social grouping in a community. They strengthen individual identity and social membership; the ethic composition also clears carries identity meanings and validation for members.

The development of global economic policies to alleviate these forms of social and economic disorder is beyond the scope of the court and of this volume, but are necessary nonetheless. The presence of a permanent and empowered ICC could also work against the belief that individuals will be able to act with impunity. Before the court, while there was a potential for tribunals to be held, this was a possibility only if your side was defeated, and even then, it was not an assured process. The problem with ad hoc systems is their deterrent value is reduced as the certainty of their existence is in question. With a permanent court whose jurisdiction covers these crimes, even successful militia endeavors face prosecution, especially if this is combined with a court's focus on the controlling transnational corporations. A track record of prosecution of corporate officers for crimes against humanity due to their complicity in actions such as we have seen in the DRC would serve to isolate the economic possibilities that a militia or standing government would have available.

Conclusion: The International Criminal Court as Control Mechanism

The discussions in this chapter have one overriding purpose—to examine the potential of the International Criminal Court to control state crimes. While the criminological literature on the deterrent effects of law in controlling street crimes shows problematic influences at best, some work has shown that among white collar offenders (or more socially bonded offenders) there is a greater potential for law to control social actors and their decision making processes. Clearly, especially within the cases discussed in this chapter and elsewhere within this volume, many of these states have engaged in criminal actions simply because they can. Current geo-political and international legal structures offer no threat of consequences; be they junta leaders in Africa or the Secretary of Defense of the United States, international law can be violated without threat of prosecution simply because there are no empowered institutions to do so. Quite simply, when actors can act with impunity, some will chose to do so.

When there are no real controls on organizational and individual behavior, especially when the criminal actors are the strongest force of social control in social location, anomic situations exhibit a strongest tendency to produce criminal behaviors. Factors such a social, economic, and geographic distance exacerbate these tendencies. Within these contexts of disorder, criminally directed organizations develop not only in response to wide-scale disorder but as the key organizing mechanisms within the landscape. When a given nation-state cannot organize itself, or at least maintain a semblance of lawful order within itself, it will increasingly fall to international social mechanisms to do so. As the cases discussed in the chapter have shown, neighbors, super powers, major NGOs (e.g., the IMF, WB), and international political institutions (e.g., the UN) have shown an inability or unwillingness to prevent and control crimes against humanity. The question of whether or not the International Criminal Court will be able to do what existing structures have been unable to do is still an open question. Moreover, as the Court stands, several limitations surrounding empowerment, crimes covered, and actors falling within the Court's jurisdiction further impede the potential to act as a control or constraint of future atrocities. In this chapter, we have attempted to highlight potentials and pitfalls for the court as it stands. Time will tell if the deterrent potentials we highlight come to bear true fruit.

Regardless of the ability to prevent or deter criminal actions, the heinous and horrific nature of the crimes under the ICC's jurisdiction demand punishment and the application of justice. Even if it has no other effects on the types of crime we have explored in this chapter, minimally it provides the possibility for resolution, justice, and restitution for victims of these crimes. Moreover, it does provide a formal historical record of the act in hopes it may remain part of the collective consciousness of humanity. Our next chapter will examine the historical attempts to create an international criminal court in response to conflicts occurring between nation-states.

Notes

1 These include operative goals, subunit goals, and managerial goals.

Chapter III

Developing an International Criminal Court

The history of proposals to establish an ICC to address conflicts within international society spans 126 years. Throughout that frame of time, several major conflicts occurred which resulted in different social relations and ideologies. The following chapter is divided according to the historical eras surrounding attempts to establish an ICC. The first section, 1872-1930, discusses the first formal attempt through World War I. The following section covers 1931-1955. This era focuses on the attempts to establish an ICC in response to World War I and as a result of World War II. From 1955-1974 the Cold War era was the dominant factor in international relations and is addressed in the third section. This is followed with a section discussing the events from 1975-1997. This section is concluded with a brief summary of the historical attempts to establish an ICC.

1872 to 1930: The Seeds for an International Criminal Court Were Planted

The first formal international attempts to establish a permanent international criminal court date back to1872. Prior to this time, many states had entered into bilateral and multilateral agreements based on violations of domestic laws (e.g., mainly extradition requests) and treaties to regulate relations for preventing war (1648 Treaty of Westphalia; Geneva Convention of 1864). Prosecution and penalization of violations remained problematic. International state parties were intent on keeping the concept of sanctions and penalties at the domestic level of states.

As pointed out in the Preface, after the Franco-Prussian war, the first attempts to establish an ICC (in 1872) by Moynier had proved futile. At the same time, the Peace Society in the United States developed an international criminal code that outlined the jurisdiction for an international criminal court (Hampson 2002). Both attempts to establish an ICC failed, as states did not support the notion of criminal sanctions at the international level. International law had been established as a tool for defining inter-state relations. However, the growing concern over violations of the Laws and Customs of War began to generate requests by independent international actors to establish an institution for prosecution of individuals that committed heinous acts at the international level.

In response to the changing nature of warfare, especially its increasing mechanization and lethality, Emperor Alexander II of Russia convened a conference in Brussels in 1874, which resulted in an International Declaration

Concerning the Laws and Customs of War. This remarkable document detailed rules for the treatment of civilians and civilian territory (occupied and unoccupied), the wounded, prisoners of war (combatants and spies), as well as the rules of surrender and treatment of those who have capitulated. Article VIII of the Declaration Concerning Laws and Customs of War provided for prosecution of violators of the Laws and Customs of War at the international level (Ferencz 1980). The International Law Association,[1] founded in Brussels in 1873, submitted a report on the feasibility of such an International code of laws (2nd Report, Geneva ILA 1874). State actors perceived the idea of international culpability with skepticism; International Law's purview was limited to inter-state relationships. The Declaration of 1874 never received enough support to be adopted. Just a few years later, General Ulysses Grant of the United States wrote to the Universal Peace Union requesting that an international court be established that "shall be recognized by all nations, which will take into consideration all differences between nations" (Grant, in Ferencz 1980: 6). Just as previous proposals for international criminal liability were met with resistance, the suggestion by Grant failed to materialize.

In 1895, the International Red Cross again attempted to establish support for an ICC in Geneva. However, the Institute of International Law rejected the formal proposal made at Geneva as it did not contain specificity for violations or the violators of the Rules of War (Ferencz 1980). Nations continued to expand their military powers hoping to provide security against competing nations. The costs of not establishing an international criminal system of laws or justice led to calls for an international solution to the growing threats to sovereign nations by other sovereign nations. This brought about the first major treaty defining (though excluding punitive measures) international law: The Hague Conventions of 1899.

The Hague Conventions of 1899 establish non-binding mediation and arbitration as the key mechanisms of inter-state conflict resolution (Article 1-19). However, the agreement also calls for the establishment of a permanent Court of Arbitration (Article 20) that "shall be competent for all arbitration cases, unless the parties agree to institute a special Tribunal" (Article 21). Even though the agreement was clear on the non-binding nature of the processes and nations had the right to select the judges to act as arbitrators, many nations in attendance adopted the principles under reservation. For example, the United States, in a sense establishing a future pattern, expressed general support for the Court and its processes, but declared that it would neither be compelled to intervene in any of the affairs of any foreign nation nor relinquish sovereignty for domestic issues (Ferencz 1980)

At this time the Law of Nations and International Law were viewed as conventional terms (Association for the Reform and Codification of the Law of Nations 1882). They were viewed in the form of inter-state relations, bilateral relations, and within an international society of independent sovereign states. Chancellor Kent stated: "That collection of customary, conventional, and judicial, which independent States appeal to for the purpose of determining their rights, prescribing their duties and regulating their intercourse, in peace and war, imposed by opinion and based on the consent of nations" (Kent, 1882: 169). The limited Treaties include the Maritime Law in Declaration of Paris, adopted by forty six States, which was seen as a uniform code of International law but with the hopes of it becoming a "permanence and fixity of principle to the Law of Nations" (Kent, 1882: 171).[2]

During the Second Hague Conference of 1907, United States representatives, Joseph Choate and James Scott, brought forth a request to establish a permanent judicial court that would exclude national interests and be based on international law (Scott 1908: UN Doc: P 35, 1920). Even though the U.S. had made this proposal, it had done so with a set of exclusions based on its own national interests, which included issues that involved vital interests and sovereignty. The proposal by the U.S. Jurists, Project of a Permanent Court of International Justice and Resolution, was to be a non-criminal and non-universal court. In response to the U.S. proposal, Mill stated: "Penal law is the essence of law: whereas the essence of Arbitration is compromise" (Utilaianism, Chapter IV, 24th Conf. ILA, 1907). The U.S. proposal never attained any support and no other provisions for a criminal court were officially proposed (24th Conf. ILA, 1907). Nations still refused to be controlled or bound by decisions of a court that they could not direct.

The 1907 Hague Conventions resulted in the furtherance of international law and customs as they related to military affairs. It restated the 1899 agreements, expanding and refining them. However, no provisions were made for a permanent ICC or enforcement mechanisms. Nations were for prosecution of treaty violations, including their own citizens or captured belligerents from other nations. Issues of sovereignty, international law, and the dominance of domestic law versus an overarching body of international law remained the custom for state practices. The concern for an international criminal court did not surface again until a retrospective evaluation of international events following WWI.

Nations soon found themselves in a decade of international battles and wars. In 1914, following the assassination of the Austrian Archduke Ferdinand and his wife in Sarajevo by a member of the Serbian-based anarchist terrorist group, the Black Hand, Austria declared war on Serbia. Germany declared war on Russia and France, then intruded into Belgium. England reacted to its commitment to protect Belgium's borders and joined the conflict. Other allies soon joined the three major powers: Turkey, Bulgaria, Japan, Italy, Romania, Greece, and, eventually, the United States. By 1914, twenty-three out of forty-eight European nations were at war. Prior treaties and conventions were put to the wayside as the war progressed; the "rules" of war were apparently deemed superfluous and flagrantly violated. November of 1918, the end of WWI, brought a time of devastation, high death tolls, a need for nation rebuilding, and a yearning for peace. Yet, this epoch of history brought a new chapter for the development of criminal responsibility of war crimes (Bassiouni 1973). The interest in an ICC was embraced by some nations and once again put on the international forum for discussion.

The Paris Peace Conference convened in Versailles in January 1919. The victors of WWI first sought a peace treaty with the defeated Germany and established two Commissions (UN Doc. A/CN.4/7/Rev.1UN No. 1949. V. 8). One Commission was to report on the plausibility for a League of Nations and the other Commission was to report all violations of international law, though limited to the defeated states (Bassiouni 1973; Ferencz 1980). The Treaty of Versailles would become a historical frame for future international law violations.

The League of Nations was established in April 1919. The atrocities and devastation of WWI prompted M. Leon Bourgeois of France to propose to the League of Nations the establishment of an ICC with an international Army to enforce the decisions of the court. The U.S. delegates refused consent to create an ICC without a precedence of international law and unknown to state practices (e.g., criminal prosecution of state leaders and expanding jurisdiction of international law beyond inter-state relations). The U.S. favored national military tribunals that followed national court precedents or the Court of International Justice and Arbitration. The Netherlands favored a Permanent Court of International Justice (UN Doc, P: 35, Article 1,14: 1920). The proposed ICC by France failed to gain enough support and had overwhelming opposition. Thus, an International High Tribunal consisting of twenty-two members was formed to address the violations of international law that had been committed by Germany and its Allies. However, this era too was plagued by conflicts between national interests, sovereignty, and international law. For example, the U.S. and Japan held strong reservations as to what should constitute international law, limitations to jurisdiction, and what was to be considered violations of the Rules of War. In spite of U.S. objections, the Commission on Responsibility of the Authors of War and Enforcement of Penalties proposed a special tribunal for the Emperor of Germany, for the "supreme offense against international morality and the sanctity of treaties" (Treaty of Peace, 1919: Article 227). The U.S. opposed concepts of criminal liability imposed for war acts that included state leaders and the waging of unlawful war; yet, the tribunal was still created but failed to be utilized as the Netherlands refused to extradite war criminals.

The Germans began diplomatic efforts to prevent the extradition of listed war criminals. The Japanese did not concede that international law was founded on penal law and would have serious "consequences that would be created in the history of international law by the prosecution for breaches of the laws and customs of war of enemy heads of states" (Bassiouni and Nando 1973: 567). The internal conflicts that arose from the non-used military tribunals and the lack of prosecution continued to illustrate the contradictions between international law and nations. These conflicts would continue to be the center of debate with the upcoming Jurists Committee's proposal.

Under Article 14 of the newly drafted Charter for the League of Nations, a permanent international court was to be created. In 1920, a Committee of Jurists was appointed to undertake the duty of attempting to fulfill Article 14 (Procèss-Verbaux of Proceedings of Committee, The Hague 1920). The Advisory Committee submitted a Resolution to establish a high court of international justice to try crimes in breach of international public order or against the universal law of nations (Hudson 1938). The concepts of international public order and a universal law of nations became highly debated and received little support from the parties to the League of Nations or the U.S. (Minutes of the Council, 10th session 1920).

Baron Descamps of Belgium, Chair of the Committee of Jurists, had remained in full support of creating an ICC. The notion of a court as a permanent international entity versus an *ex post facto* (after the fact) creation seemed to be the solution to the previous failings of the prosecution of German high officials. The Norwegian Jurist was adamantly opposed to an ICC and suggested the proposal fell out of the Committee's authority. Japan's member reiterated this objection. Holland's member, Mr. Loder, wanted an agreed upon definition of international crimes before consenting to such a proposal. Member after member viewed the attempt to establish an ICC without the definition and codification of international law as violating *nullem crimen sine lege*[3] (no crime without law). Thus, an ICC was perceived as premature (Ferencz 1980). Elihu Root, from the U.S., had participated in attempts to establish an ICC several years earlier. Just as his previous proposals had reservations founded on the U.S. concerns of its sovereignty and national interests, Root's participation in the Committee of Jurists was a diplomatic maneuver. Root's recommendation was to implement a High Court of Justice as a part of the League of Nations (Procès-Verbaux 1920 The Hague). The First Assembly of the League of Nations accepted the outcome of the Committee of Jurists: an ICC was premature and the concept was again put on the shelf. As the world had entered a momentary phase of peace, public and political pressure for an ICC temporarily subsided.

While the concept of an ICC was met with little enthusiasm by many nations, the International Law Association (ILA, founded in 1873) continued to promote the concept along with many scholars (ILA Report of 1873). In September 1924, the League of Nations resolved to create a special committee for codification of international law in attempt to halt many of the previous arguments against an ICC (Fifth Assembly Resolution 1926). In Vienna, 1926, the ILA again met with Committee members appointed by the Executive Council of the League to discuss the matter of an ICC. The conclusion drawn was that a court was "not only expedient but also practicable" (International Law Report, 1926: 34: 109). In 1926 the ILA approved a plan for an ICC and proposed codification of international law. A draft by Hugh Bellot was used and modified as a premise for an ICC. Bellot had established himself as the leading proponent for an ICC; however, his efforts were not fulfilled within his life as he died at a Conference in Warsaw in 1928 (Ferencz 1980). The Association recommended that the proposed court also be a penal court and be situated at The Hague; however, the concept of states being culpable for offenses outside of their territory was still at the center of controversy over issues of sovereignty and a court's jurisdiction remained unresolved (International Law Report, 1926; 34: 106). The leading nations were not ready to comply with a court that demanded compulsory jurisdiction.

The underlying contradiction of an international system (an ideology of an international society) versus sovereign nations (existing international relations) remained a fixture of conflict for the next several decades. As an ICC failed to materialize, nations relied on conferences, treaties of non-aggression, conventions, and potential codification meetings as a medium for addressing international relations (e.g., Paris Pact of 1928; Kellogg-Briand Pact 1928; Resolution of the Sixth Pan-American Conference 1928; Convention on the Definition of Aggressor, London 1933; Anti War Treaty of Non-aggression and Conciliation, Rio de Janeiro 1933; Geneva Conventions of 1925; and International Conventions on Amelioration of the Wounded, Geneva 1929) (Bassiouni 1973). These reinforced the common practice of international law as an inter-state tool versus a system of universality; essentially international law was operating as a system of diplomatic agreements, not a binding regulatory institution. Negotiations or discussions for an ICC would not arise again until the next major international conflict occurred. Yet, the very existence of these accords served the purpose of continuing to build a framework for and a body of international law—which provided an a priori enhancement of the legitimacy of the ICC notion itself.

In summary, these initial attempts to create an ICC met with resistance. States held to the ideology of sovereignty and international law as a tool for inter-state relations all the while forming an alliance of an international society (League of Nations and International Law Association). As conflicts arose, international organizations, charters, and treaties were formed to try to resolve these. As will be discussed later, these issues are one of the primary conflicts and compromises of the ICC jurisdictional powers (a complimentary system of justice).

After WWI, the League of Nations was formed to attempt to resolve the earlier conflicts of enforcing violations of inter-state relation treaties in the form of a system of universal international law. The unsuccessful outcome for an ICC and the end result of a non-materialized IMT was an example of how a conflict (between an ideology and need for universal international law) and the political cooperation of the international society (composed of different sovereign states) created further conflicts and resulted in new international laws proposed within a system of international justice. The ability for the Netherlands to refuse to extradite, thus harboring the German criminals, and Germany's diplomatic maneuvers to use international law as complimentary to and within their domestic legal system were the result of these contradictions not being resolved. The establishment of a permanent ICC was unacceptable in the form of universality and the contradictions of international society and the growing body of international law remained. Laws continued to become *jus cogens* but the concept of *erga omnes* remained unfulfilled as law was still seen as inter-state, thus not flowing to all.

1931 to 1955: Global Crisis and the Birth of the United Nations

An economic crisis engulfed the world beginning in 1929; states concentrated on their own affairs, ignoring existing concerns about an international court or the codification of international law. Nations focused on reducing expenditures in the form of limiting their military armaments. The Worldwide Disarmament Conference, convened in 1932, focused on economics and disarmament allowed some nations to briefly consider that the era might be ripe for the empowerment of the League of Nations. While this was met with less enthusiasm than previous attempts by some states, other states considered the empowerment of the League necessary due to the perceived vulnerability of nations at this time (Ferencz 1980). Germany, a large source of opposition, walked out of the conference and abstained its membership in the League of Nations. The notions of disarmament and a permanent ICC were further limited by the existing major powers. Most were unwilling to define aggression or subjugate themselves to international constraints of their power. Rather, nations turned back to rebuilding their armaments, ending the brief period that was focused on reducing expenditures or attaining disarmament; violence again took center stage in 1934.

On 9 October 1934, King Alexander of Yugoslavia and the Foreign Minister of France were killed while the King was on a visit to France (Ferencz 1980). The Romanian Minister Duca and the Austrian Chancellor Dolfuss were assassinated. Just as the murder of the Archduke Ferdinand in Sarajevo sparked international war, these unfortunate acts of terrorism (assassination) contributed to political destabilization; however, they sparked a renewed interest in establishing international justice. The French Government sent word to the League of

Nations calling for a convention to elaborate on the repression of crimes (Bassiouni 1975).

In December 1934, France submitted a memorandum supporting the condemnation of terrorism and for the establishment of an international penal court. The League responded and formulated a committee of eleven members to begin work on a draft that was proposed for the repression of terrorist acts. The eleven members represented Belgium, the United Kingdom, Chile, Spain, France, Hungary, Italy, Poland, Switzerland, and the USSR. This committee was referred to as the Terrorism Committee (Ferencz 1980). The Commission proposed a resolution that defined terrorists' acts and proposed punishment by an ICC. The first draft contained Articles 7, 8, and 9 which proposed an ICC (Committee for the International Repression of Terrorism, 1935). The second part of the draft included the structure and function of said court. Romania was one of the leading proponents of the Draft. The U.S. diplomatically suggested the concept was a noble effort; however, they had no need to consider or participate in this Draft. Guatemala gave its complete support for France's proposal and the subsequent 1935 Draft. Other nations included their own suggestions or technical changes suited to their nations' interests and current judicial system.

The second session of the Committee on Terrorism met in 1936 to discuss observations, objections, and support of the proposed treaty. Egypt supported an ICC and the concept of compulsory jurisdiction of the court. The Netherlands refuted the jurisdiction, as its nations practice was to grant "hospitality to political refugees." The Dutch contingently accepted the draft of jurisdiction but wanted clarification of "foreseen" problems. The Committee considered these responses and revised their original draft (Committee for the International Repression of Terrorism 1936). Part of this revision was the separation of the Terrorism Treaty into two separate Treaties: (1) the Repression of Terrorism Convention, and (2) a treaty for an ICC. This allowed any states that objected to an ICC to adopt the Terrorism Convention; but, no state could adopt the ICC Treaty without adopting the Terrorism Prevention Treaty. Bolivia supported the final Drafts that were completed in 1936; Australia, Hungary, Norway, Venezuela, and Poland opposed the establishment of a permanent ICC (Ferencz 1980). British India had problems with the geographic location of the court since it would be inaccessible for their representatives and domestic issues of coinciding legislation. Austria would only consider jurisdiction of said court if the laws broken fell under Austrian domestic law. The USSR believed the Draft should have been limited to terrorist acts that endangered the world as a whole. The United Kingdom wanted to abandon the idea of an ICC as premature and unnecessary at that time (Committee for the International Repression of Terrorism 1936). The eleven-member committee met again for its final session to modify their draft in response to the nations' comments. The concept or mention of an ICC was vacated from the Terrorism Treaty: two separate treaties had been officially formed (Creation of an ICC and Repression of Terrorism).

In May of 1937, the Council convened a conference on the Repression of Terrorism. Thirty-six nations attended. The Final Act of the international conference was signed November 1937 (League of Nations Proceedings of the International Conference on the Repression of Terrorism 1937). By May 1938, thirteen states had signed the Convention for the Creation of an International Criminal Court: Belgium, Bulgaria, Cuba, Spain, France, Greece, Monaco, Netherlands, Romania, and Czechoslovakia. However, no state ratified this Convention, leaving it another unfulfilled attempt to establish an ICC (only one state ratified the Terrorism Convention: British/India) (League of Nations Proceedings of the International Conference on the Repression of Terrorism 1937).

The underlying obstacles of the contradiction between an "international society," sovereignty, and inter-state relations versus intra-state relations mediated by an ICC were still viewed as impermeable. Simply stated, states were unwilling to have any domestic interference by way of international jurisdiction. Nation-states would not submit themselves to the compulsory authority of another organization. The conflicts between different forms of judicial systems of states created yet another impasse for the potentiality of an ICC to be established. These conflicts, coupled with the escalating violence and emergence of wars, again, tabled the establishment of an ICC.

During the 1930s the Spanish Civil War broke out, Italy invaded Abyssinia (Ethiopia), and by 1938 Germany had begun its aggressive and militaristic policies (Bassiouni 1999). The Rhineland, located along the middle Rhine River in Germany, had again been militarized by German forces. German troops invaded Austria, Czechoslovakia, and Poland. Again, Britain and France declared war on Germany. The Soviet Union moved into the Eastern part of Poland. Russia invaded Finland. Finland in turn called upon the League of Nations for help. The Minister of France, Paul-Boncour, who had staunchly supported an ICC, believed the events in the world were a "tardy awakening of public conscience" (League of Nations Record, in Ferencz 1980: 55). Ironically, the League of Nations that had been called upon for support was in the midst of disintegrating as its members were involved in mass world conflicts. By 1940, Germany invaded Denmark, Norway, the Netherlands, Belgium, Luxembourg, and France. By 1941, Germany had invaded Greece, Yugoslavia, and finally the Soviet Union. The Hitler regime had already begun its mission of genocide. Japan attacked the U.S.; Germany (bound with Japan) declared war on the U.S. Nearly the entire world was involved in WWII. Hindsight was becoming a vision of lost opportunity.

The response to a major conflict once again brought together another body to promote an ICC. While the war was occurring, state delegates (from Belgium, Czechoslovakia, France, Greece, the Netherlands, and Luxembourg) met in London proclaiming a need for international prosecution for the atrocities being committed that were in blatant violation of international treaties, charters, and customary law. In January 1942, twenty-six nations that were at war with Germany and Japan signed a Declaration in Washington stating their allegiances and cooperation to not make peace with any of the German Axis (Italy, Japan, and Germany) (Ferencz 1980). The title of this meeting was the Declaration by United Nations. In Moscow, 1943, the United Kingdom, Soviet Union, and the United States proclaimed to be the voices of thirty-three United Nations warning Germany that prosecution at the international level was imminent (Bassiouni 1973).

During the world crisis, an unofficial group called the London International Assembly (operating under the old auspices of the League of Nations), convened to discuss the punishment of war crimes and creation of an apparatus to do so (Ferencz 1980). The members consisted of designated delegates in exile such as Dr. Benes of Czechoslovakia, Renè Cassin of France, and Dr. Marcel of Belgium. They began working on a proposal for codification of international law, as this was one of the major stumbling blocks to previous attempts to establish an ICC (UNWCC 1942). In June 1943, the London International Assembly prepared a final convention proposing an ICC be created by the newly emerging United Nations to be empowered by an International Constabulary (Historical Survey of the Question of International Criminal Jurisdiction, UN 1949). Much of their work was incorporated into the future war crime trials of German's military; however, their proposals for an ICC did not proceed much further than the past attempts, except perhaps, to remind the "international society" that the contradictions within "international society" and international law must be resolved, vis-à-vis a compulsory ICC.

Past attempts to resolve these conflicts had only successfully been addressed by settling conflicts temporarily via conventions, multilateral agreements, and treaties until the next major conflict occurred. The resolve to try German war criminals by an International Military Tribunal versus a permanent ICC was another reminder of the inability or unwillingness of state leaders to commit themselves to a higher legal authority as well as their unwillingness to submit their own ideology of sovereign nations to a system of universal international law.

The impetus for an International Military Tribunal (IMT) served three key functions: (1) bringing vindication for the atrocities of the Nazis, (2) establishing a thorough historical record of Nazi atrocities, and (3) to generate deterrence against future genocides and war crimes (Ferencz 1980). Yet, even an *ex post facto* ad hoc form of international justice was ridden with conflicts over the technicalities of procedure and precedence of international law. Conflicts emerged over the contradictions of divergent national systems in this newly arranged international society. The drafting of the IMT Charter proved a difficult task. The contrasts between civil law, adversarial common law, and "Socialist Justice" brought about a mixture of processes. The problematical outcomes that arise from divergent systems of justice will again resurface in conflicts during the establishment of the Rome statute and the ICC. Once the procedural and legal issues were resolved, the charter of the IMT was appended to the London Agreement in August 1945.

At nearly the same time in 1945, representatives of fifty states assembled in San Francisco to agree on a charter for an international organization to maintain peace and security called the United Nations. This included the role of the Security Council in the UN and a bitter debate over an ICC (United Nations Conference on International Organization 1945). The U.S. and the Soviet Union led the opposition for an independent judicial organ with compulsory jurisdiction. Just as the U.S. Senate had doused the U.S. membership in the League of Nations, it also squashed the jurisdiction of the Court of Justice unless it was in U.S. interests (Ferencz 1980). The result of this Conference led to the Ad hoc and International Court of Justice with limited powers.

At the end of the Nuremberg trials, 1 October 1946, a long effort to create an ICC began. The United Nations now replaced the League of Nations. The UN appointed the Economic and Social Council (ECOSOC) to report on the advisability of bringing under the UN all activities previously carried out by the League of Nations and the International Penal and Penitentiary Commission (ESC Res 7(1)). The UN Charter continued a precedent formulated by the League to develop international law and its codification. The first steps to codify international law and to establish a permanent ICC had begun. The stated vision was for a permanent, competent and empowered ICC to adjudicate war crimes and crimes against peace. Designed to remove the longstanding argument of *ex post facto*, it was hoped a codified standard of international law would be developed (Harris 1999).

The International Congress (IC) (composed of international lawyers from twenty-two states and the prosecuting powers of the IMT) convened in Paris to call for an ICC. Leading the initiation for an ICC was Judge Henri Donnediu de Vabres, the French Judge on the IMT. He made two proposals. One was for a permanent ICC and the other was to establish a criminal chamber within the existing Court of Justice. The Dutch representative fully supported the French proposal for an ICC. Russia, Yugoslavia, Poland, and Egypt believed that an attempt to establish an ICC was out of the jurisdiction of the Committee's mandate and that it would be contrary to Article 7 of the UN Charter (the Court of Justice without mandatory jurisdiction is mentioned) (Ferencz 1980). Article 7 states, "such subsidiary organs as may be found necessary may be established in accordance with the present Charter." Since the U.S. had reservations about the court, the U.S. representative suggested the matter be transferred to a commission of experts.

In the wake of the holocaust, the Economic and Social Committee (ECOSOC) was also working on a mandate to study and formalize a convention dealing with genocide. The Secretary General consulted with members of the International Penal Law Association and other international law experts (Ferencz 1980). A first draft included the proposal for an ICC. The proposal provided for two types of courts: a permanent ICC or an ad hoc Tribunal to address crimes of genocide. This was submitted to states to choose the most acceptable form of court according to their interests and willingness to support (UN Doc

A/332 and A/336 1947). State responses were both favorable and unfavorable to a permanent ICC. Many included their own interests and suggestions to the proposal. Haiti favored the proposal but suggested the Court of Justice at The Hague be given mandatory jurisdiction over international crimes. Venezuela adamantly opposed any form of compulsory jurisdiction or extradition requirements. The U.S. supported an International Court in the form of ad hoc Tribunals and recommended the matter be given to the International Law Association (ILA) for deliberation (Ferencz 1980). France was in full support of a permanent ICC that would have mandatory jurisdiction. Other states including the USSR, Egypt, Brazil, and the United Kingdom failed to respond, as they believed the subject of an ICC required further study.

In the interim, the United Nations General Assembly considered the proposals made by the IC and the ECOSOC including transferring the proposal for an ICC to the ILA, when they convened for the drafting of the Convention on the Prevention and Punishment of Genocide (Harris 1999). This resolution was coupled with another resolution by the U.S., Netherlands, and several other states that had been active in the aforementioned draft of genocide. The second resolution requested an International Law Commission study the desirability for a criminal chamber of the Court of Justice.

In December 1948, the General Assembly passed the proposal on and requested the International Law Commission (ILC) consider the possibility of creating a permanent ICC and/or creating a chamber within the Court of Justice, while they were formulating the principles of international law (Ferencz 1980).

The efforts advanced by some international organizations to create an ICC as a part of the Genocide Convention ended in 1948. The hope for an ICC did not completely wither as the ILC would continue the battle to establish an ICC. The UN appeared to be fully committed to an international society, international law, and an ICC. This is traced with the attempts of codification of international crimes and with the draft statute for an ICC (Bassiouni 1999). The UN Charter also institutionalized social representation and allowed NGO's a consultative role (Hampson 2002). This historic change to integrating civil society in a formal international institution would play a significant role in the future development of an ICC.

The International Law Commission (ILC) (composed of fifteen members) convened their first annual session in April 1949 to tackle the responsibility the General Assembly had passed on to it (Ferencz 1980). This included the formulation of the principles of international law, a code of offenses against peace and security, a code of international crimes, and a judicial organ. At the same time the Rapporteurs of the ILC were working on their agenda, several Conventions were signed in Geneva that would aid the ILC in attempts to carry out its mission: most significant was the acknowledgment of a foreign court having jurisdiction over war criminals of another state. This proposal cut right into the issue of state sovereignty. If a useful and independent ICC was to be established, states must transfer some of their autonomy to the body. A court, which cannot act on its own, which nations did not submit to, would have little ability to control or punish the actions of criminal individuals and organizations.

The ILC formed subcommittees to tackle the demands of the UN General Assembly. A special Rapporteur was appointed to prepare a draft Code of Offences Against the Peace and Security of Mankind, and another Rapporteur was assigned to formulate a draft for an ICC (Bassiouni 1999; UN Doc A/CN.4/15 (1950). The first report submitted to the ILC was a report on an ICC. This report condemned the separation of formulating a substantive criminal code and a statute for an ICC, as they were complimentary. A second Rapporteur was then appointed to develop a draft for an ICC. The two Rapporteurs were Jean Spiropoulos and Emil Sandstrom. They had separate agendas and ideologies, which not only conflicted but reflected two trends within the world: idealism and political realism. The issues of national sovereignty, classical law of nations, and a general mistrust of any international constraints fueled conflicts for an ICC. The Soviet Union feared for its sovereignty upon the establishment of such a court, the U.S. would not accept a court at the height of the Cold War, France supported the concept of an ICC but did not attempt to use political weight to ensure its position, and the United Kingdom regarded the matter as politically premature (Bassiouni 1999). These positions were not new in the bitter battle to establish an empowered ICC. One of the defining features of the classic nation-state is its right to self-regulate; making its own laws; establishing its own courts; determining its own foreign, economic, and domestic policy agendas: all seen as the sole purview of a state itself. The existence of an external legal body by its very nature limits a state's liberty to pursue its interests in its own fashion.

The General Assembly formed another Special Committee in 1950 that was composed of seventeen states to draft a convention to establish an ICC. This Committee completed its first draft in 1951 that modeled the International Court of Justice (UN Doc A/2136, A/2186, A/2186/Add 1, November 1952). The Committee agreed, "the court should be a permanent body but should only function in case of need, and that it would be concerned with individuals, not bodies corporate" (UN Doc A/2136, A/2186, A/2186/Add 1, November 1952). The court should be conceived through a Convention but remain linked with the United Nations. There remained many objections to the clarifications of the role of the court. For example, the U.S. wanted the court open only for signatory states and France wanted the court to address international crimes and lesser crimes involving states and crimes of international concern. Despite high hopes, the Sixth Committee was not able to resolve the issue. The reference to the General Assemblies note in Resolution 489 (V) reminded all that the "General Assembly had stated that it had not yet been able to take a final decision regarding the setting up of such a court. It would remain a political decision" (UN Doc A/2186 Add.1: Article 46).

The Committee's mandate was extended, memberships changed, and in 1953 it produced a revised text (Bassiouni 1999). The revised text was even less optimistic and added provisions that limited jurisdiction and did not bind states.

One provision also gave states the ability to withdraw jurisdiction when the court was conferred. The Draft was submitted to the General Assembly. However, the General Assembly felt compelled to first consider the ILC's Draft Code of Offences, which to date was not completed. The outcome of the 1953 Committee's proposal put a damper on hope for an ICC that many held (Francis Biddle, Justice Jackson, Henri Donnedieu de Vabres, Sir Fyfe, and Telford Taylor). Many states had succeeded in again postponing accountability at the international level. Only three of the seventeen representatives (the Netherlands, France, and Israel) advocated a permanent empowered ICC. The statute for an ICC was thus tabled again until the completion of the Code of Offences.

In 1954, the ILC completed the draft Code of Crimes Against Peace and Security; however, a consensus could still not be reached on a draft for an ICC (Hampson 2002). The Final Draft Code consisted of only four articles (UN Doc A/2693, 1954). Article 2 of the draft code outlines thirteen offenses including unprovoked state aggression on another state, generating civil strife in another state, political or economic coercion, genocide and other human rights violations, and violations of the laws of war. Article 3 refuses to excuse someone acting as Head of State from culpability. Article 4, in direct response to issues which arose in the Nuremberg trials, clearly states that: "The fact that a person charged with an offense defined in the Code acted in pursuant to an order of his Government or of a superior does not relieve him of responsibility in international law, if the circumstances at the time, it was possible for him not to comply with that order."

Now, under international law, not only is a citizen theoretically or morally obligated to question orders to engage in aggression or illegal acts, but also they are legally responsible to do so if they want to protect themselves from prosecution. Such a condition greatly bothered many nations, like the United States, that continued to seek immunity from the culpability of their actions on the international stage.

Missing from this draft was any mention of an ICC as well as the controversial definition for aggression (UN Doc A/2693, 1954). What appeared as hope for the Committee for establishing an ICC would soon disintegrate. The Sixth Committee of the UN reviewed the Draft and the only consensus that could be reached was that no decision could be made on the Code of Offences. The Committee further requested that an enlarged Committee should be created to define aggression. This committee was composed of nineteen members who were to report back in 1956 (Ferencz 1999). This further extended the 1953 Committee's draft for an ICC for consideration.

In summary, following WWII the "international society" became distended. International law was viewed as essential for more than inter-state relations. The realization that no court had been formed to penalize the mass atrocities and international violations of WWII due to previous conflicts between states over issues of international law and issues of sovereignty was more than evident for the "victor allies." The position of the U.S. on international law and penalization had taken a turn for the first time since the late 1800s. The U.S. Representative, Justice Robert Jackson, headed the IMT. Jackson believed fully in the rule of law and sought to establish the same standard for international law through forming the Nuremberg Principles: universal international law that was viewed as both *jus cogens* and *erga omnes*. For the Victors, issues of sovereignty for Germany no longer were significant enough to allow Germany to prosecute their own under domestic law. An international body to penalize was viewed favorably. The form it was to take, however, remained a topic of controversy and the result again was an *ad hoc* IMT.

The codification of the Nuremberg Principles reflected a changing ideology—one of universally applied international law. An image of an international society became more predominant. This included language used by non-governmental organizations that focused on international humanitarian laws perceived as an inherent right for all mankind. The Nuremberg Principles conveyed a cultural message even though there was not a permanent ICC for enforcement. The Nuremberg Trials and the creation of the United Nations brought with it the continuation of previous attempts to create an ICC and an enlargement of "international society" as NGOs joined the political realm and membership in the UN expanded. The argument of international law as inter-state was no longer a prevailing ideology. However, issues of jurisdiction, sovereignty, and *erga omnes* remained sources of conflict for many states.

1956 to 1973: The Cold War Intermission

Although many other committees were formed every few years (1954-1957, 1959-1967, and 1967-1974) with the task of defining aggression and formatting a Draft of Offences, the political climate only hampered their success (Bassiouni 1997). During this time the Draft for an ICC lay dormant. As different bodies worked separately in Geneva and New York, divergent texts were produced and submitted at different times. It became an easy solution for the General Assembly to table successive drafts as one or the other committees had not finished its task. Another reason the Drafts were continually tabled was due to the political will of the five "superpowers" (e.g., China, France, the UK, the U.S., and the USSR) that were in conflict and mostly in opposition to the establishment of an ICC as the world was at a position of division and at risk for war. It was the era of the Cold War; mistrust ran rampant. The French were involved in a bitter conflict with Vietnam, which the U.S. supported financially and militarily. Many states, the Soviet Union, Ukraine, United Kingdom, Venezuela, Poland, and Czechoslovakia were concerned that an ICC would interfere with their internal affairs.

International conflicts continued to erupt. War between the North and South Vietnam exploded. Soviet troops invaded Hungary. War broke out in the Middle East. The French sent troops to the Suez. The Cuban Missile Crisis occurred. Cyprus erupted in violence. The U.S. invaded Cambodia. Pakistan and India were in conflict. The Six-Day War occurred. Pakistan was involved in mass atrocities. Bangladesh suffered the loss of thousands that were massacred. Wars for independence raged across the African continent. It appeared that the last agenda for this epoch in history was to define aggression or establish an ICC, as so many states were busy committing aggression, ensuring their interests, and refusing to consider a higher legal authority of constraint against them. In the interim, the UN consistently pointed to atrocities in the world that violated the Nuremberg Principles. Due to their lack of enforcement power the UN was limited to the purely symbolic gestures of vocal condemnation and patronizing the violators.

Many of the political and historical forces at play during this period can be seen in the examination of one military conflict: the war between North and South Vietnam. Originally begun as a war of independence from colonial French dominance, this conflict developed into a staging area for existing Cold War tensions between the U.S. and USSR. Both super-powers poured military personnel into the two countries, extending and intensifying the civil war. Ignoring the UN charter and the working definition of aggression and aggressor states, the U.S., the USSR, and their allies devastated the lands and peoples of the small South Asian nation. War crimes in the form of violations of the Geneva Conventions were committed by both sides (e.g., U.S. troops' destruction of My Lai, routine torture of prisoners in the so-called "Hanoi Hilton"). The war also poured over Vietnam's borders, with the U.S. illegally invading Laos and bombing Cambodia. Any optimism for an international court of justice or for true peaceable international cooperation generated by the post-World War II experience evaporated as the Cold War, and its many inspired "hot" conflicts, ranged around the world.

To sum up, during the Cold War the U.S. fell back on its earlier positions of self-interest, sovereignty, and inter-state international law. The role of the Security Council in the UN is an illustration of these concerns. The work toward an ICC continued in the Commissions set forth by the UN, which included the processes of codifying international law and defining the Crimes Against Humanity Offences over the next decade. However, the U.S. remained adamant that it would not accept or support an empowered permanent ICC at the height of the Cold War. In the interim, conflicts arose and the international society again found itself in strife as states committed aggression on other states, pursued their interests, and invaded territories of others.

1974 to 1997: International Ideology Begins to Shift

With the end of the Vietnam War, some of the tensions between the major powers subsided; however, violence still erupted in the Middle East. Public outcries, involvement of NGOs, and efforts by scholars and statesmen seemed to spark the movement of the Special Committee to Define Aggression (Ferencz 1999). On 14 December 1974, the Definition of Aggression made it to the UN General

Assembly and was accepted by consensus. Although the definition was ambiguous and left itself open for individual state interpretation, the barrier to consider an ICC had been "officially" removed. The Legal Counsel of the UN, Professor Suy, approached the delegates with the reminder that the time for considering the Draft Code (now over twenty years old) and an ICC was upon them. Many states responded. The U.S. considered expanding the jurisdiction of the International Court of Justice in a Senate Resolution. The State Department recommended the U.S. repeal the Connally Amendment and accept jurisdiction of the World Court (Ferencz 1999). Of course, this would still fail to achieve what other states were attempting to establish: a permanent criminal court with compulsory jurisdiction and empowerment. Secretary General Waldheim presented a report to the Assembly for all states to accept compulsory jurisdiction and "to withdraw the extensive and self-defeating reservations" (Waldheim 1974: in Ferencz 1999: 77).

In July of 1977, the ILC reminded the General Assembly that Resolution 1186 (xii) of 1954 had been deferred until aggression had been defined and suggested it should review the topics for a Draft Code of Offences and a Draft for an ICC again (Ferencz 1999). Several states, Mexico, Panama, Syria, the Philippines, Barbados, Fiji, Nigeria, and Cyprus agreed and pushed for the reopening of attempts to conclude the Drafts. The proposal sat until 1978 for reconsideration. The International Association of Penal Law continued to promote a criminal code and an ICC. Among its members, M. Cherif Bassiouni and Ved Nando of the U.S. were the strongest supporters to further the work that had began over twenty years ago. The General Assembly again tabled the suggestion to reopen the Committees work on a Draft Code of Offences and an ICC due to the underlying controversy surrounding the growth of the UN (from less than sixty members in the 1950s to over 150 members in the late 1970s) (UN Doc A/33/45 Supp No. 45, 1978/79).

In 1981, the General Assembly again formally requested that the ILC work on the Draft Code of Crimes. Members of the ILC reiterated the need to establish a mechanism to act as a constraint and enforcement of the upcoming implementations. Continuous appeals to the General Assembly were made by the ILC to consider again the Draft for an ICC. However, it would take several more years, filled with changes in geopolitical relations, before the GA reacts to the ILC's requests.

The 1980s indicated a change in world attitudes among many states. The U.S.-Soviet hostilities had declined. The USSR General Secretary Gorbechev sent a letter to the UN proposing the establishment of a global security plan that included strengthening enforcement of the rule of international law. Transnational Corporations were expanding at a rapid pace and many states felt a legal mechanism needed to be formed for constraint and control of transnational actors (Hampson 2002). New forms of perceived security threats encouraged states to consider an ICC to control terrorism, drug trafficking, and hijacking. In December 1988, the General Assembly asked the ILC to consider the Code of

Offences implementation. In 1989, a Coalition of sixteen Latin American and Caribbean states (headed by Trinidad and Tobago) requested the UN address the growing problem of drug trafficking (Sadat 2002). The General Assembly convened a special session addressing these problems. Trinidad and Tobago proposed that a specialized international criminal court be created. The General Assembly made an official request for the ILC to prepare a report on establishing an ICC for drug trafficking offenders.

Contemporaneously, the International Institute of Higher Studies in Criminal Sciences in conjunction with the UN (Chaired by M. Cherif Bassiouni) prepared a draft statute for an ICC with jurisdiction over all international crimes. This draft was submitted to the Eight United Nations Congress on Crime Prevention and Treatment of Offenders in 1990 and further recommended that the ILC consider this draft (Bassiouni 1999). The ILC had also completed their report that the General Assembly had assigned them in 1989 and submitted it to the forty-fifth session of the General Assembly. The report did not limit the concept of a court to drug trafficking, but was expanded to include a more universal criminal court that would cover other forms of international crimes (Bassiouni 1999). The General Assembly requested the ILC continue to prepare a comprehensive statute for an ICC. The ILC had also adopted a Draft code of Crimes in 1991 (Sadat 2002).

In 1992, the ILC created a working group, chaired by Abdul Koroma of Sierra Leone, to specifically work on a statute for an ICC. The ILC working group submitted a report composed of several propositions which included: an ICC be established in the form of a treaty agreed upon by state parties; the court's jurisdiction would only cover crimes defined by international treaties in force; should not be compulsory; should be in the form of an *ad hoc* body; and must guarantee due process, independence, and impartiality (Sadat 2002). The proposals were primarily based on the work of the 1951 and 1953 committees and were later adopted into the 1994 Draft statute issued by the ILC. The General Assembly received the 1992 recommendations of the ILC at its Forty-Seventh session. The General Assembly granted the ILC a mandate to elaborate the statute as "a matter of priority" (UN GA Res 47/33 in Sadat, 2002:39). The Draft Code of Crimes had met the usual support and resistance that was to coincide with the development of an ICC. The U.S. was one of the objectors; its dissatisfaction centered on issues over the lack of a definition for aggression.[4] Some revisions did occur between the 1992 draft and the 1994 draft—primarily jurisdiction limitations and other technical changes to suit political objections by the major world powers made at the General Assembly session (Bassiouni 1999).

During 1993 and 1995 the Security Council was addressing atrocities and war crimes committed in the former Yugoslavia, mass genocide that occurred in Rwanda, and Iraq's violations of International Humanitarian Law (IHL) which aided the sense of urgency for the General Assembly to create an ICC (Bassiouni 1999). Ad hoc Tribunals were eventually established for Yugoslavia and Rwanda. This was the first time since WWII that the states came together as a body to provide investigations and prosecutions of violations of international law. However, the Security Council was becoming less willing to continue the processes of ad hoc Tribunals due to the complexities of reaching consensus on the procedures or desires for an International Military Tribunal (IMT) and because of the veto power of the Security Council which allowed the selectivity of cases that would be eligible for IMT. The growing concerns about creating IMTs brought many members of the United Nations to support a permanent ICC. Many states still held reservations on the plausibility for acceptance of an ICC without a universal desire of state leaders (especially since the U.S. was reluctant to provide any support or leadership in the development or acceptance of an ICC). During George H. W. Bush's Administration (1989-1993), such hesitancy was a matter of U.S. Foreign Policy. The concern was intensified with the International Court of Justice's adverse ruling in the Nicaragua case as well as the potential threat of undermining the State department's existing international "law enforcements" (Bassiouni 1999). The ICJ found that the United States violated international law by supporting Contra guerrillas in the war against the Nicaraguan government and by mining Nicaragua's harbors. The Clinton Administration (1993-2001) displayed a diplomatic interest in the development of an ICC and participated in the creation of an ICC that would also be suited to U.S. interests (this entailed ensuring limitations on jurisdiction and the Security Council's decisions for charges of crimes). Essentially, the U.S. played a role to ensure it would not be subjected to the jurisdiction of the court's power or authority without state consent to protect itself from prosecution against any violations of international law that occurred as the U.S. pursued its economic and foreign policy interests. The insistence on the Security Council having a role in the cases to be tried under the ICC jurisdiction was to ensure veto power for the U.S. to exercise if a case was brought forward against the U.S., its current allies, or foreign policy interests.

Two drafts for an ICC were drawn up by the ILC in 1994 addressing different political concerns. The final agreed upon report was ready to be submitted to the General Assembly. However, the report remained ambiguous about certain controversial topics such as the financing of the court, definition of crimes to be covered by the court, jurisdictional matters, and the organizational structure (Sadat 2002). The 1994 ILC's final report on the statute for an ICC was submitted to the Forty-Ninth Session of the General Assembly (GA), which tabled consideration until the Fiftieth Session (Bassiouni 1999). However, the GA did form an ad hoc committee to discuss the substantive and administrative issues of the ILC's report: the 1995 Ad Hoc Committee for the Establishment of an International Criminal Court (chaired by the Ministry of Foreign Affairs for the Netherlands) (Res 49/53). In the Resolution forming the Ad Hoc Committee, the GA separated the ILC's 1994 Draft Statute for an ICC and its 1991 Draft Code of Crimes Against Peace and Security of Mankind. This was done in response to the amount of members working on each draft as well as the number of participants (NGOs and GOs not formally in committee membership but able to put forth proposals).

The Ad Hoc Committee met twice in 1995 (April thru August) to review the Commission's report on the establishment of an ICC and rendered their report back to the GA (Sadat 2002; Bassiouni 1999). Upon receiving the results from the Ad Hoc Committee, the GA set forth to establish the 1996 Preparatory Committee on the Establishment of an International Criminal Court. The Ad Hoc committee continued to focus on the feasibility of establishing an ICC while the Preparatory Committee focused on the text of such a court.

The meetings held by the Preparatory Committee consisted of an open forum for all members of the United Nations, and for specialized agencies in international law or humanitarian efforts (Bassiouni 1999). These groups consisted of the International Institute of Higher Studies, members of the Bureau and working group from the Netherlands, NGOs (thirty organizations began the Coalition for a Criminal Court in 1995 and grew to over eight hundred NGOs within three years), Australia, Austria, Argentina, Belgium, Canada, Chili, Croatia, Denmark, Egypt, Finland, Germany, Greece, Guatemala, Hungary, Ireland, Italy, Lesotho, Netherlands, New Zealand, Norway, Portugal, Samoa, Slovakia, South Africa, Sweden, Switzerland, Trinidad, Tobago, Uruguay, and Venezuela (Bassiouni 1999, Vol 3:623; Shelton 2000). All of them played significant roles in advancing the concept for an ICC.

A preliminary report that compiled various proposals was submitted to the General Assembly at the Fifty-First session in 1996 requesting an extension for the Preparatory Committee to negotiate proposals made to them to consolidate into a text for a statute. The GA complied and extended the original date of 1996 to 1998 passing Resolution 51/207 for holding a diplomatic conference of plenipotentiaries in 1998 (Cooper 2002). With the renewed mandate from the GA, the Preparatory Committee set about formulating the list and definitions of crimes, principles of law and penalties, court's organization, procedures, trigger mechanisms, state cooperation, relationship of court to the UN, and financial matters. The potential for establishing an ICC was viewed in a more positive light, which sparked a stage of negotiations over the next two years. The Preparatory Committee had six official meetings between those years. In April 1998, the Committee had finalized a draft statute to be considered at the convening 1998 Diplomatic Conference (Cassesse 2002). The range of participation to establish an ICC by states, inter-governmental, and non-governmental organizations indicates the assortment of interests. The variety of interests from multiple actors will later result in lengthy and contentious discussions over the complexities involved in establishing an ICC in lieu of the existing conflicts contained within the realm of contradictions of an "international society."

To sum up, by the 1970s and 1980s many of the conflicts of international society had lessoned and members of the international society continued to push for an empowered ICC. This included NGOs, the ILC, International Institute of Higher Studies in Criminal Science, the USSR, Trinidad, and Tobago. However, the issues of a court with universality and an international society composed of sovereign states, some unwilling to relinquish their impermeable borders to a system of universal international law, remained a conflict and ensured major obstacles for the work on the ICC in the 1990s.

The 1990s represent a major historical contingency: new legal approaches to the conflicts of international society resurfaced with a renewed verve. During the 1996 PrepCom Reports, a large number of contending proposals were submitted. These contained various national positions regarding sovereignty, common law systems, civil law systems, divergent crimes to be covered, penalties applied by the Court, role of the Security Council, the role of the Prosecutor, and other major issues that had divided earlier progress for an ICC (GA Fifty-first Session 1996). These same controversial topics were again at the center of debate during the 1998 conference of plenipotentiaries. Although the U.S. was an active participant in the negotiations and formation of proposals for an ICC in the 1990s, the position of the U.S. during the Clinton Administration remained intent on ensuring the ICC did not impede upon the sovereignty of the U.S. or interfere with any U.S. foreign policy or practices. Much of the U.S. support could be viewed as self-interested or symbolic. Many of the political gestures that were made during the negotiations were designed to appease the conflicting LMS positions. The result of the six PrepCom meetings was the disaggregating of the former proposals into a workable set of compromises for the 1998 Plenipotentiaries Meeting.

Summary

From the onset, attempts to establish an ICC were met with resistance. To relinquish territorial domestic law to a universality of international law would have required states to accept universal jurisdiction versus international law governing only inter-state issues. The result would have endangered the sovereignty that many states saw as essential for their safety, political interests, and political or national ideologies. The core element of this conflict arises from the contradiction of an "international society." Territories, borders, government, and domestic judicial systems have fundamentally been viewed as the foundation of states. International law was founded on and with acceptance of statehood and state sovereignty.

The earliest international treaties, charters, customs, and laws were based solely on inter-state relations (UN Doc 2003). The attempt to create a universality of international common good, international common law, and an ICC with universal jurisdiction for an international society implied a need for porous state borders. The contradiction of sovereign of states structuring an international society versus the ideology of a unified international society has resulted in decades of conflicts over the attempts to establish an ICC.

These conflicts and the fundamental contradiction of international society led to *ad hoc* international systems of justice (IMT, World Court of Justice,

Court of Arbitration, and non-empowered international organizations) rather than an empowered universal criminal court. All of these international organizations are the result of attempts to address specific conflicts (Franco-Prussian War, WWI, WWII, Assassination of Leaders, Terrorism, Drug Trafficking). Customary international law, treaties, and charters have historically been viewed as *jus cogens*. However, international law was initiated and advanced under the premise of independent sovereign states and as a frame for inter-state relations. Thus, it often failed to achieve the level of *erga omnes*. This coupled with a non-empowered universal system of justice resulted in the failure of these organizations to constrain future conflicts.

Historical attempts to establish an international system of justice that is empowered and universalistic have illustrated how the contradictions of an international society constrain the potential outcome for such an institution. What has resulted from the conflicts that arose as a result of these international contradictions are *ad hoc* entities, non-empowered systems of justice, and the establishment of new international laws without a corresponding change in ideology within international society and/or international law (during the late 1800s through the 1930s).

As contemporary efforts were made to establish an ICC, the presence of a changing ideology yielded new principles used to guide international law. This change in values or principles is evident in the rhetoric used within international organizations such as the UN, Amnesty International, Human Rights Organizations, and the International Law Association, which refer to international society and existing relations as a community. This expresses a naturalistic view as well as common goals, interests, values, and ethos that are shared among all members. However, this new ideology (principle and value) remains in direct conflict with the composition of international society and the relations between states. At the base of the contradiction between international society and the ideal type or ideology of international society are the issues of sovereign rule (Austinian concept) and jurisdiction. Rather than attempting to resolve the underlying contradiction of the structure and ideology of international relations, the ideological principles and goals for a unified international society was injected into attempts to establish an ICC.

Notes

1 The ILA is composed of lawyers in private practice, academia, government, and the judiciary, to non-lawyer experts and has consultative status, as an international non-governmental organization

2. It should be noted that the U.S. did not become a signatory to this or participate in the process of the Maritime Paris Peace Treaty because of issues of sovereignty.

3. There can be no crime without a preceding law.

4. Aggression had been defined by the Special Committee to Define Aggression in 1974 and was accepted with consensus by the UN. However, it remained vague and

ambiguous. The definition for aggression was not codified within international law, treaties, or a resolution.

Chapter IV

The Rome Statute of the International Criminal Court

The previously discussed Prepatory Committee Meetings (held during 1995-1997) provided the frame for the Rome Statute Diplomatic Conference of 1998. This chapter begins with a discussion of the Rome Conference focusing on the contentious subject of jurisdiction and state sovereignty. Then, we provide a section giving a descriptive account of the current status of the Rome Statute of the International Criminal Court. This is followed by a segment examining the U.S. reaction to the ICC, followed by a brief summary of the chapter.

The Rome Conference

15 June 1998 marked the end of decades of work to establish an ICC and the commencement of a five-week Diplomatic Conference that resulted in the Rome Statute of an International Criminal Court. The large number of delegates presented many difficulties for the process of the Conference. Informal working groups and "informal-informal working groups" were created to address various articles of the working draft statute (Bassiouni 1999: 628). The piecemeal construction of these articles and working in six languages made it difficult for the Committee to maintain consistency and attain consensus. The most contentious subject matters (Part II, Articles 5-21) were not discussed until the final sessions. These included all the major political issues that created conflict: definition of crimes, jurisdiction, the role of the Security Council, and the role of the prosecutor (Bassiouni 1999).

Significant conflicts occurred over resolving issues of the Court's jurisdiction and its ability to exercise that jurisdiction (Cassesse 2002). States held incompatible views regarding the role of the Court. As previously mentioned, the issue of jurisdiction was a major constraint that inhibited previous attempts to establish an ICC as well as a major contention in the development of the Rome Statute. This is due to several factors. From the theoretical frame of critical international law, jurisdiction symbolizes the root of the contradiction between international relations (international society as it is) and the ideology or ideal type of international society presented in principle (the ought, not the is, of international relations). This includes the current composition of international society (independent sovereign states based on self governing and ultimate authority: the Austinian model of positivism) and the principles that are portrayed as consensus, common values, goals, and interests (naturalism and the innate consciousness of absolute norms).[1]

Many states supported universal jurisdiction of the Court, ensuring a universal justice while other states (mainly the U.S.) insisted that the acceptance of the ICC's jurisdiction by states was a necessary precondition to jurisdiction. These two positions were heavily debated and resulted in a compromise that was not fully satisfactory to either of the conflicting forces; the "Like-Minded states" (LMS[2]) that wanted universal jurisdiction and the U.S. (the main challenger) that wanted a system based on compliance at will. The U.S.'s position was grounded in the Austinian concept of sovereignty, which holds to the traditional composition of international relations and international law. Article 1, The Court, lays out the concept of jurisdiction in the form of a complimentary Court to national courts. It states: "An International Criminal Court ('the Court') is hereby established. It shall be a permanent institution and shall have the power to exercise its jurisdiction over persons for the most serious crimes of international concern, as referred to in this jurisdiction and functioning of the Court shall be governed by the provisions of this Statute."

The dialectical processes reflected in this Article portray how both sides of the underlying contradiction (between the tradition of sovereign state relations and the principles representing the ideology of a consensual society) can be represented within the creation of new laws to which can then lead to further conflicts (Chambliss 1993).

Although there was a general consensus that crimes of genocide, war crimes, and crimes against humanity should be covered by the court's jurisdiction, there were conflicts over the scope of crimes covered under war crimes, crimes against humanity, and the definition for crimes of aggression. Despite the fact that precedence had been set for the definition of aggressive crimes during the IMT of the Nuremberg defendants and in the General Assembly Resolution 3314 (XXIX) of December 1974 (passed with a consensus for the definition of aggression), it remained an irresolvable issue for the Committee Meeting members. This precedent definition was "the use of armed force by a State against the sovereignty, territorial integrity or political independence of another State, or in any other manner inconsistent with the United Nations" (quoted from Harris 1999: 579).

During the process of negotiations of the Rome Statute in June 1998, U.S. Ambassador Bill Richardson reminded conference members that while the U.S. supported the IMT trials of Yugoslavia and Rwanda, the acceptance of any definitions or attempts to further define acts of aggression was premature for purposes of individual criminal responsibility (Harris 1999). He suggested it be tabled and the court limited to jurisdiction for genocide, crimes against humanity, and war crimes to prevent reoccurrences of those crimes. Due to an inability to produce a compromise, jurisdiction over crimes of aggression was dismissed until a final provision is adopted that defines aggression, thus the Court's jurisdiction. To date, this remains undefined. This declaration is included within Article 5 (2) (described below).

Crimes of aggression were not the only controversial crime debated during the Conference. U.S. delegates insisted that the Court's jurisdiction should only occur if a state was signatory when war crimes were committed on a large scale (Sadat 2002). This would mean that war crimes would essentially also have to be crimes against humanity before the Court could interject its jurisdiction. The U.S. was triumphant in this debate and the condition of jurisdiction over war crimes was included in Article 8 (1) as a part of Part 2 Jurisdiction, Admissibility and Applicable Law. Article 8 (1) states: "the Court shall have jurisdiction in respect of war crimes in particular when committed as part of a plan or policy or as part of a large-scale commission of such crimes."

The other crimes falling under the Court's jurisdiction that was agreed to include genocide and crimes against humanity. These are included in Article 5, crimes within the jurisdiction of the court that states:

> (1) The jurisdiction of the court shall be limited to the most serious crimes of concern to the international community as a whole. The Court has jurisdiction in accordance with this Statute with respect to the following crimes: (a) The crime of genocide; (b) Crimes against humanity; (c) War crimes; and (d) The crime of aggression.
>
> (2) The Court shall exercise jurisdiction over the crime of aggression once a provision is adopted in accordance with articles 121 and 123 defining the crime and setting out the conditions under which the Court shall exercise jurisdiction with respect to this crime.

These crimes are defined in Article 6 (genocide), Article 7 (crimes against humanity), and Article 8 (war crimes) of the Rome Statute. Crimes against humanity are reinforcement to the ideological principles of inalienable rights (naturalism) and the ethos of an international society, while at the same time are limited by an "enforcement jurisdiction which is paltry at best" (Sadat 2002: 103). The weak enforcement jurisdiction is the result of the conflict between this ideology and the traditional structure of international relations and international law.[3]

Crimes listed within the Rome Statute specifically refer to individual culpability versus an organization or state. This is defined within Article 1 and Article

25 of the Rome Statute. However, the ability of a state or organizational entity to be prosecuted has been a long-standing point of debate going back to the Nuremberg IMTs where it was argued "international crimes are committed by men not by abstract entities" (Sadat 2002: 778). During the process of meetings, the French delegate introduced a proposal for the inclusion of organizations. Thus, one Draft Statue contained an Article that would subject legal entities to the Court's jurisdiction if the crimes were committed on behalf of such legal persons or their agencies or representatives. In the end this was dismissed as contradictory to the principle of a complimentary system (Sadat 2002). The result is Article 25 (1, 2, 3, and 4) Individual Criminal Responsibility which states:

(1) The court shall have jurisdiction over natural persons pursuant to Statute.
(2) A person who commits a crime within the jurisdiction of the Court shall be individually responsible and liable for punishment in accordance with this Statute
(3) In accordance with this Statute, a person shall be criminally responsible and liable for punishment for a crime within the jurisdiction of the Court.
(4) No provision in this Statute relating to individual criminal responsibility shall affect the responsibility of States under international law.

Even though concerns regarding the contradiction of a complimentary system were addressed, Part 4 of this Article does ensure that the Court's exclusion of state responsibility is not precluded from customary international law or treaties obligations. Again, this represents the traditions of international law and international relations based on sovereign rule as the dominant principle guiding new laws while being placed within a system that represents the ideology of an international society with common ethos, goals, and principles.

Matters of jurisdiction regarding the role of the ICC and national prosecution for crimes were also a contentious subject as many states believed supporting national prosecution would enable impunity and shield perpetrators of crimes to protect their state interests (Cassesse 2002). The U.S. circulated an informal "paper" questioning whether the ICC should include domestic amnesty under jurisdiction (Meintjies 1999). This issue was viewed by some as an opportunity for states to grant impunity to individuals that had committed heinous crimes and by others as a resource for healing the nation (e.g., Truth and Reconciliation Commissions held in South Africa). The inclusion of this would have further limited the jurisdiction of the Court and given greater powers to decisions of states regarding perpetrators of the most serious crimes listed in Article 5. While Domestic Amnesty was omitted from the Rome Statute, the concerns over its misuse were indirectly covered under Article 17 (b) Issues of Admissibility. It states: "the case has been investigated by a state, which has jurisdiction over it, and the State has decided not to prosecute the person concerned, unless the decision resulted from unwillingness or inability of the State genuinely to prosecute."

Other modifications entered into the Rome Statute as a result of the five weeks of meetings included providing a format for challenging jurisdiction of the Court or admissibility of a case. This is included in Article 19 (2). It states: "Challenges to the admissibility of a case on the grounds referred to in Article 17 or challenges to the jurisdiction of the Court may be made by (b) A State which has jurisdiction over a case, on the ground that it is investigating or prosecuting the case or has investigated or prosecuted."

This Article ensures a state its rights of sovereignty for its domestic legal system and re-emphasizes the complimentary nature of the Court. This supports the tradition of international relations and sovereign determinism while negating the principle behind ensuring impunity does not occur.

The support for traditions of inter-state relations and international law that conflict with the ideological principles of universality and the mission of the Rome Statute is also evident in Article 98, The Cooperation with Respect to Waiver of Immunity and Consent to Surrender. Many of the delegates within the Prepatory Commission to the Rome Statute had apprehensions regarding conflicts between Article 98 of the Rome Statute with previous international agreements. It is for this reason Article 98 recognizes previously dated bilateral agreements concerning the surrender of an individual from a state party to an alternative third party. Article 98 of the Rome Statute states: "The court may not proceed with a request for surrender which would require the requested state to act inconsistently with its obligations under international agreements pursuant to which the consent of a sending State is required to surrender a person of that state to the Court."

The intention of Article 98 was to allow the court the attainment of waivers of immunity for prosecution *prior* to individuals being surrendered over to the ICC if that individual was covered under an existing international agreement (CICC Publication 2002). The delegates intended to address any conflicts between the Rome Statute and pre-existing international agreements or new agreements based on ones with set precedence such as Status of Force Agreements (SOFA)[4] or the Vienna Convention on Diplomatic Relations (UN Doc.A/CONF.20/13 1961).[5] This Article later becomes the focus of debate for the international society (and will be discussed in the section of the U.S. reactions to the ICC).

The position of the U.S. for supporting the ICC was evident during the final days of the Rome Conference. On 16 July 1998 the U.S. submitted a proposal, which would have further limited the Court's jurisdiction "over all acts committed in the course of official duties and acknowledged by the State as such" (Scheffer 1998, in Cassesse 2002: V.I: 601). The U.S. would not bend on its insistence that the acceptance of state nationality was a necessary pre-condition to the Court's jurisdiction (Sadat 2002). The final compromise was that the exercise of criminal jurisdiction be limited to territorial state signatories or state of nationality signatories. This compromise became Article 12 of the Rome Statute called the Precondition to the Exercise of Jurisdiction. Article 12 states:

(1) a State which becomes a Party to this Statute thereby accepts the jurisdiction of the Court with respect to the crimes referred to in Article 5,
(2) in case of Article 13,[6] paragraph (a) or (c), the court may exercise its jurisdiction if one or more of the following States are Parties to this Statute or have accepted the jurisdiction of the Court in accordance with paragraph 3): (a) The State on the Territory of which the conduct in question occurred or, if the crime was committed on board a vessel or aircraft, the State of registration of that vessel or aircraft; (b) The State of which the person accused of the crime is a national

The only exception to this Article is when the Security Council, which then gives universality of jurisdiction, refers a case (Article 13 (b)). This compromise (at the insistence of the U.S.) fulfilled two issues. One was the demand for the Security Council to have a role. This is a significant compromise when one considers the veto power of the "Five Members" of the Security Council in ensuring their interests or referral for a case that can be eliminated vis-à-vis veto power. It compromises the Like-Minded State's desire for universal jurisdiction while at the same time satisfying the U.S. with the second part of Article 12, which is the precondition of a state to consent to being a participant of the ICC (the complimentary court to national proceedings versus the universal court). Article 13 proclaims how the Court may exercise these jurisdictional rights on the territory of a State Party with four subsections. These include jurisdiction of the Court if a referral by a state party or the Prosecutor is made and/or the Security Council makes a referral. The second condition is for crimes committed on the territory of a non-State Party, which includes jurisdiction if a referral by a State Party or the Prosecutor is initiated and/or a referral from the Security Council.

Article 12 is also a manifestation of the sovereignty principle. As a complimentary system, states have primacy over their own territories, which limit the territory of the Court's jurisdiction. The aspect of a complimentary system will vastly restrain the Court's jurisdiction and limits the authority and legitimacy[7] of the Court. In effect, the Court has resulted in being a consent-based system versus a universal system based on *jus cogens* and *erga omnes*. The U.S. was one of the greatest objectors to a universal court and had attained a portion of its interests by the compromises that resulted in Article 12. Yet, even with the concessions for the pre-condition of state consent regarding jurisdiction, Article 12 was still viewed as highly problematic for the U.S. (as we will discuss in greater detail in the next chapter). As previously stated, the compromises of jurisdiction have greatly weakened the jurisdictional powers of the Court and the U.S. opposition is at best ill placed. This is stated well by Cassesse (2002: VI:614), "against this background it remains astonishing that the United States continues to oppose the weak compromise of Article 12 and has, since the Rome Conference, explored various ways and formulas to alter Article 12 or to make it inapplicable with regard to U.S. Nationals."

With jurisdiction, the concept of automatic authority for the Court upon signature remained an issue. The U.S.—and a limited number of other states including France—wanted an opt-out option for the Court's jurisdiction (Sadat 2002). This would further limit the court's jurisdiction and strengthen the position of sovereign state determinism. The final outcome was a compromise promoted by Japan—Article 124 of the Rome Statute called the Transitional Provisions. It states:

> Notwithstanding article 12, paragraphs 1 and 2, a State, on becoming a party to this Statute, may declare that, for a period of seven years after the entry into force of this Statute for the State concerned, it does not accept the jurisdiction of the Court with respect to the category of crimes referred to in article 8 when a crime is alleged to have been committed by its nationals or on its territory. A declaration under this article may be withdrawn at any time. The provision of this article shall be reviewed at the Review Conference in accordance with article 123, paragraph 1.

This appears to address both the tradition of state sovereignty and international law as consensually based inter-state contracts.

Beyond the concerns for an opt-in/opt-out option, states were concerned about their past actions being subject to the Court's jurisdiction. The concern over *ex post facto* is not a new trend. The claim to immunity for acts committed ex post facto was used as the defense for the Nazi war criminals during the International Military Tribunals. It is not surprising that these concerns resurface during the creation of an ICC. The concerns are addressed in Article 11, which limits the Court's jurisdiction to crimes committed after the Statute enters into force (for the ratifying State Party). Article 11 states:

> (1) The Court has jurisdiction only with respect to crimes committed after the entry into force of this Statute
> (2) If a state becomes a Party to this Statute after its entry into force, the Court may exercise its jurisdiction only with respect to crimes committed after the entry into force of this Statute for that State, unless that State has made a declaration under Article 12, paragraph 3.

Many compromises had been made; however, this does not mean that these compromises were acceptable to the opposing actors. Instead many of these compromises represent Chambliss's (1998) concept of symbolic politics which incorporates the adaptation of a proposed law by making it malleable to other proposals and erroneously consecrated as shared interests. This was manifested in the final hours of the Rome Conference.

17 July 1998 was the final day for the delegates of the Committee of the Whole to finalize the most contentious articles. At the deadline hour, the U.S. and India attempted to introduce amendments to the proposal which would have collapsed the Conference and ended the chance for an ICC (Bassiouni 1999). India requested limitations on the role of the Security Council and a prohibition

of all nuclear weapons. The U.S. requested further limitations on the Court's jurisdiction, only supported by China and Qatar, to restrict the compromises of jurisdiction already made and to call for unrecorded votes at the last minutes on 17 July (Cassesse 2002). Had the U.S. been successful in attaining action, the ICC conference would have been shut down and rescheduled for later. The last minute effort to thwart the establishment of an ICC by the U.S. was only the first of many to come (Bassiouni 1999).

A no action vote was introduced and the U.S. and India proposals were not addressed: out of 161 registered delegates 155 voted for the no action motion and acceptance of the proposed draft of the Committee. The Committee of the whole adjourned and the final session of the Plenary was convened for a quick formal session to adopt the Rome Statute (Bassiouni 1999). The U.S. held to its opposition and requested another vote on the previous last minute proposals (Harris 1999; Bassiouni 1999). At the insistence of the U.S., a final vote was taken; 120 delegations voted in favor of the Rome Statute, 7 voted against, and 21 abstained on The Final Act of the Diplomatic Conference, and to open for signature 18 July (CICC 2003). Those opposed to the Rome Statute included India, Iraq, Israel, Libyan Arab Jamchiriya, Qatar, China, and the U.S. The final vote represented the end of years of efforts to establish a Statute for an ICC.

In summary, during the process of negotiations of the Plenipotentiaries Meeting no one state (including the U.S.) was a monolithic obstacle. The proceedings were divided rather conspicuously among those Like-Minded States—over sixty states headed by Canada, Australia, and the United Kingdom—who wanted universal jurisdiction, expanded definition of war crimes, an empowered prosecutor, and the exclusion of the Security Council in the Court's decision, versus the non-Like-Minded States, such as the U.S., Iraq, Qatar, and China. One of the major concessions made with the insistence of the U.S. was the inclusion of a complimentary court. This ensured that the concept of universality would be diminished by the recognition of the primacy of domestic courts. Another major compromise made at the insistence of the U.S. was the need for a state to be a signatory. This ensured state willingness to participate in the court versus a court empowered under a universal system of international law governing all of international society. Again, this reiterates the contradiction of an international society composed of sovereign states but guided by an ideology of consensus as well as an international system of laws that are being viewed as both *jus cogens* and *erga omnes.*

The Rome Conference was the result of compromises and efforts from the PrepCom and Plenipotentiaries Meetings. However, the issues and conflicts remained last minute battles as states attempted to form the ICC to their ideology and interests. The same LMS held to their positions and the U.S. continued to oppose many of the Articles being formed that involved jurisdiction, empowerment, and universality. The creation of the Rome Statute was a step to address conflicts occurring between and within states. However, just as the structural contradiction model illuminates, attempts to address conflicts vis-à-vis law creation, can lead to further conflicts as they ignore the larger structural contradictions.

As jurisdiction represents the core contradiction within international society and international law,[8] it is often the central foci of further conflicts. This was the case with jurisdiction and sovereignty for the Rome Statute development and the ICC. As international law is a part of the international system, it reflects *the* fundamental contradiction, which then becomes inserted into charters, treaties, and resolutions. International law is the language that states use to attempt to resolve competing legal interests. This is further complicated with the distinction between law that finds its origin in a normative will—binding because it is imposed by that will—and positive law—multifaceted idealistic requirements that are asserted by social conscience (Austin, J. 1867). Thus, the issue of jurisdiction is at the root of a contradiction within international law.

According to Chambliss, the passage of the Rome Statute displays the symbolic use of politics wherein proposed law (an entire legal institution) is made malleable to existing proposals and erroneously consecrated as a culmination of shared interests.[9] This is done through consciously designing compromises that do not hold to the original intentions of the political or legal issue to appease the opposition. It is the alteration of a proposed legal system that is made malleable to opposing legal proposals and then consecrated as "shared interests" (Chambliss and Katz 1993). The central compromise involved weakening the court's jurisdiction to appease the U.S. while maintaining a portion of the original principle and intention of the Rome Statute: an international criminal court with universality for the most serious crimes against humanity and those that threaten the very order of international society.

The passing of the Rome Statute does indeed signify a major change in political ideology of the international society and for international law. However, many of the same obstacles that blocked earlier attempts to establish a court were temporally resolved, not by addressing the contradiction of international society or international law, but by compromises and the creation of a new system of laws and justice that is only as strong as the compromises allow. The Rome Conference was a point in history that revised the existing relationships between states, political interests, and institutions such as the UN. However, the process of appeasing conflicts by making malleable the proposals for a universal Court does limit the potentiality of the ICC (all the while being conveyed as an institution that is a culmination of shared interests). This revision of political and state relationships has created conflicts due to the structure and ideology of the ICC in opposition to existing international law and international societal relations. Thus, new conflicts will and have arose that are centered on issues of sovereignty, jurisdiction, and *erga omnes*. These contentious factors are discussed fully in Chapter V.

Structure and Function of the International Criminal Court

The Rome Statute required sixty states to become signatories by 31 December 2000 (Article 126) for the Statute to enter force. That goal was far exceeded with 139 state signatories at the closing date. The International Criminal Court became a reality on 1 July 2002 with more than 120 nations attending the final Prepatory Commission Meetings. The endorsement of the Rome Statute requires states to be signatories and ratified members. The ratification of a state's signature varies with each state's domestic legal system. For example, the U.S. would need the approval of the Senate for the international signature to be ratified. Support of the ICC stands to become stronger as the 139 states that have endorsed the Rome Statue with their signature become ratified members; as of December 2004, 97 states have become ratified members in accordance with their domestic legal systems. This number excludes the two states that were signatories but withdrew all support for the ICC: the U.S. and Israel. A few states have failed to become signatories due to domestic strife, but are willing to participate in the ICC, such as Kazakhstan, Indonesia, and Malaysia. Other states are adamantly opposed to the ICC such as the Libyan Arab Jamchiriya, India, Pakistan, Saudi Arabia, Turkey, Iraq, and Myanmar (Mullins, Kauzlarich, and Rothe 2004).

The ICC consists of ninety-seven states forming the Assembly of States Parties (ASP) to the Rome Statue. The Assembly of States Parties is the management oversight and legislative body of the International Criminal Court. It is composed of representatives of the States that have ratified and acceded to the Rome Statute. The Assembly of States Parties has a main Bureau, consisting of a President, two Vice Presidents and eighteen elected members for a three-year term (ICC 2004). Ambassador Bruno Stagno has been elected to serve as its next President to commence November 2005. The Permanent Secretariat of the Assembly is headed by Dr. Medard Rwelamira (South Africa). The ASP's role is to decide on items such as the adoption of normative texts and of the budget, the election of the judges, the Prosecutor, and the Deputy Prosecutor(s). According to article 112:7 of the Rome Statute, each State Party has one vote and every effort has to be made to reach decisions by consensus both in the Assembly and the Bureau. If consensus cannot be reached, decisions are taken by vote.

The International Criminal Court consists of four Chambers: (1) the Presidency; (2) Judicial Court (An Appeals Chamber, Trial Chamber, and a Pre-Trial Chamber); (3) Office of the Prosecutor; and (4) the Registry. Each of these play a significant role in the Court's processes; consequentially, we briefly visit each Chamber.

Court Chambers: The Presidency and First and Second Vice Presidency

The Presidency is an elected office serving terms of three years and holds responsibility for the administrative duties of the court, excluding the office of the Prosecutor. The Presidency will coordinate and seek the concurrence of the Prosecutor on all matters of mutual concern. The President serves a six-year term on the Appeals Court. The First and Second Vice Presidents serve nine-year terms on the Trial Division. The judges composing the Presidency also serve on a full-time basis. The President and First and Second Vice Presidents are to elected by an absolute majority of the eighteen Judges of the Court.

On 11 March 2003 the elected President and First and Second Vice Presidents were chosen: President Judge Philippe Kirsch (Canada), Judge Akua Kuenyehia (Ghana) as First Vice-President, and Judge Elizabeth Odio Benito (Costa Rica) as Second Vice-President of the Court.

Registry

The Registry is solely responsible for the administrative and non-judicial aspects of the Court and for creating a Victims and Witness Unit providing protective and security measures for witnesses, victims or others at risk due to testimony given to the court. More specifically, the Registrar is responsible for the administration of legal aid matters, court management, victims and witness matters, defense counsel, detention unit, finances, translation, and personnel. In relation to victims, it is the Registrar that is responsible for providing notice to of the case to victims, assisting them in obtaining legal advice and representation and if necessary provide agreements for relocation and support services (Rule 16 of the Rules of Procedure). The Registrar is also responsible for receiving, obtaining and providing information with States and as the main channel of communication between the Court, States, Inter-governmental Organizations and Non-Governmental Organizations. The Registrar is elected by the Assembly of State Parties by an absolute majority. On 24 June 2003, the Bureau of the Assembly of States Parties appointed Mr. Bruno Cathala from France as the first Registrar of the Court. He will hold office for a renewable term of five years.

Judicial Chambers

The functions of the Judicial Court are divided into Chambers, which allows the judges to be on more than one chamber if it serves the functioning of the court in a more efficient manner. The Appellate Chamber is exempt from this, as an Appellate Judge is prohibited from serving on other chambers (Article 39, Rome Statute). Under Resolutions 2 and 3 of the ICC adopted on September 2002 the procedures for nominations of candidates for judges is outlined; the process begins with the Secretariat of the Assembly of State Parties (Dr. Medard Rwelamira of South Africa) circulating invitations for nominations of judges amongst state party members. State parties include those states that have started ratification processes, accession or acceptance of the Statute and that with the intent of having deposited its ratification with the Secretary General of the United Nations before the nomination period. The nomination period is a fixed term decided by the Bureau of the Assembly of State Parties. State parties may then communicate nominations through diplomatic channels to the Secretariat of the Assembly of State Parties. Once nominations were made, the Secretariat placed them and all supporting documentation on the ICC website as well as circulating paper copies to all state members. The nomination period could only have been extended beyond the 30 November 2002 deadline under the following conditions: (a) There are insufficient candidates; (b) The number of candidates from a regional group is less than one-fourth the number of state parties in that group or if the number of state parties of any region is less than three-eighteenths the total number of state parties of the Rome statute; (c) If the number of candidates from one gender is less than one-fourth the total number of candidates with a minimum of ten candidates from each gender.

The persons elected to the Court shall have obtained the highest number of votes with a two-thirds majority of state parties present and voting. However, during the process of elections, state parties must take into account the need for representation of the principle legal systems of the world, equitable geographic representation, and expertise in specific legal issues such as violence against women and children. From this, each state party votes for a maximum number of eighteen candidates. This is broken down into Groups to which each state party must vote for three candidates from the Group of African States; three from the Group of Asian States; three from the Group of East European States; three from the Group of Latin America and Caribbean States, and three from the Group of Western European and other states. Prior to Election Day, the President of the Assembly of State Parties distributes to all state parties copies of instructions for voting and sample ballots.

During its first resumed session held in New York from 3 to 7 February 2003, the Assembly of States Parties elected the eighteen judges. The judges constitute a forum of international experts that represents the world's principal legal systems. Seven were elected from the Western European and others Group of States (WEOG), four from the Latin American and the Caribbean Group of States (GRULAC), three from the Asian Group of States, three from the African Group of States, one from the Group of Eastern Europe.

The judges were elected from two lists: (1) candidates with established competence in criminal law and procedures, with the necessary relevant experience, whether as judge, prosecutor, advocate, or in another capacity in criminal proceedings; (2) candidates with established competence in relevant areas of international law including international humanitarian law and the law of human rights, and extensive experience in a professional legal capacity which is of relevance to the judicial work of the Court.

After the election of the judges, the Court organized itself into Appeals, Pre-Trial and Trial Chambers of the Court. As of December 2004, the Pre-trial Chambers consist of: Chamber One—Presiding Judge Claude Jord, Judge Akua Kuenyehia, and Judge Silvia Steiner; Chamber Two—Judge Tuiloma Neroni Slade, Judge Mauro Politi, and Judge Fatoumata Dembele Diarra; and Chamber Three—Judge Tuiloma Neroni Slade, Judge Hans-Peter Kaul, and Judge Sylvia Steiner.

Prosecutor

The Office of the Prosecutor is a separate division of the Court with the responsibility for the investigation of referrals on crimes covered by the ICC. The Prosecutor has full authority over the administration of the Prosecutorial Division (Article 42, Rome Statute). Cases brought to the ICC are handled independently by this office, unlike the system used by the United Nations' Security Council where there must be joint agreement to charges brought forth against individuals for crimes covered under international laws and treatises. A state may refer cases to the Prosecution, or the Prosecutor can initiate the investigation based on information of a crime being committed within the jurisdiction of the Court (Article 14 and 15 Rome Statute). The Assembly of State Parties (ASP) will further define the relationship agreement between the United Nations and the Court over disputes regarding how referrals will proceed and if the wording of the Rome Statute will allow an advisory opinion from the International Court of Justice, especially regarding the Acts of Aggression (Coalition for International Criminal Court—CICC 6, 2002). The Assembly of States Parties may also elect one or two Deputy Prosecutors from a list of candidates provided by the Chief Prosecutor (ICC 2004).

As a consequence of its mandate, the Office comprises both Investigation and Prosecution Divisions. The former is mainly responsible for preliminary examinations and the conduct of investigations, such as collecting and examining evidence, questioning persons being investigated as well as victims and witnesses. In this respect, the Statute requires the Office to extend all investigations so that they cover both incriminating and exonerating facts. This is to be done to ensure the Prosecutor recognizes, and fulfills, their responsibility to strive to and uncover the truth in every case. The Prosecution Division has a role in the investigative process, but will have principal responsibility for the litigation of cases before the various Chambers of the Court.

Nominations of candidates for Prosecutor follow the same guidelines as for the judges. The Bureau of the Assembly of State Parties fixes the election date for the Prosecutor's position. Moreover, the election process is done with the intention of consensus. In absence of consensus, the Prosecutor is elected via secret ballot by an absolute majority of the members of the Assembly of State

Parties. The Prosecutor then nominates three candidates for each position of Deputy Prosecutor, that must all be of different nationalities, based upon where they exercise civil and political rights. The Secretariat then posts the list of candidates on the ICC web and distributes hard copies through diplomatic channels to all state party members. The election process itself is a replication of the procedures outlined for the Prosecutor.

Currently, the Chief Prosecutor is Mr. Luis Moreno-Ocampo of Argentina, who took office on 16 June 2003. As of the end of 2004, 120 staff members are a part of the Prosecutor's office. Deputy Prosecutor Serge Brammertz heads the investigative staff. The Deputy Prosecutor for Prosecutions is Ms. Fatou Bensouda of Gambia. Other staff members include professionals and NGO investigators with an international background.

Processes of Investigations

The Chief Prosecutor may start an investigation upon referral of situations in which there is a reasonable basis to believe that crimes covered by the Rome Statute have been or are being committed. Such referrals must be made by a State Party or the Security Council of the United Nations. In accordance with the Statute and the Rules of Procedure and Evidence, the Chief Prosecutor has to evaluate the material submitted to him before making the decision to proceed. In addition to State Party and Security Council referrals, the Chief Prosecutor may also receive information on crimes within the jurisdiction of the Court provided by other sources, such as individuals or non-governmental organizations.

The Prosecutor then conducts a preliminary examination of the information in every case. To aid in this process, the Legal Advisory Section (LAS) of the Office of the Prosecutor (OTP), implemented legal "tools" and services to provide frameworks for consistency and efficiency of the OTP. This included a "case matrix" application to provide overviews of elements of crimes and legal requirements of modes of liability for all offenses in the Rome Statute. This matrix contains a comprehensive list of elements of proof necessary or relevant for each specific case. If the Prosecutor decides not to pursue a case due to lack of credible information or facts he or she must provide prompt notice informing the State or States that referred the situation under Article 14 or the Security Council under Article 13 (b).

If the Chief Prosecutor decides that there is a reasonable basis to proceed with an investigation, he will request the Pre-Trial Chamber to authorize such. The prosecutor evaluates the information and investigates to determine whether or not there is sufficient basis to prosecute. The Prosecutor is solely responsible for the retention, storage, and security of all information and physical evidence obtained during the course of investigation (Rule 10 of Rules of Procedure and Evidence). If the prosecutor decides to proceed with the investigation, he or she must first obtain authorization from the pretrial chamber. Formal prosecution then begins once a pretrial chamber judge issues an arrest warrant or summons for the accused individual to appear before the Court based on the charges filed by the prosecutor.

Once the accused appears, a hearing is held to determine whether sufficient evidence exists to proceed to the trial stage. It is at this point that the domestic states of those individuals may appear to the Court to challenge its jurisdiction or the admissibility of the case based on state primacy to prosecute. Moreover, at this stage the defendant is ensured of legal defense. The defendant can either choose the lawyer(s) or have legal assistance assigned by the Court, without payment if the accused lacks sufficient means. As in all jurisdictions of the Court the accused also has the right to have adequate time and facilities for the preparation of his/her defense. Hence, the accused has the right to legal assistance under all conditions and with due to for proper representation; however, the accused may also represent his/herself in the process. He/She can either choose the lawyer(s) or have legal assistance assigned by the Court without payment if the accused lacks the means to pay for it. Once a defense has been chosen, the Office of the Registrar is responsible for ensuring a fair trial by providing the defense assistance and information necessary for professional investigators to conduct the defense of the accused. The possibility also exists for the detained accused to request an interim release pending trial upon the first appearance and at least every 120 days. This request must be made in writing. Then, the Pre-Trial Chamber makes a decision or holds a hearing. If no requests are formally given, a hearing must still be held at least once a year on behalf of the accused.

When the pretrial chamber has confirmed the prosecutor's charges and jurisdiction of the Court, a three-judge trial chamber conducts the trial in public proceedings. The court may find an accused guilty when two out of the three judges are convinced of the suspect's guilt beyond reasonable doubt. Thus, the decision of guilt or innocence need not be unanimous. The court can then fine or imprison those convicted and possibly order reparations to victims. The maximum sentence allowed by the Rome Statute is life imprisonment. Sentences of imprisonment will be served in The Netherlands or in another country that voluntarily accepts the prisoner. At this point, the prosecution or the defense may appeal the verdict or the sentence to the appeals chamber. The appeals chamber would hear the case and make a final ruling regarding any contentious matter such as sentencing or the verdict.

The Court also has provisions or oversights for allegations of misconduct pertaining to the Prosecutors, Judges, Deputy Prosecutors, or the Registrar. "Serious Misconduct" is any conduct that occurs in the course of official duties and is incompatible with the official functions of that Chamber or an act that causes, or potentially can cause, serious harm to the administration of justice in a case. This includes such things as disclosing facts or information that may be prejudicial to any person or proceedings, concealing information, abuse of judicial office to obtain "favors" from authorities or officials, gross negligence in the performance of their "official" duties, or causes unwarranted delays in the processes of a case. Under Article 46 (1), 47, and rules 24 and 25, a complaint may be lodged concerning misconduct to the Presidency. Based on provided information, the President may initiate proceedings with the assistance of one or more judges or may consider the complaint frivolous and dismiss the charges.

Crimes Covered

The intention of the ICC is to provide an international system of justice that would address heinous crimes against humanity when a state is unable or unwilling to investigate or prosecute any individual accused of the crimes specified in the Rome Statute (Mullins, Kauzlarich, and Rothe 2002). Crimes that are subject for prosecution under the Rome Statute are defined in Articles 5, 6, 7, and 8.

Article 5 of the Rome Statute lists the crimes within the jurisdiction of the ICC: crimes of genocide, crimes against humanity, war crimes, and crimes of aggression still to be defined by the ASP (Article 5, paragraph 2, Rome Statute). Crimes of genocide refer to "acts committed with intent to destroy, in whole or in part, a national, ethnical, racial, or religious group" (Article 6, Rome Statute).

Article 7 defines crimes against humanity as acts that are widespread or a systematic attack against a civilian population. This includes acts of torture, intentional causing of great suffering to bodily or mental health, murder, and attacks directed against a civilian population. Crimes against humanity are not as inclusive as previously recognized Human Rights Law (HRL). The HRL applies in times of peace or war, but is primarily conscious of protecting people against governmental violence against their recognized civil, political, economic, social, and cultural rights (Universal Declaration of Human Rights, GA. Res.217A (III0, UN Doc A/810 at 71 (1948)).

War crimes are defined by breaches of the Geneva Conventions of 8/1949 (Article 8, Rome Statute). These include torture or inhumane treatment, biological experiments, extensive destruction and appropriation of property, and willfully denying a prisoner of war or other protected person the right to a fair and regular trial.

The ICC is limited in its investigative reach, being unable to subpoena any state or their records. While the Court may request a warrant or subpoena, the Prosecutor and the Court lack an empowered policing agency to ensure the fulfillment of either request (Article 54-58 Rome Statute). However, on 22 December 2004 a cooperation agreement between the Offices of the Prosecutor (OTP) by Deputy Prosecutor Serge Brammertz, and the International Criminal Police Organization (Interpol) by Secretary General Roland K. Noble was signed. The agreement establishes a framework for cooperation between the Office of the Prosecutor and Interpol. The agreement enables the OTP and Interpol to exchange police information and criminal analysis, and to cooperate in the search for fugitives and suspects. Moreover, the agreement gives the OTP access to Interpol telecommunications network and databases.

The Prosecutor is limited to requesting the presence of persons being investigated, victims, and witnesses. The Court must seek the cooperation of a state in fulfilling the Prosecutor's requests. It must rely on the compliance of a state or state party to relinquish any evidence, suspects, or witnesses that are relevant to the ongoing investigations carried out by the Prosecutorial Branch. The Court is unable to enforce its decisions without voluntary state compliance.

The Court also has limited jurisdiction, inclusive only of a state party to the treaty or by agreement of a state not a party to the Statute. The criteria listed in Article 12 for the exercise of jurisdiction requires a state to become a party to the statute or accept the jurisdiction of the Court if the crime occurred on the State territory, its vessel, or aircraft, or if the State of which a person accused is a national (Article 12, a-b). No person can be held liable by the court unless the crime occurred within the jurisdiction of the court. Compliance by a non-party state is highly unlikely and non-compliance can act as a detriment to the ability of the ICC to be an effective measure of international justice.

Current Cases

As of February 2005, three States Parties have referred potential cases and/or grievances to the Office of the Prosecutor. The Office of the Prosecutor, as of February 2005 has accepted three cases with investigations and two referrals. The first case to be investigated and charged by the ICC was decided on 23 June 2004: the Democratic Republic of Congo. States, international organizations, and non-governmental organizations have reported thousands of deaths by mass murder, summary execution, a pattern of rape, torture, forced displacement, and the illegal use of child soldiers, all of which fall under the purview of the Court. This case, once brought forward will occur in the Pre-Trial Chamber I under the Presiding Judge Claude Jord. This case will be thoroughly explored in Chapter V.

The second case brought to and accepted by the Prosecutor is Northern Uganda and the Lord's Resistance Army. The alleged crimes being committed in the region include conscription or enlisting of children under fifteen years into the army, willful killing, rape, sexual slavery, forced pregnancy, and forced displacement of civilians which may constitute crimes against humanity under the Rome Statute. This case, once brought forward will occur within the Pre-Trial Chamber II with Presiding Judge Tuiloma Neroni Slade.

The third case was brought to the prosecutor on 6 January 2005. Moreno-Ocampo received a letter sent on behalf of the government of the Central African Republic. At this time, in accordance with the Rome Statute and the Rules of Procedure and Evidence, the Prosecutor will carry out an analysis to determine whether to initiate an investigation or to drop the case. Currently it is in the early investigative stages where the Prosecutor is seeking additional information in "including the gravity of alleged crimes, any relevant national proceedings, and the interests of justice" (ICC 2005).

Summary

The mission statement of the Rome Statute personifies the new ideology of an international society, with common goals, values, and interests, and the ideological principle of universal jurisdiction. The Rome Statute describes an ability to have jurisdiction over the most serious crimes but realistically has limited jurisdiction. Indeed, the ICC does represent a change in international relations and international law. The degree to which the ICC will affect international law is set within the treaty. However, the question remains to what extent the ICC will influence the relations of international society without addressing the underlying contradiction between the ideological international society and current trends of international relations. Simply stated, the potential for the ICC is reflected in the conflicts that arose in its establishment over issues of jurisdiction and state sovereignty. Moreover, to fully understand the impact of these contradictions upon the Court and inter-state relations, we must also explore international law. The following chapter addresses international law and its impact on inter-state relations as well as the impact of states on international law.

Notes

1 See Appendix for chart

2 Like-Minded states include those states that want a court based on universal jurisdiction and have legal traditions based on civil law This is discussed in greater detail in the following analysis regarding the debate and compromise of jurisdictional matters during the Rome Conference

3 This is the same ongoing philosophical and legal debate between naturalism and positivism that has occurred for centuries Under international law, positivism has been the traditional form of interpretation However, the issue of jurisdiction remains at the heart of these conflicting paradigms and at the center of debate at each attempt to establish an ICC

4 SOFA are jurisdictional agreements that give the sending state or receiving state a primary right to exercise its jurisdiction over certain crimes If a state party would have an obligation to surrender an individual (e g U S national) to the court the individual would be transferred to U S jurisdiction versus an international World Court or third state

5 For more detailed information on the Article 98 impunity agreements see the CICC This includes states reactions and detailed analysis on the bilateral agreements

6 Article 13 details the Court's jurisdiction for prosecution of crimes under Article 5

7 Legitimacy in its simplest form refers to conformity with the law "Unlike legality, legitimacy refers to the ought and not just the is of law" (Carty 1998) It also refers to the perceived view of an institution as valid and acceptable (Scott, et al 1986)

8 See Appendix for chart illustrating this contradiction and the place of jurisdiction within this system

9 To revisit Chambliss's model see Chapter IV

Chapter V

The Contradictions of International Law

The development of, and conflict over, the International Criminal Court reflects broader tensions and contradictions within international law itself. Previously, we have discussed the historical trends and forces leading up to the creation of the ICC, as well as many of the specific conflicts that drove the negotiations of the Rome Statute itself. We will now turn our attention to conflicts that continue—and will continue—to plague the implementation and operation of the court. The passage and ratification of the Rome Statute, and the court's initial operations, has not ended the conflicts between certain nations and international society as whole over the nature and jurisdiction of the court. These tensions arise out of key conflicts and contradictions within international law itself. To better understand the current controversies and conflicts, we will first outline and explore key ideals and practices within the development and operation of international law. Then we frame continued resistance to the court in light of these principles and possibilities. More specifically, we address the U.S. reaction to the ICC, international law, and issues of jurisdiction.

International Law, National Sovereignty, and Universalism

The evolution of the modern nation state, along with changes in the level of international commerce, presented practical and ideological challenges to conceptualizations of international law and international relations. Natural law, embodied in the principle of the social contract, was *the* major organizing principle of intra and inter-state relations. Natural law, as a conceptualization of social control, has subsisted for 2,500 years in a variety of forms. This tradition dates back to the system of Roman law, the Court of Chancery, and to philosophers such as Aquinas, Grotius, Locke, and Hume (Friedmann 1967). It is rooted in the ideal that there exists an objective, Natural Law, not one of human origin, rooted in norms of conduct seen to be an essential part of human nature and found "existing in the reason and conscience of every human being" (Brown 1960: VI). The rise of the modern nation state and the expansion of international commerce produced numerous minor and major conflicts which began to erode the core of Natural Law. The base tenants of the philosophy were variantly replaced by core ideologies of nationalism, capitalism, relativism, modern science, positivism (also known as utilitarianism and pragmatism), and the rise of the Austinian jurisprudence (Brown 1960).

The Austinian model drew upon Kant's rejection of attaching law to morality, an objective moral law (Friedmann 1967; Koskeniemi 2003). Austin insisted that supreme power as embodied in a state limited by positive law is contradictory. The sovereign state, by its very nature, can impose positive law on itself vis-à-vis treaties, but is not under obligation to be fully bound by such self-imposed limitations. Thus, a polity can abrogate these mutual agreements regardless of positive law. With the acceptance of the positivistic legal philosophy that began to guide international law and international relations, legal scholars (e.g., Max Hubor and N. Politis) refused to recognize the existence of an international code of conduct external to a nation-state (Reuters 1957). Such a position in and of itself stymies the development of an international society as, "if all states claim to be sovereign, then there can be no higher authority, no international law, or restraint of any kind" (Ziegler 1977: 103). Attempting to resolve these contradictions, a movement toward establishing such boundaries arose.

Most clearly seen in the development of the Hague and Geneva conventions' articulation of "rules" of war, the process was hastened by Europe's collective horror at the devastation of World War I. By 1919, the first international political organization developed as an attempt to organize and encourage interstate relations and peaceful settlement of international disputes (Reuters 1958). The League of Nations was formed with the purpose of unifying an international arena composed of sovereign states with divergent political interests, economic interests, cultural disparities, religions, state practices, and traditions (Carty 1991). However, even with the establishment of the League, international relations deteriorated. An economic crisis engulfed the world beginning in 1929. Conflicts increased and European powers found themselves at the core of another world conflict.

The end of World War II brought new alliances and new attempts to generate and legitimate an international institution designed to foster peaceful cooperation among nations. In 1945, representatives of fifty states assembled in San Francisco, U.S.A, to develop the charter of an international organization to maintain peace and security called the United Nations (UN) and to dissolve the failed League of Nations. With the development of the UN, international relations and law began to take on a fundamentally different character.

The expansion of codified international law reflected a change in ideology—one that emphasized a universal tone previously only reflected in customary law. The doctrine of universal jurisdiction asserts that some crimes are so heinous that their perpetrators should not escape justice by invoking doctrines of sovereign immunity or the sacrosanct nature of national frontiers. The attainment of international social control and collective security were forefronted in the international political agendas. Yet, this required state consensus. Based on the historical relations of sovereign states, the mission of the UN represented the competing principles of a higher moral and legal authority—the legitimation of which would require creating a collective identity and consciousness—the same need seen in state formation requiring the development of nationhood: the reification of nationalism (see Brubaker 2004). As stated by Secretary General Waldheim (1987): "The United Nations is the symbol of a higher and more ambitious political and social aim, the evolution of an international community with interests, aspirations and loyalties of a far more wide-ranging kind." Just as nationalism is not engendered by nations, but rather produced by political fields of power, internationalism is not engendered by the existence of an international arena (Brubaker 2004). It is international organizations, operating through the principles of international law that must act to regulate inter-state relations. However, attempts to internationally regulate states' behaviors have historically been met with the same objections: state sovereignty.

Thus, as international law continues to evolve towards a universalistic practice and interpretation, sovereignty becomes a central wedge used to ensure international regulation is limited. This was the case with the resultant system of complimentary jurisdiction in the Rome Statute.

As we discussed in Chapter IV, the processes leading up to the final draft of the Rome Statute involved several contentious issues. One of the leading factors was centered on the desire to have a universal system of control versus the position that state sovereignty had primacy over any international regulation. Moreover, the contentious matter of universal jurisdiction, state sovereignty, and the ICC continues to play a major role in international dialogues. Despite the limitations places on the court's jurisdiction, there are potentialities within international law for the court's jurisdiction to, over time, become universal. It is this possibility which has driven some nations, led by the U.S., to pursue a powerful and continued resistance to the court. We now turn to these legal traditions and then explore how the U.S. has attempted to shield itself from a court were it to be universalized.

Customary Law, *Jus Cogens*, and *Erga Omnes*

Customary laws are based on common and constant practices of states out of a sense of *opinio juris*—an ideal of natural law based upon legal obligation and principles. Simply stated, the fundamental principles behind customary laws are founded on willing state participation and a historical recognition of consistent state practices. Customary laws are viewed as *jus cogens*—a compelling law—in that they are internationally accepted principles, norms, and binding without exception. Unlike treaties, charters, and resolutions (which are codified laws and compelling for the signatory states), customary or *jus cogens* laws may or may not be *erga omnes*—or law which flows to all. Many times customary law becomes codified into treaties or statutes between states; however, the compulsory nature of customary law and general principles remain as the scaffold of international law. Moreover, the principles of *jus cogens* which is "compelling law" and *erga omnes* which is "flowing to all" can often be conflicting (Bassiouni 1991; Danilenko 1991). If a law is *jus cogens* it should follow that it is *erga omnes* (Bassiouni 1991). When something is compelling to and for everyone, it would stand to reason that it should be expected for all. However, this is not always the case.

For example, International Human Rights Laws are compelling but not necessarily flowing to all. This is, in part, due to pre-existing agreements which can cover specific situations. In the case of Human Rights Law, they are not applicable during a time of war, as these legal conditions are addressed by the Geneva Conventions, which articulate similar principles as they are to play out within a theatre of combat. As stated, customary laws, *jus cogens*, often find their way into multilateral treaties. For example, nine treaties, along with the principle of customary *jus cogens* law, have substantiated crimes of aggression. Thus, crimes of aggression can be viewed as customary and codified via *jus cogens* and *erga omnes*. The significance for understanding the role of customary law and the terms of *jus cogens* and *erga omnes* are central to the potential of the ICC to attain customary status.

Potential for the ICC as Customary

The establishment of the ICC, regardless of its limited jurisdiction, presents an optimistic prospect: it can become a customary law to the echelon of *erga omnes*. A treaty, such as the Rome Statute, can become a part of customary law according to previous precedence set by international law and the International Court of Justice. The International Court of Justice states:

> With respect to the other elements usually regarded as necessary before a conventional rule can be considered to have become a general rule of international law, it might be that, even without the passage of any considerable amount of time, a very widespread and representative participation in the convention might suffice of itself, provided it included that of states whose interests were especially affected (ICJ. Continental Shelf Case, 1969)

Therefore, the Rome Statute in the future may be conceived as general customary law, just as the Nuremberg Principles are. If this were to occur, the Court would reach a level of universal jurisdiction regardless of the wording or limitations of jurisdiction within the Rome Statute itself.

There are elements within the Rome Statute itself which allow for such future reconceptualizations. The phrasing of the Treaty can then be altered under Article 123 of the Rome Statute. This article calls for the review of the Statute and allows for changes deemed necessary by the international society. Article 123 states:

> 1 Seven years after the entry into force of this Statute the Secretary-General of the United Nations shall convene a Review Conference to consider any amendments to this statute Such review may include, but is not limited to, the list of crimes contained in article 5 The conference shall be open to those participating in the Assembly of States Parties and on the same conditions
> 2 At any time thereafter, at the request of a State Party and for the purpose set out in paragraph 1, the Secretary-General of the United Nations shall upon approval by a majority of State Parties, convene a Review Conference
> 3 The provisions of article 121, paragraphs 3 to 7, shall apply to the adoption and entry into force of any amendment to the Statute considered at a review Conference

The potential for a treaty or practice to become customary law is also perceived as not being limited to state practice but that *opinio juris* is sufficient for instant customary law (Morris, 1999). This is founded on the principle that instant custom, customary law, can be considered with virtual consensus of a Treaty. The potential of the ICC to become universal would be the first of many steps necessary to resolve the contradiction of international society. A universalistic system of justice would help to remove the underlying contradiction of an international society composed of sovereign states without legal permeable borders. It may also allow the emerging ideology of an international society, complete with new values of a united system, to be articulated, accepted, and legitimized. Clearly, this could give further legitimacy to the ICC and its stated mission: an international system of justice to put an end to impunity and the most atrocious crimes against humanity.

On the other hand, the potential of the ICC is hindered by the limitations of jurisdiction based on issues of sovereignty. This was the case of the often-embittered negotiations of the Rome Statute and is evident by the U.S. withdrawal, opposition, and flagrant actions aimed to impede the ICC. Due to the conflicts and the contradiction of an international society the ICC has limited ability to exercise jurisdiction. This can mean that many of the most heinous crimes will potentially not fall within the jurisdiction of the Court. These include the crimes of the past, Article 11, those committed in the territory of a non-party state or by a national of a non-state party, Article 12, and certain war crimes, Articles 8 and Article 124. The Articles as they stand are indeed limiting for the ICC; however, had the U.S. attained all of its positions the Court would only be empowered vis-à-vis the Security Council. This would make the court no different from previous international courts: symbolic tools for the victors and superpowers. Previous courts have had jurisdiction over state parties only. In general, states have not relinquished jurisdiction to these courts concerning themselves and were only utilized for the "others" or as *ad hoc.*

These future potentials may help to partially explain the U.S.'s vehement and voracious opposition to the court. While on the surface, such continued attacks seem merely mean spirited, as the U.S. opted-out of the court's jurisdiction, continued attempts to undermine the court flow out of the very nature of international law itself and the underlying contradiction between principles of sovereignty and universality of international norms and law. We now turn specifically to the nature, dynamics, and purposes of U.S. opposition.

The United States' Position and Proceedings

A consistent pattern of U.S. objections exist throughout the historical efforts to establish an ICC, the development of the Rome Statute, and recent U.S. policies aimed at thwarting the efficacy of the ICC. While historically the U.S. has maintained that an international system of justice was desirable (recall General Grant's position discussed in Chapter III); each formal proposal made for an ICC brought intense U.S. opposition; it has always claimed that state sovereignty trumps any international system of justice. For example, France's post-WWI proposal for a court was met with reluctance and opposition by the U.S., the U.S. also failed to become a member of the League of Nations at this time. In 1945, after WWII, the U.S. held a momentary position of support for a universal system of justice and universal jurisdiction. However, this support was limited to the German perpetrators of genocide and war crimes and was quickly retracted when the proposed court would pertain to the U.S. The U.S. failed to support the establishment of an ICC throughout the "Cold War era" as it pursued its own self-interests, economic gains, and strategic and military expenditures. Issues of sovereignty, universality of jurisdiction, a system of complimentary, and pre-conditions of consensus have been the political and ideological stand for the U.S.'s previous objections and lack of support in establishing an ICC.

Moreover, the ideology behind establishing an ICC for the U.S. was not all-inclusive. The U.S. wanted a court for the rest of the world, but insisted the jurisdiction could not impinge on the U.S., its policies, or its own state actors. The issue of sovereignty has served two primary functions for the U.S. First, it has served as an impetus of protection against subjection to a universal system of international law. Second, it has served as a tool for justification and neutralization for the recent U.S. domestic and foreign policy aimed to ensure the U.S. would be free from prosecution for even the most heinous crimes against humanity.

To further ensure U.S. military, foreign ambassadors, and other U.S. officials remained out of the reach of international jurisdiction, two key pieces of domestic legislation were passed. As negotiations over the court were taking shape in 1996, the U S. took measures to ensure its citizen would be outside the court's jurisdiction by creating the War Crimes Act (18 U.S.C § 2441). This legislation further enforced the State's position that, as a sovereign nation, it could, and would, domestically prosecute its own citizens for breaches of international war crimes to be included in the Rome Statute. Ensuring jurisdiction of an ICC would not be imposed upon the U.S., the War Crimes Act of 1996 states:

> (c) Definition —As used in this section the term "war crime" means any conduct—
> (1) defined as a grave breach in any of the international conventions signed at Geneva 12 August 1949, or any protocol to such convention to which the United States is a party,
> (2) prohibited by Article 23, 25, 27, or 28 of the Annex to the Hague Convention IV, Respecting the Laws and Customs of War on Land, signed 18 October 1907,
> (3) which constitutes a violation of common Article 3 of the international conventions signed at Geneva, 12 August 1949, or any protocol to such convention to which the United States is a party and which deals with non- international armed conflict, or
> (4) of a person who, in relation to an armed conflict and contrary to the provisions of the Protocol on Prohibitions or Restrictions on the Use of Mines, Booby-Traps and Other Devices as amended at Geneva on 3 May 1996 (Protocol II as amended on 3 May 1996), when the United States is a party to such Protocol, willfully kills or causes serious injury to civilians

A year later, the U.S. decided that this was not a strong enough or an exclusive enough set of protections and, in 1997, passed The Expanded War Crimes Act, 18 U.S.C & 2401 (SEC. 583). The primary goal was to amend and redefine the circumstances that were necessary for State prosecution and recognition of international law:

> (1) in subsection (a), by striking "grave breach of the Geneva Conventions" and inserting "war crime",
> (2) in subsection (b), by striking "breach" each place it appears and inserting "war crime", and
> (3) so that subsection (c) reads as follows
>
> (c) Definition —As used in this section the term "war crime" means any conduct—
> (1) defined as a grave breach in any of the international conventions signed at Geneva 12 August 1949, or any protocol to such convention to which the United States is a party,
> (2) prohibited by Articles 23, 25, 27, or 28 of the Annex to the Hague Convention IV, Respecting the Laws and Customs of War on Land, signed 18 October 1907,
> (3) which constitutes a violation of common Article 3 of the international conventions 12 August 1949, or any protocol to such convention to which the United States is a party and which deals with non-international armed conflict, or

(4) of a person who, in relation to an armed conflict and contrary to the provisions of the Protocol on Prohibitions or Restrictions on the Use of Mines, Booby-Traps and Other Devices as amended at Geneva on 3 May 1996 (Protocol II as amended on 3 May 1996), when the United States is a party to such Protocol, willfully kills or causes serious injury to civilians

In essence, this legislation provides the necessary domestic law guaranteeing precedence for prosecution of any U.S. party, thus further ensuring the Court would not have jurisdiction over individuals accused of war crimes. Moreover, the legislation enforces previous agreements of international treaties to which it is a signatory while ensuring U.S. primacy of jurisdiction.

The U.S. withdrawal and legislative undermining of the ICC not only reflects the ambiguous relationship the U.S. has with international law, but also reveals some of the inherent limitations of the ICC as an international institution of formal social control that is to represent the common good of the international society vis-à-vis international law. These limitations are reflected in the previous compromises that were made in the development of the Rome Statute and are centered on the fundamental contradictions of international society (issues of sovereignty) and international law (compelling and flowing to all).

The position of the U.S. towards the ICC is contentious at best. The U.S. takes the dubious position that humanity is best served by the U.S. remaining free from the limitations imposed by the Rome Statute. U.S. Ambassador Scheffer argued at the international level that the consequence imposed by Article 12, particularly for non-parties to the treaty, will be to limit severely those lawful, but highly controversial and inherently risky, interventions that the advocates of human rights and world peace so desperately seek from the United States and other military powers. The U.S. position then claims that there will be significant new legal and political risks in such interventions. However, this grossly misrepresents the nature of such activities and the nature of the Court itself. When interventions are approved by the UN Security Council, the obligations of aggression determination are met and thus such actions would not automatically be considered under the rubric of the Court. If U.S. troops engaged in atrocities while betrothed in an UN-sanctioned military endeavor, of course they would still be subject to the Statutes and Court's jurisdiction. The only foreseeable rationale behind such a protest is the desire of the U.S. to engage in war crimes with impunity, not being able to intervene in humanitarian missions when needed.

On 23 July 1998, the position of the U.S. was boldly stated in the Committee on Foreign Relations of the One Hundred Fifth Congress Session. The members present included Senator Jesse Helms, Phil Gramm, John Ashcroft, Dianne Feinstein, and Joseph Biden and Ambassador David Scheffer. The International Operations Committee began their deliberation of the ICC with a statement made by Senator Helms. In his opening proclamation Helms states:

> given this Court claims universal jurisdiction—in other words, the right to prosecute United States citizens even though the U S is not a party to the treaty—it is important for Congress and the American people to become appraised of the details regarding the Court Now, while I am relieved that the administration voted against the Treaty in Rome, I am convinced that it is not in itself sufficient to safeguard our Nation's interests The United States must aggressively oppose this court each step of the way, because the treaty establishing an international criminal court is not just bad, but I believe it is also dangerous The fact remains the most effective deterrent is the threat of military action, and this court is undermining the ability of the United States to do that very thing (Senator Helms 1998 2-3)

The ideological position of Helms, and the Bush administration, is clear. Yet, as typical of many of the administrations public statements especially in regards to the court, it is deceptive. Quite simply, under UN charter, the right of a nation to utilize their military in self-defense is not removed from any state party. Helm's statement makes clear the Neo-Conservative desire to wield U.S. military might as the first diplomatic tool in its international relations. This is indeed the sort of behavior the UN charter, as well as the International Criminal Court, is designed to curtail and prevent While the U.S. cites the issue of sovereignty as its key protection, national sovereignty has never given a nation the right to impinge upon the sovereignty other others. This is exactly what Helms desires and it is the core implication behind his statement. The U.S. should be able to use military force whenever and wherever it desires. This principle is in core violation of all international law as it relates to warfare and inter-state aggression.

While President Clinton, as a political gesture, signed the Rome Statute on 31 December 2000, this proved to be a mere façade. The former President claimed the treaty was "significantly flawed," based on his ongoing concern over the court's jurisdiction. Clinton de-legitimized his symbolic support further by recommending to his successor that the Senate not ratify the treaty. His actions reflect the use of symbolic political gestures, which are designed to appease a conflicting force that was not ignorable: the U.S. Delegate (e.g., Scheffer), members of Congress (e.g., Senators Helms and Gramm) and members of international society (e.g., NGOs and allies that were in support of the court).

President Clinton had originally intended on supporting the Rome Statute with a vote in favor on 17 July 1998. However, the U.S. Delegate and Ambassador Scheffer failed to do as the Administration wanted. Senator Gramm, addressing Ambassador Scheffer, revealed this in the Congressional Hearings as he stated:

> It is no secret that the United States walked away from this treaty negotiated in Rome to establish an permanent United Nations international criminal court That was certainly the right thing for you to do I appreciate you having done that I am aware that the Administration was eager to sign that treaty, so the

> very fact that you, Mr Ambassador, declined to do so speaks volumes about how unwise this treaty really is

The overwhelming lack of support by the U.S. Congress helps to explain Clinton's last minute signatory to the Rome Statute with reservations (American Bar Association 2002). The presence of Senator Ashcroft and his position further displays the ideology which would strongly emerge during the Bush Administration. It further illustrates key issues contradiction of an international society. Ashcroft states (1998: 8): "If there is one critical component of sovereignty, it is the authority to define crimes and punishment. This court strikes at the heart of sovereignty by taking this fundamental power away from individual countries and giving it to international bureaucrats." Ashcroft is being disingenuous in his discourse. The court does nothing to affect a state's ability to define crimes and punishments *within its own borders*. Sovereignty has never allowed a given state to do so outside of its own national boundaries. This is little more than an argument that it is the right of U.S. troops to commit war crimes when it is deemed fit.

While at the time these statements were made, they represented the position of the party controlling the U.S. federal legislatures. Especially, they represented the more conservative positions within the Republican Party. They were neither U.S. policy nor reflective of mainstream U.S. governmental or public opinion. However, when George W. assumed the mantle of the Presidency in January of 2001, these ideologies would shift from a minority opinion within the legislature and become the core principles structuring U.S. foreign and military policy.

The Bush Administration and the ICC

The Bush Administration's determination to undermine the ICC is demonstrated by the political and legislative maneuvering that has taken place during their term in office. The actions of the Bush Administration reflect the dialectic nature of international law as a system that incorporates the broader political system. The establishment of the ICC hindered the political interests of the Administration, thus the U.S. responded with a number of attempts to thwart the Court. In an effort to restrict cooperation with the Court, on 28 November 2001, President Bush signed into law H.R. 2500 (Departments of Commerce, Justice, State, the Judiciary, and Related Agencies Appropriations Act) that contains amendment Section 630 which prohibits the use of appropriated funds for cooperation with, assistance, or other support to the International Criminal Court or its Preparatory Commission. The legislation of HR 2500 was a political move by the U.S. to restrict the use of military finances that supported any action for the ICC.

In March 2002, Pierre Prosper, U.S. Ambassador at large for War Crimes, testified before the House International Relations Committee calling for abolishment of war crime tribunals in The Hague and Arusha by 2008 (CICC Monitor, 9-2002). His position coincides with his appointment by G. W. Bush as

Ambassador and in support of the Administration's policies of detention and treatment of Afghanistan prisoners as enemy combatants not qualified for protection of the Geneva Conventions The Bush Administration then submitted a letter to the UN on 6 May 2002 that "formally declared U.S. intention not to ratify the Rome Statute, and renounced any legal obligations arising from its signature of the treaty."

The Bush administration attempted to exempt former U.S. Ambassador to the UN, Richard Holbrooke, from testifying before the International Criminal Tribunal for the former Yugoslavia in the trial of Slobodan Milosevic. The Bush administration was reported as being "wary of setting any precedent of senior U.S. officials testifying before international courts, particularly with regard to the International Criminal Court" (CICC Monitor 9-2002).

On 2 August 2002, President George W. Bush signed the Supplemental Appropriations Bill, making the American Servicemembers' Protection Act binding U.S. national law. The American Servicemembers' Protection Act (ASMPA) has been dubbed the "Hague Invasion Act" (CICC 2002, Documents). The ASMPA restricts: (1) U.S. cooperation in any comportment with the ICC, (2) Participation in UN Peacekeeping, and (3) giving military assistance to most countries that ratify the Rome Statute. Section 2005 of the ASMPA restricting the U.S. from UN Peacekeeping missions is broken into several aspects providing the U.S. "legitimate legislation" for a coercive tool to de-legitimize the efficacy of the ICC. This includes (1) the UN Security Council exempting U.S. armed forces from international prosecution, (2) U.S. troops to only operate in non-party states of the ICC, or (3) a state wanting participation in peacekeeping efforts must enter into the U.S. Article 98(2), or (4) U.S. national interests supersede its opposition to the ICC. Section 2007 prohibits U.S. military assistance unless that state would enter into a bilateral agreement by singing onto Article 98(2). The ASMPA had been in the works for nearly two years, as the U.S. feared the jurisdiction of the ICC. On June 14 2000 in the U.S. Senate the discussion of servicemen and issues of jurisdiction was opened. The opening statement made by Chairman Helms displays the concern over jurisdiction with: "Now then, with the establishment of a prominent International Criminal Court drawing nearer and nearer, the fact that American Servicemen and officials may one day be seized, extradited and prosecuted for war crimes is growing. And indeed, that day may have come" (Chair, Senator Helms, 6/2000: 1).

The U.S. National Security Strategy Policy was released in September 2002 with a direct reference to undermine the ICC:

> We will take the actions necessary to ensure that our efforts to meet our global security commitments and protect Americans are not impaired by the potential for investigations inquiry, or prosecution by the International Criminal Court (ICC), whose jurisdiction does not extend to Americans and which we do not accept We will work together with other nations to avoid complications in our military operations and cooperation, through such mechanisms as multilateral and bilateral agreements that will protect U S nationals from the ICC We will

> implement fully the American Servicemembers protection Act, whose provisions are intended to ensure and enhance the protection of U S personnel and officials

Clearly, the intention of the Bush Administration was to de-legitimize the authority of the ICC and to continue the road of impunity.

On 7 Decembei 2004 the Nethercutt Amendment was added to the 2004 Omnibus Appropriations Bill. This Amendment cuts assistance and funding for states that are signatories or Party members to the ICC unless a bilateral agreement is entered into with the U.S. thus, granting immunity for U.S. personnel, U.S. Nationals, Non-Nationals, and Contractors from ICC prosecution. The types of funding at risk include economic aid for counter-terrorism projects, peace process programs, anti-drug trafficking programs, truth and reconciliation programs, and HIV/AIDS education programs. Some of the States most threatened by this Amendment include Jordan, Ireland, Cyprus, Peru, Venezuela, and South Africa (ICC 2004).

The U.S. did not stop at domestic maneuvering to suppress the efficacy of the ICC. The Bush Administration put substantial pressure on the UN to ensure immunity from the ICC's jurisdiction by threatening to end all relief aid to Bosnia and Herzegovina. The timing of the U.S.'s demands for immunity was enhanced by the costs of U.S. aid withdrawal to the renewal of the United Nations Transitional Administration in East Timor (UNTAET). The result of the pressure put on the UN and the international community resulted in a controversial UN resolution. On 12 July 2002, the Security Council voted on Resolution 1422 granting peacekeepers from non-state parties a one-year immunity from prosecution by the ICC. Resolution 1422 has been viewed as an attempt by the U.S. to undertake a multifaceted approach in its efforts to prevent the functioning of the ICC as it was intended (U.S. Ambassador John Negroponte, 7-12-02). On 12 June 2003, Resolution 1422 was up for renewal at the UN. The proposed Resolution 1487 would offer the U.S. the same privileges of impunity granted in 1422. Ambassador James Cunningham, Deputy United States Representative, presented the U.S. position (U.S. UN Press Release #85 (03) June 12, 2003). The U.S. concerns over sovereignty, jurisdiction, and laws of *jus cogens* and *erga omnes* are evident in Cunningham's speech to the UN. He states:

> The resolution is consistent with the fundamental principle of international law, the need for a state to consent if it is to be bound, is respected by exempting from ICC jurisdiction personnel and forces of states that are not parties to the Rome Statute It is worth noting that the resolution does not in any way affect parties to the Court, nor the Rome Statute itself Nor does it, as some today suggested, elevate an entire category of people above the law The ICC is not "the law" It is important that Member States not add concern about ICC jurisdiction to the difficulty of participating I would suggest that even one instance of the ICC attempting to exercise jurisdiction over those involved in a UN operation would have a seriously damaging impact on future UN operations The U S has been and will continue to be a strong supporter of the

> tribunals established under the aegis of this Council But unlike the ICC, those tribunals are accountable to the Security Council (U S UN Press Release #85 (03) June 12, 2003)

Moreover, the actions of the Security Council were easily controllable by the U.S. due to its veto power. The UN approved extending the U.S. exemptions for another year in Resolution 1487. Kofi Annan warned that this should not become a yearly ritual for the U.S. Resolution 1422 and 1487 further weakens the jurisdictional powers of the ICC and ensures further conflicts within the international society.

Other Security Resolutions exempting U.S. personnel include Resolution 1497, adopted 1 August 2003. Resolution 1497 authorized the deployment of a stabilization force in Liberia; however, the U.S. used its veto power to ensure a paragraph was included granting exclusive jurisdiction to troop contributing states not party to the ICC, thus further opening the door for immunity from the ICC for crimes of genocide, war crimes, and crimes against humanity. Resolution 1502 was adopted by the Security Council addressing the need for protection for humanitarian workers and UN personnel after the bombing of the UN office in Baghdad. Yet the adoption of the resolution was significantly stalled due to the U.S. insistence that any reference to or of the Rome statute and the ICC be omitted.

The U.S. established bilateral agreement, known as Article 98(2), is a response by the U.S. to Article 98 of the Rome Statute. The precautions taken by the Prepatory Commission to recognize pre-dated international agreements resulted in a perceived weakness within the text of the Rome Statute (Article 98). This resulted in the misuse and misinterpretation that the U.S. seized to pursue U.S. interests and to further the de-legitimization of the ICC and limits the Court's already limited jurisdictional powers. The U.S. has drafted and circulated to over one hundred countries a version of Article 98 (98, 2) that would literally render the ICC ineffective in attaining jurisdictional authority over U.S. nationals, military, and peacekeepers abroad as well as any national the U.S. allowed into its own territory.

The U.S. Article 98 Agreements (98, 2) begins with the U.S. "Reaffirming the importance of bringing to justice those who commit genocide, crimes against humanity and war crimes." The Agreement continues with the affirmation by the U.S. of its intention to investigate and prosecute "appropriate acts." However, the U.S. is unable to prosecute persons covered by immunity agreements for all crimes that are included in the Rome Statute and the second state is not obligated to prosecute in its own court persons covered by this agreement. Crimes against humanity committed abroad are not crimes under domestic Federal law. Federal courts have jurisdiction over genocide committed abroad if committed by U S. nationals, but not U.S. members of the Armed Forces or persons not U.S. nationals.

Beyond the legalist jurisdiction that formulates a contradiction in the U.S.'s statement of ability and willingness to prosecute, the wording of 98 (2) states "where appropriate." Amnesty International claims this is "indicating the decision to investigate and prosecute is a matter solely within the discretion of the U.S.A and not a matter of a law" (AI 8/2002). Additionally, Article 98 (2) prevents U.S. nationals and others from voluntarily serving as a witness in cases of genocide, war crimes, and crimes against humanity (AI 8/2002). One of the larger points of concern in the text of this Agreement is E (1) which defines persons as former Government officials, employees (including contractors), military personnel, and nationals of one party. This expands Article 98 (2) to include individuals that would not fall under the agreement's purview. The U.S. Agreement continues with E (a-b) by proclaiming no person present in the territory of the Party be surrendered to the ICC, a third country, or expelled to a third country for purpose of aiding the ICC in its proceedings. The Agreement has made provision that if one party terminates the agreement, the agreement would still be valid for one year. The U.S. has clearly expanded the definition and attempted to enlarge the scope of persons covered under Article 98 of the Rome Statute. The CICC states the delegates' choice of terminology regarding "Sending State" was to ensure a consensus that this terminology would limit the use of Article 98 to those states that sent someone to another country under international agreement such as SOFA or an extradition treaty. Interestingly, the Rome Statute specifically addresses competing requests for the surrender of a person in Article 90 (4) that states: "If the requesting State is a State not Party to this statute, the requested State, if it is not under an international obligation to extradite the person to the requesting State, shall give priority to the request for surrender from the Court."

The Bilateral Agreements, Article 98 (2) are also based on the U.S. fears of being held accountable to the ICC even though the issues of Universal Jurisdiction were limited by compromises. The U.S.'s political and military interests required impunity. The solution sought out of fear was the impetus for returning back to inter-state relations with bilateral agreements. The U.S. fear of prosecution was reflected in the 2000 Senate Hearings:

> The FBI has warned several former U S officials not to travel to some countries, including some in Europe, where there is a risk of extradition to other nations interested in prosecuting them Moreover, this year for the first time we have seen an international criminal tribunal investigate allegations that NATO committed war crimes during the Kosovo campaign And a month ago, in May, NATO Secretary General Lord Robertson submitted to a degrading written interrogation by a woman named Carla Del Ponte, chief prosecutor of the Yugoslavia War Crimes Tribunal (Helms, 6/2000 2)

These seem to be little more than a tacit acknowledgement that if U.S. troops commit war crimes, they should be allowed to do so with impunity. President Bush, 1 July 2003, announced suspension in military aid to thirty-five state parties to the ICC. However, waivers for the ASPA prohibition of military assistance could be provided to ICC parties that conclude in the BIA Agreements (98(2)) (see also Appendix D). The Bush administration has effectively circulated over 100 Bilateral Article 98 (2) Agreements. This includes seventy-seven officially documented states that have signed, including seventeen state signatories of the ICC, thirty-seven state party members of the ICC, and twenty-three non-state parties (CICC 2003). The documented seventy-seven states that have signed these impunity agreements are listed along with dates and relative comments in Appendix D.

The Bilateral Article 98 (2) Agreements reflect the limited Jurisdiction of the ICC but they also reflect the larger contradiction based on issues of sovereignty within the international society and existing contradictions within the system of international law. These contradictions have led to conflicts that were addressed by establishing the ICC. However, the ICC was formed through mass compromises without addressing the aforementioned structural contradictions. The newly formed international system of justice and its corresponding laws led to further conflicts which were attempted to be resolved (for the U.S.) with the creation of a Bilateral Agreement (Article 98 (2)). This in turn, has led to further conflicts within the international society, as members disagree with the U.S.'s actions. Indeed, the political nature of international law coupled with the creation of new laws often results in new international conflicts. Not only is the U.S. pursuing immunity from the ICC, but also it is assertively "persuading" other states to ignore the legitimacy and jurisdiction of the ICC. Many of these "new" conflicts arise from the basic contradiction of international law as universal and the constructed image of sovereign states.

In reference to the International Criminal Court, the doctrine of universal jurisdiction continues to be disputed, though mostly by non-state parties and by political leaders who are at potential risk of being subjected to the Court's purview. For example, in July 2001, Henry Kissinger—who has been accused of war crimes—wrote a piece disclaiming universal jurisdiction and the legitimacy of the ICC. He argues that the concept of universal jurisdiction, which allows people who commit the most severe human rights crimes can be tried wherever they are found, is faulty as is the role and structure of the ICC. First, Kissinger is misguided in his belief that the ICC is universal. As we have shown in previous chapters, the ICC is a complimentary system and has limited jurisdictional scope. Beyond this, Kissinger attempts to de-legitimize the court itself based on the notion of universalism. He contends that "definitions of the relevant crimes are vague and highly susceptible to politicized application," a point the Bush Administration has also attempted to make. Kissinger criticizes the "extraordinary attempt of the ICC to assert jurisdiction over Americans even in the absence of U.S accession to the treaty" (Kissinger 2001). However, as we have seen, the ICC will assert such power only if an U.S. citizen commits a specified atrocity on the territory of a government that has joined the ICC and has thus delegated its prosecutorial authority to the court. This argument is central to the U.S. 98 (2) agreements. The role of the ICC, universalism, and the draconian ideology of state sovereignty granting impunity continue to surface within the international arena. We believe this could be because the practices and acceptance of customary laws could potentially be a factor in the future potential of the ICC to attain universalism.

We have discussed several issues centered on the ideologies of complimentary versus universal in past sections; however, the issue of customary law and its use within the universal ideology should also be explored. Let us begin with Article 25:4 of the Rome Statute which states: "no provision in this Statute relating to individual criminal responsibility shall affect the responsibility of States under international law." This Article acts to ensure that the Court's exclusion of state responsibility is not precluded from customary international law or treaties obligations. Thus, the role of customary law takes a significant stance for ensuring state sovereignty does not take precedence even when the jurisdiction of the ICC is limited by its very structure.

Chapter VI

The Illegal War on Iraq: The "Role" of the International Criminal Court

with Ronald C. Kramer

The Rome Statute, which established the International Criminal Court (ICC), is potentially the most significant development in international law and social control to date. The ICC is a promising progression towards the control of the most heinous crimes against humanity. The Preamble to the Rome Statute states:

> Mindful that during this century millions of children, women, and men have been victims of unimaginable atrocities that deeply shock the conscience of humanity determined to put an end to impunity for the perpetrators of these crimes and thus to contribute to the prevention of such crimes . establish an independent permanent International Criminal Court with jurisdiction over the most serious crimes of concern to the international community as a whole (Rome Statute, July 1999)

Thus, the fundamental goal of the ICC is to prosecute and punish those responsible for the most serious of crimes. Moreover, the most fundamental norm of international law is the prohibition of the use of force by nations. This norm is codified in the United Nations Charter and the Nuremberg Charter, which declared that waging a war of aggression, was the "supreme international crime." In this chapter, we argue that the invasion and occupation of Iraq in 2003 by the United States and its allies was a state crime, a flagrant violation of the UN Charter, the Nuremberg Charter, and other forms of international law: namely crimes of aggression, war crimes, and crimes against humanity. As all three of these categories are listed under the purview of the ICC, it would stand to reason that the Court would be committed to prosecuting and punishing those that committed such acts. However, as the ICC is based on a multilateral treaty—states volunteer their subjectivity to the Court's jurisdiction—its role as a universal institution of social control is limited to participating states. Moreover, the United States and Iraq are among the handful of states that refused to be under the ICC's jurisdiction.

First, we will explore what it could mean "if" the United States or Iraq had ratified the Rome Statute Treaty. A detailing of the United States violations under international law follows this. We then offer the following "what if" scenario: if the ICC was indeed a universal court, what influence could it have diplomatically? More specifically, as the court currently stands, universal or via consensus, what influence or constraint could it have, remembering that Britain is a ratified member state and primary ally of the U.S. war on Iraq? In conclusion, a brief narrative on the development of the court is provided.

What if the United States or Iraq Were Parties to the Rome Statute?

As we will see in later chapters, the International Criminal Court is a complex system based on states willing submission to its jurisdiction. Neither Iraq nor the United States are members to the Rome Statute Treaty. But, let us suppose the United States was a signatory. Granting that the war on Iraq is illegal according to international law and the "crimes" committed fall under the purview of the court, which we argue below, what role could the court assume? According to the Rome Statute, cases may be brought against a state by two means: (1) a state may refer cases to the Prosecution, or (2) the Prosecutor can initiate the investigation based on information of a crime being committed within the jurisdiction of the Court. Realistically, the United States would neither bring its own illegalities to the court, nor is it likely that any state (other than Iraq) would bring charges against the lone "superpower" of the world for fear of retaliation and/or economic harm. Moreover, since Iraq is not a member state to the Rome Statute, it would not be able to bring allegations to the court against the United States for aggressive intervention and attack either. That leaves the option up to the prosecutor to bring indictments against the United States, which, for our hypothetical case, we will assume occurs.

However, as this is a complimentary system, prosecutorial charges do not result in immediate court action. Once allegations have been made against a state, that state has the right and duty to first investigate and prosecute its own citizens—including heads of state—before the court may intervene. If *and only if* the United States refused to investigate and legitimately prosecute those accused of crimes listed under the ICC could the jurisdiction of the court be employed. Let's suppose the U.S. refused to act on the charges brought forth. The

ICC is still limited in its investigative reach, being unable to subpoena any state or their records. While the Court may request a warrant or subpoena, the Prosecutor and the Court lack an empowered policing agency to ensure the fulfillment of either request (Article 54-58 Rome Statute). The Prosecutor is limited to requesting the presence of persons being investigated, victims, and witnesses. The Court must seek the cooperation of a state in fulfilling the Prosecutor's requests. Again, if the U.S. refused cooperation with the court, the only option left would be for an alternative state member to extradite those accused of the crimes. For this to occur, those listed under the charges brought by the prosecutor must be in the domestic territory of another state member to the Rome Statute.

While the goal of the ICC is to prosecute those that commit the most heinous crimes against the international society, it is able to do so only under perfect conditions of consensus. From this exercise, it becomes clear that the only means to prosecute the U.S. by the ICC, after its own domestic failure to do so, is via its own agreement to be prosecuted or a situation in which the heads of state and top military officials left the U.S. and entered another state member's territory and that state was willing to arrest and extradite them to the court. Thus, as it current stands, the ICC's potential deterrent threat is very limited.[1]

So, what if Iraq had been a signatory to the Rome Statute and not the United States? Once the U.S. aggressively attacked Iraq, the Iraqi Regime could have requested the prosecutor to investigate U.S. actions. However, under these conditions, Iraq would have had to still have its legitimate government in place. As the U.S. quickly dismantled the Iraqi government and military, it is highly unlikely that Iraq could have brought charges immediately to the court. Currently, the interim government in Iraq could potentially bring charges against the U.S. While this is a highly unlikely scenario (as the interim government is a U.S. placed political apparatus), let's assume they did. Once allegations had been made against the United States by the Iraqi regime, the issue of the ICC's empowerment remains a central point. Just as the previous scenario outlined, those accused must be willing to participate with the court. However, compliance by a non-party state is highly unlikely (Mullins, Kauzlarich, and Rothe 2004; Rothe and Mullins 2004; and Rothe 2004). So again, we would need for those accused of the crimes to be within the territory of Iraq before they could then be arrested and extradited to the court.

From these scenarios we can see the complexities involved in using the ICC as an international institution of social control. Moreover, we can see that a state's willingness to participate by becoming a member state or through compliance with the prosecutor's requests and submission to the court's proceedings is a key impediment for the court to aggressively seek out those accused of the "supreme crimes against humanity." As we previously noted, the role of the court is one based on a system of complimentary jurisdiction: meaning all member states have the duty to first prosecute their own for atrocities as recognized under state sovereignty. Thus, the role of the court is secondary to state members' own domestic judicial system. The ICC is further limited in its jurisdiction to its member states. Hence, the scenarios we played out here illuminate the complexities of this court which the previous chapters explored.

To continue with our hypothetical case, we can envision the sort of legal argument that the prosecutor would make against the U.S. concerning the war on Iraq. Many scholars have identified and explored the violations of international law that were committed by the invasion and occupation of Iraq (Boyle 2004; Falk 2004; Kramer and Michalowski 2005; Kramer, Michalowski, and Rothe 2005; Mandel 2004; Sands 2005; Weeramantry 2003). These researchers are not the only ones to declare the war criminal; in fact, in an interview with the BBC, United Nations Secretary-General Kofi Annan stated that the war "is not in conformity with the UN Charter, from our point of view, and from the Charter point of view it was illegal" (UN News Service 2004:1). In the following section we review the legal arguments for declaring the war on Iraq to be illegal under international law. These are the arguments that a potential ICC prosecutor would have at their disposal if they wished to pursue a case concerning the 2003 U.S.-led invasion of Iraq.

Why the U.S. War on Iraq Was Illegal

Violating the U.N. Charter

With the creation of the United Nations in 1945, the UN Charter became the bedrock document of the international legal system. The Charter is considered to be the highest treaty in the world, the embodiment of international law that codifies and supersedes all existing laws and customs (Normand 2003).[2] The Nuremberg Charter is a part of the UN Charter. It is important to note that the UN Charter is also a treaty entered into and ratified by the United States and as such becomes part of the "supreme law of the land" within the United States under Article VI, Clause 2 of the Constitution. Thus, a violation of the Charter could also be considered a domestic crime in the United States.

At the heart of the U.N. Charter is the moral and legal prohibition of war. As C. G. Weeramantry (2003), a former Judge of the International Court of Justice, points out: "It would be true to say . . . that by its very structure, by its express provisions and by its underlying intent the U.N. Charter completely outlaws unilateral resort to armed force." The specific prohibition of aggressive war is found in Article 2(4) of the Charter which reads: "All members shall refrain in their international relations from the threat or use of force against the territorial integrity or political independence of any state, or [behave] in any other manner inconsistent with the purposes of the United Nations." Article 2(4) is a peremptory norm having the character of supreme law that cannot be modified by treaty or by ordinary customary law.

On its face, the U.S. war on Iraq is a clear violation of Article 2(4). However, U.S. and British state officials have argued that the invasion of Iraq can be legally justified by reference to various exceptions to Article 2(4) that are found in the UN Charter and in the emerging concept of humanitarian intervention. To determine whether or not the Iraq war was a state crime, we must determine whether or not these exceptions are valid.

Exceptions to Article 2(4)

There are three possible exceptions to the Article 2(4) general prohibition on the use of force. Two can be found within the UN Charter itself: Article 51 (the right of self-defense) and Article 42 (collective enforcement authorized by the Security Council). Article 51 of the UN Charter recognizes that states have an "inherent right" to use force in self-defense. The triggering condition for the exercise of self-defense under Article 51 must be the occurrence of an actual armed attack (see Rai 2003). With regard to the situation in Iraq, clearly there was no armed attack by Iraq against the U.S. or UK, and no evidence that Saddam Hussein had any intention of attacking either country. Thus, it would seem that Article 51 can not be used to justify the unprovoked invasion of Iraq.

The Bush administration, however, implied on numerous occasions that there was a strong connection between Saddam Hussein and the Al Qaeda terrorist organization that was responsible for the September 11, 2001 attacks in the United States. While they never stated it directly, administration officials repeatedly implied that Iraq was somehow involved in the 9-11 terrorist attacks. During the build up to the war, no major statement on Iraq by the Bush administration was made without multiple references to terrorism in general and Al Qaeda specifically (see Prados 2004). Attacking Iraq, they argued, was part of the broader war on terrorism. This campaign was highly successful as evidenced by the fact that prior to the start of the invasion, 70 percent of U.S. citizens believed that Iraq was responsible for 9-11 (see Corn 2003). The clear implication of the administration was that Saddam Hussein was responsible for the terrorist attacks against the U.S. and that war on Iraq was a legitimate form of self-defense.

There is, however, *no evidence* that Iraq had any ties to Al Qaeda or any responsibility for the 9-11 terrorist attacks. The Bush administration claims concerning Iraqi connections to Al Qaeda have been thoroughly investigated, most recently by the 9-11 Commission, and found to be false (see Rampton and Stauber 2003; Scheer, Scheer, and Chaudhry 2003). Richard Clarke (2004), the Counterterrorism expert who has served four presidents, reported that he personally informed President Bush that Al Qaeda was responsible for the terrorist attacks and that Iraq had no connection to Al Qaeda (see also Dorrien 2003; Suskind 2004). Yet statements implying such a connection became a staple of the prewar campaign to build public support for an invasion. In late 2003, both President Bush and Secretary of State Colin Powell were finally forced to admit in public that there was no evidence connecting Saddam Hussein to 9-11. Thus, the war on Iraq cannot be justified as self-defense against an actual armed attack under Article 51.

However, some scholars interpret Article 51 more broadly to allow for preemptive or anticipatory self-defense in response to an imminent threat (Slomanson 2003). In 2002 the Bush administration promulgated a new National Security Strategy that claimed the United States has the right to use force preemptively against any perceived threat to U.S. security (Mahajan 2003). This new strategic doctrine was then asserted as a legal justification for the use of force against Iraq. Testifying in front of Congress on 19 September 2002 Secretary of Defense Donald Rumsfeld rejected the idea that a U.S. attack would violate international law and evoked a right of anticipatory self-defense against Iraq's alleged weapons of mass destruction. In the build up to the war, U.S. and Britain officials repeatedly claimed to have intelligence that showed that Iraq had stockpiles of biological and chemical weapons, an active nuclear weapons program and the potential to hand these weapons off to terrorist groups for use against the West. Iraq thus constituted a "grave and gathering threat" of imminent harm, they argued, a threat that required the U.S. and UK to launch a preemptive strike in self-defense.

There are several major problems with the claim that the invasion of Iraq was covered under the legal concept of self-defense. First, the doctrine of anticipatory self-defense is only legally justified when the necessity for action is, in the words of U.S. Secretary of State Daniel Webster regarding the 1837 Caroline Affair,[3] "instant, overwhelming, and leaving no choice of means, and no moment for deliberation" (quoted in Gardner 2003). That is, the threat must be imminent. There was no evidence of an imminent threat from Iraq in 2003.

But the biggest problem with the claim of anticipatory self-defense, of course, is that Iraq did not, in fact, have any remaining biological or chemical weapons or an active nuclear weapons program. Prior to the war there was a considerable amount of evidence that Iraq no longer possessed prohibited weapons (Pitt 2002; Rai 2002, 2003; Ratner, Green, and Olshansky 2003; Solomon and Erlich 2003). The United Nations Special Commission (UNSCOM) inspection process operated in Iraq from 1991 to 1998 and verified that all or nearly all of Iraq's biological and chemical weapons had been destroyed, and that its nuclear weapons program had been dismantled (Pitt 2002; Ritter 2003). An Iraqi defector, Hussein Kamel, who was Saddam Hussein's son-in-law and a manager of Iraqi weapons programs, reported that Iraq had destroyed its stockpiles of weapons and the missiles to deliver them (Prados 2004; Scheer, Scheer, and Chaudhry 2003). The UN Monitoring, Verification and Inspection Commission (UNMOVIC), headed by Hans Blix, and the International Atomic Energy Agency (IAEA), directed by Mohammed ElBaradei, operating in Iraq right up to the time of the invasion, were reporting that they could find no operable weapons of mass destruction, nor any viable facilities to produce them (Blix 2004).

During the invasion the Iraqi military did not use chemical or biological weapons and, after the war, coalition troops found no prohibited weapons. The final blow to the U.S./UK claims concerning Iraqi weapons of mass destruction came from the report of the CIA's Iraq Survey Group, headed first by David Kay and then by Charles Duelfer. In January 2004, Kay reported that no evidence of any stockpiles of Iraqi weapons had been found. "It turns out we were all wrong," he stated. Then in October 2004, Duelfer reported that Iraq had destroyed its illicit weapons stockpiles within months after the Persian Gulf War of 1991, and its ability to produce such weapons had significantly eroded by the time of the U.S. invasion in 2003. Thus, the available evidence makes it clear that Iraq had, in fact, disarmed, was in compliance with UN Security Council resolutions, and had not posed any threat that would justify war under the legal doctrine of anticipatory self-defense (see Allman 2004; Eisendrath and Goodman 2004; Gellman 2004; Hiro 2004; Rai 2003; Rampton and Stauber 2003). Furious debates erupted in both the U.S. and the UK about whether the pre-war intelligence was flawed or whether officials had manipulated the reports. With the release of the famous Downing Street memo (Danner 2005), the bulk of the evidence points to deliberate manipulation of the evidence concerning the threat of Iraqi weapons in order to build public support for the war (also see Cirincione, Matthews, Perkovich, and Orton 2004; Dreyfuss and Vest 2004; Eisendrath and Goodman 2004; Pollack 2004; Prados 2004).

The Bush and Blair administrations then reframed their justification for the invasion around the claim that Iraq had "weapons related programs" or the "intent" to develop weapons of mass destruction in the future. These were not, however, the claims they used to mobilize public support for the war in the months prior to the invasion of Iraq. Moreover, claims about intent and future possible programs have no legal standing as justifications for preemptive war. They do not constitute an imminent threat; the war cannot be justified on the basis of self-defense

UN Security Council Authorization

A second exception to the Article 2(4) prohibition of war is found in Chapter Seven of the Charter that sets out the collective security structure of the UN. When the UN Security Council determines, under Article 39, that there is a threat to, or breach of, international peace and security, it may authorize various measures to respond to the threat or breach. If all of the non-military measures allowed under Article 41 have been exhausted, then, and only then, can the Security Council authorize the use of force under Article 42 to restore or maintain international peace and security. There was no such authorization for the use of force against Iraq in March 2003. The U.S., the UK, and Spain had sought a Security Council resolution in early 2003 that declared that Iraq was in violation of an earlier resolution (1441), and that this noncompliance posed a threat to international peace and security. This draft resolution did not explicitly authorize force, but it was clear that the drafters intended to use such a resolution to legally justify their planned invasion. Despite intense pressure from the Bush and Blair administrations, and amid charges of U.S. and UK efforts to spy on other Security Council members, the draft resolution was withdrawn when the sponsors decided that it would not pass. As Hans Blix (2004) concluded: "By withholding an authorization desired if not formally requested, the Council dissociated the UN from an armed action that most member states thought was not justified-at any rate, not at this stage."

Even though there was no formal UN Security Council resolution authorizing war against Iraq, U.S. and UK officials argued that a series of previous Security Council resolutions could be read in such a way as to provide legal justification for the invasion of Iraq. This argument avers that these earlier resolutions concerning Iraq provided a continuing authorization for war. The resolutions in question are 678 (1990), which authorized the use of force to repel Iraq from Kuwait, 687 (1991), which set out the terms of the cease fire at the end of the first Gulf War, and the more recent 1441 (2002), which sent UNMOVIC to Iraq to establish an enhanced inspections regime.

In essence, the U.S. and UK argument was that any material breach of the disarmament requirements of 687 or 1441 either "revived" the authority to use force under 678, or triggered a new authorization for any member state to use all necessary means (military force) to enforce the disarmament resolutions. According to a number of legal critics (see Charlesworth 2003; Franck 2003; Normand 2003; Ratner 2002; Sands 2005), these assertions required a "selective," "misleading," "creative," "problematic," and ultimately "unsustainable" interpretation of the resolutions in question. First of all, the 1990 authorization of force against Iraq ended with Iraq's withdrawal from Kuwait. Second, neither 687 nor 1441 contains an automatic trigger for the use of force. In both resolutions the Security Council declared that it "remained seized of the matter" meaning that if there were any problems with the enforcement of the resolutions the issue would have to come back to the Council for further consideration. While 1441 expresses concern that the government of Iraq may have failed to comply with its commitments pursuant to resolution 687, it responded to this concern by establishing "an enhanced inspection regime." That inspection process (UNMOVIC) was in place and, according to Hans Blix (2004), was operating with reasonable cooperation from the Iraqi government at the time of the invasion. Furthermore, the decision to enforce a Security Council resolution must always be a collective decision of the Council itself, not a unilateral decision of any particular member state or coalition of member states. Most importantly, as we noted earlier, overwhelming evidence has established that Iraq did not have weapons of mass destruction and was, in fact, in compliance with its disarmament obligations under 687 and 1441. If Iraq was not in material breach of its obligation to disarm, then this legal justification for war is null and void, and even if they had been in material breach, it would still have required a Security

Council resolution expressly authorizing the use of force to render the invasion other than an illegal war of aggression.

Humanitarian Intervention

The third possible exception to Article 2(4) can be found in what Normand (2003) calls "the legally dubious doctrine of humanitarian intervention, a new concept that has not gained the support of the international law community." The U.S. and the UK argued that they had a right and a duty to use military force for the humanitarian purpose of liberating Iraq and saving the Iraqi people from the human rights violations of the brutal tyrant Saddam Hussein. There are good reasons to doubt that this was a primary motive for the war. In most of the major statements the Bush administration made justifying the invasion, the liberation of Iraq was barely mentioned. As Falk (2003) notes, "War is too serious a matter to allow it to be declared on one basis and justified after the fact on another."

Furthermore, in the past the U.S. had strongly supported and supplied Saddam Hussein, particularly during his war against Iran in the 1980s (see Chomsky 2003; Zunes 2003); the invasion and occupation of Iraq was planned by the neoconservatives in the Bush administration as the first step in their grand geopolitical strategy to enhance U.S. imperial domination of the world (Dorrien 2004). But even if we put those doubts aside and accept humanitarian intervention as the true motive for invading Iraq, the question remains as to the legality of such an intervention under international law (Chesterman 2001). As Normand (2003) points out: "This concept has aroused considerable skepticism from most international lawyers, in part because it circumvents well-established procedures and principles of the UN Charter and international law. Even supporters concede that humanitarian intervention is a moral argument and not a legal right."

If a situation involving gross human rights abuses exists and requires a humanitarian intervention, the UN Security Council is already empowered, under Chapter Seven, to respond with force if necessary to maintain international peace and security. But if the Security Council is unable or unwilling to intervene in such a situation, can "a coalition of the willing" use force to respond to the crisis? Some legal scholars say "yes," citing the NATO intervention in Kosovo in the 1990s as a prime example. This action violated the UN Charter's rules on the use of force. Still, the Independent International Commission on Kosovo later concluded that the intervention was, in a memorable phrase, "illegal, but legitimate" (Faulk 2003). Lest this conclusion be interpreted as an overly broad cover to allow individual states a right to intervene and use force without accountability to general principles of law, the Commission suggested that several conditions must apply for a humanitarian intervention to be legitimate. Faulk further states: "The troublesome elasticity of this doctrine was conditioned in two ways, first by suggesting the need for the intervening side to bear a heavy burden of persuasion" and as a secondary condition with a checklist of duties "that need to be fulfilled . . . emphasizing the protection of the civilian population . . . and a convincing focus on humanitarian goals, as distinct from economic and strategic aims."

According to the logic of this doctrine, although a military intervention undertaken for a humanitarian purpose would be technically illegal if not authorized by the Security Council, it would be spared the label of state criminality if the intervention met certain legitimating conditions that outweighed the illegality of the act in the eyes of the international society. The question is, did the war on Iraq meet these legitimating conditions? Most legal analysts say no (Boyle 2004; Charlesworth 2003; Falk 2003; Mandel 2004; Normand 2003; Sands 2005).

There is no public evidence that a humanitarian crisis existed in 2003 in which a large-scale loss of human life was being caused by the Iraqi government (Charlesworth 2003; Roth 2004). While it's certainly true that Saddam Hussein's government had a record of political repression, human rights abuses, and chemical weapons use, most of these crimes occurred in the 1980s and early 1990s when the U.S. and other Western nations were either supporting and supplying Iraq or standing idly by (Samir al-Khahil 1990; Amnesty International 2002). After the Gulf War of 1991, the Iraqi government was kept in check by UN weapons inspections, Security Council sanctions, and U.S. no fly zones. While the Hussein government remained a brutal and repressive regime, Human Rights Watch concluded that at the time of the U.S. invasion, political killings in Iraq were "not of the exceptional nature that would justify such intervention," nor was invasion "the last reasonable option to stop Iraqi atrocities." The Bush administration chose to risk invasion and occupation despite widespread concern around the world that this choice would result in more rather than less death, injury, and material destruction for Iraqis. The heavy burden of persuasion to justify a humanitarian invasion was not met, and subsequent events have made it clear that the intervention has unleashed an even greater humanitarian crisis for Iraq.

In addition to bearing the burden of persuasion, the legal and moral legitimacy of humanitarian interventions depends, at a minimum, on protecting civilian populations. This was not done. The use of indiscriminate weapons (such as cluster bombs, napalm, and depleted uranium shells) and indiscriminate tactics (such as decapitation strikes) by the invading forces killed thousands of Iraqi civilians. Charlesworth (2003) notes: "If the human rights of the Iraqis were the primary motive for the invasion, given the destruction of civilian life and infrastructure that it caused, questions can be raised about whether the means used to protect Iraqi human rights were proportionate." That is, even if the liberation of the Iraqi people was a just cause, we must examine the morality of the means that are selected to accomplish that goal. Shalom (2004: 1) points out: "Basic morality and international law specify that not all means are permissible even in the pursuit of a just cause." War is rarely a permissible means to accomplish any goal. "Talking about the world, or at least Iraq, being better off . . . avoids the civilian carnage caused by the war" (Savoy 2004: 16).

Violations of International Humanitarian Law

Given that the invasion of Iraq was illegal under international law, the deaths and destruction it caused are war crimes. Beyond these crimes, however, it has been documented that during the invasion and subsequent occupation, the U.S. engaged in a number of specific violations of international humanitarian law (IHL), also known as the law of armed conflict. IHL stems from a variety of sources, particularly the 1907 Hague Regulations, the four Geneva Conventions of 1949, and the First Additional Protocol of 1977 to the 1949 Geneva Conventions (Protocol I). This body of international law is also built on the broad moral principle that innocent human life must be protected at all costs. IHL requires parties to an armed conflict to protect civilians and noncombatants, limits the means or methods that are permissible during warfare, and sets out the rules that govern the behavior of occupying forces. Violations of IHL are considered war crimes. The U.S. Congress expressly incorporated the 1949 Geneva Conventions into U.S. law with the ratification of the Geneva treaties and the passage of the War Crimes Act of 1996 (Slomanson 2003).

Protecting Civilians

The most important moral principle of International Humanitarian Law is the protection of innocent civilians. IHL forbids direct assaults on civilians and civilian objects, and it prohibits indiscriminate attacks that, in the language of Protocol I, are "expected to cause incidental loss of civilian life, injury to civilians [or] damage to civilian objectives . . . which would be excessive in relation to the concrete and direct military advantage anticipated from that attack." Yet, tens of thousands of Iraqi civilians have died as a result of the invasion and subsequent occupation. One estimate puts the number of excess deaths since the invasion at 100,000 (Roberts, et al., 2004). A Human Rights Watch (2003) report documents that the widespread use of cluster bombs and numerous attempted "decapitation" strikes targeting senior Iraqi officials—often based on scanty or questionable intelligence—were responsible for the deaths of hundreds of Iraqi civilians. Coalition forces have also exposed Iraqi civilians to significant "collateral damage" through the deployment of Mark 77 firebombs, which are similar to napalm bombs (Buncombe 2003), and the indiscriminate use of depleted uranium munitions that release dangerous radioactive debris in the short term (Miller 2003), and pose long-term environmental hazards to people exposed to uranium-contaminated soil or water (Michalowski and Bitten 2004).

Violations of IHL during the Occupation

In addition to the use of weapons and military tactics that brought devastating lethality to Iraqi's civilian populations during the period of "active hostilities," four other sets of war crimes were committed by the Bush and Blair administrations during the occupation phase of the campaign: (1) the failure to secure public safety and protect civilian rights, (2) the illegal transformation of the Iraqi economy, (3) indiscriminate responses to Iraqi resistance actions that resulted in further civilian casualties, and (4) the torture of Iraqi prisoners.

Once the U.S. and UK became occupying powers, a new set of legal obligations were incurred under international law. In the first instance, under the Fourth Geneva Convention, the occupying power must ensure public safety and order, and guarantee the civilian population's fundamental rights to food, health care, education, work, and freedom of movement. The lives and property of civilians must be respected at all times. If the occupying power fails to assure these rights, it is a violation of IHL and is considered a war crime. The evidence is clear that the occupiers failed to meet these legal obligations.

Amnesty International reports (AI) (2004) revealed that across Iraq, disorder, fear, and insecurity prevailed in the first year of the occupation. In the early weeks following the overthrow of the Hussein government, UK and U.S. troops stood by as most important public buildings were looted and destroyed. The immediate outlawing of the Iraqi Army and criminalization of key governmental leaders meant that at the point of defeat, there was no one in a position of authority to surrender to invading forces while providing a continuity of government services. The elimination of low-level Baath party members from public positions, including policing, had additional consequences for Iraq's security situation. The wholesale blacklisting of large numbers of Baathist public employees significantly weakened Iraq's police forces. Left leaderless, and without an effective police apparatus, Iraqi cities, particularly Baghdad, made a swift descent into not only looting and chaos, but a free-for-all of private retribution and routine criminality. As AI noted:

> The Coalition Forces had removed the previous government's authority, but had demonstrably failed to provide the protection and assistance they were obligated to give the people whose land they were occupying Under international humanitarian law as occupying powers it was their duty to maintain and restore public order, and provide food, medical care, and relief assistance They failed in this duty, with the result that millions of Iraqis faced grave threats to their health and safety

The U.S. effort to privatize Iraq's economy constitutes a second set of war crimes. The objective of the Bush administration is to transform Iraq from a state-controlled economy into a showpiece market economy characterized by free trade, supply-side tax policy, privatization of key economic sectors, and widespread foreign ownership in those sectors (Bacon 2004; Juhaz 2004; Krugman 2004b). However, as journalist William Greider (2003) notes, international law prohibits an occupying state from unilateral transformation of the economic or social structure of the occupied country. The obstacle is the Fourth Geneva Convention of 1949, which codified in greater detail the principles of "occupation law" first framed by the Hague Convention of 1907 rules of warfare meant to prevent a military power from plundering a defeated nation or reordering the country (as Hitler repeatedly did) to conform to the conqueror's ideology and economics. Occupation law requires the occupying power to respect the domestic laws of the subjugated country unless absolutely prevented from doing so by military necessity. Yet in a series of Orders in 2003, L. Paul Bremer, the head of the Coalition Provisional Authority at the time, ignored Iraqi law and opened the country up for foreign investment and ownership. As economist Antonia Juhasz (2004) notes:

> These orders include the full privatization of public enterprises, full ownership rights by foreign firms of Iraqi businesses, full repatriation of foreign profits, the Flat Tax, the opening of Iraq's banks to foreign control, national treatment for foreign companies and elimination of nearly all trade barriers

This transformation of the Iraqi economy, what Bremer called "reconstruction," has been handed over primarily to U.S.-based corporations, with Halliburton and Bechtel being major winners of multi-billion dollar contracts. Amid charges of "war profiteering," these companies have received contracts without competitive bidding or even minimal oversight (Hartung 2004). The Bush administration has also systematically blocked proposals to have Congressional auditors oversee spending, or to impose severe penalties for fraud (Krugman 2004b).

In addition to opening the door for war profiteering (see Rothe 2006) and corruption, the consequences of this economic colonization for the Iraqi people have been devastating. Privatization led to 70 percent unemployment (Klein 2003). There is no unemployment insurance or welfare system. According to journalist David Bacon (2004), the violence of poverty "exacerbated by economic sanctions after the first Gulf War, has been deepened by the U.S. invasion. Every day the economic policies of the occupying authorities create more hunger among Iraq's working people, transforming them into a pool of low-wage, semi-employed labor, desperate for jobs at almost any price." Moreover, it is clear that the CPA, at the highest levels, was aware that the economic changes responsible for these conditions were illegal under international law. In a 26 March 2003 controversial leaked memo, British Attorney General Lord Peter Goldsmith, informed Prime Minister Blair that the transformation of the Iraqi economy was illegal (Innes 2003; Mate 2004).

The third category of war crimes concerning the occupation involves the U.S./UK response to the Iraqi resistance. The occupation has provoked fierce armed resistance by militant Sunni and Shiite sectors of the Iraqi populace. The result has been the death of thousands of Iraqis and hundreds of coalition military personnel. There is strong evidence that the occupying powers have engaged in numerous violations of IHL as they attempt to handle the Iraqi resistance, which has only served to fan the fires of insurrection and deepen the daily security crisis for average Iraqi citizens (Andersen 2004). In their attempts to control the resistance, U.S. and British forces have shot and killed demonstrators, bombed civilian areas, and used other types of excessive force resulting in the death of innocent civilians, demolished homes, and destroyed property in acts of collective punishment (Amnesty International 2004; Packer 2004). Coalition forces have used hostage taking as way of rooting out insurgents, effected arbitrary arrests, and held detainees indefinitely without charges or access to lawyers (ICRC 2004). Iraq's occupiers have, in effect, stripped Iraqis of the most basic protections of due process rights, protections they are enjoined to guarantee by existing International Humanitarian Law.

The final set of war crimes we will consider concerns the torture of Iraqi prisoners being held by Coalition forces. A Pentagon report, prepared by U.S. Major General Antonio Taguba, detailed the "systemic and illegal" torture and humiliation that occurred inside the infamous Abu Ghraib prison. Specifically, Taguba found that there were numerous instances of "sadistic, blatant, and wanton criminal abuses" at Abu Ghraib. Photos released by CBS's 60 Minutes II on 28 April 2004 documented both physical and psychosexual abuse inflicted on Iraqi detainees by U.S. military personnel at the prison (Hirsch 2004; Taguba 2003). Cohn (2004), executive vice president of the U.S. National Lawyers Guild, points out: "These actions are not only offensive to human dignity; they violate the Geneva Convention, and the Convention Against Torture and Other Cruel, Inhuman or Degrading Treatment or Punishment."

Bush administration officials tried to downplay the torture scandal by suggesting that the crimes were the work of just a few "bad apples" among the Military Police (MP) Brigade working at Abu Ghraib; individual crimes perhaps, but not state crimes. The Taguba report, however, documents the involvement of higher-level state officials and private contractors hired by the U.S. government. The criminal liability for the Abu Ghraib torture and abuse, as for all the violations of IHL during the invasion and occupation of Iraq, does not stop with those immediately guilty of the crimes. As Cohn (2004) observes, the well-established doctrine of "command responsibility," enshrined in both international law and U.S. military law, "provides criminal liability for commanders whose underlings commit war crimes. Even if the superior officer did not personally carry out the criminal acts, he/she would be liable if he/she knew or should have known of the conduct, yet failed to take reasonable measures to prevent or repress the criminal behavior." In the case of Iraqi prisoners in U.S. custody, there is significant evidence that immediate superior officers were aware that prisoners were being tortured, and that these practices were not limited to the Abu Ghraib prison (see Jehl and Schmitt 2004a; Wilkinson and Rubin 2004; Zernike 2004a, 2004b). And as the "torture memos" and other documents show, responsibility for these abuses does not stop with superior officers in Iraq, but goes right to the top of the Pentagon and the White House (Danner 2004; Greenberg and Dratel 2005; Hersh 2004).

If the International Criminal Court Had Universal Jurisdiction

Above, we have set forth the case that the invasion of Iraq and subsequent acts of war and occupation constitute war crimes under existing international law. If this is true, then George W. Bush, Tony Blair, and their core military and political advisors are war criminals whom should be subject to removal from office, prosecution, and punishment. But no legal proceedings are likely to occur with regard to these crimes. The U.S. is not a signatory to the International Criminal Court, and as permanent members of the UN Security Council, the U.S. and UK can veto any move to censure their illegalities. While The UK is indeed a signatory to the Rome Statute, it remains unlikely that any action will be taken in the current political climate. However, while the ICC remains a complimentary court, let us again imagine what potential the court could have if it had universal jurisdiction—over every state and territory of international society.

Under these conditions, the scenarios we explored of the U.S. or Iraq as signatories would not be relevant. The court would automatically have over both states and be able to bring charges and initiate an investigation. However, the issue of the court's empowerment is still relevant; the court is not equipped with a policing enforcement agency. Thus, it would still require state compliance to be subjected to the court's proceedings unless those accused left their domestic territory enabling another state to arrest and extradite them to the court.

An example of these weaknesses is best seen with the current Iraq war and Britain. While the Court does not have universal jurisdiction, it does retain authority over Britain. The British, as key participants in the Iraq war, are subject to prosecution under the Rome Statute. Most obviously, the potential of the court to act as a deterrent was not a significant catalyst in the decision-making process by Britain before joining the U.S. in its act of illegal aggression. However, the British Administration could potentially be brought before the ICC once Britain itself rejects charging the state leaders with international crimes under the purview of the ICC as the court cannot intervene if a case is being prosecuted in national courts: it can intervene only if those national courts are unable or unwilling to act. This clause, which would present the ICC prosecutor with formidable problems of proof, does at least require the British courts to act.

By the end of 2003, several groups had attempted to utilize the ICC to bring forth charges against the British government. The Athens Bar Association of Greece, led by attorney Dimitris Paxinos, formally lodged a complaint with the ICC prosecutor. The complaint outlines 110 violations of the international criminal code. The charges are against Prime Minister Tony Blair; the foreign secretary, Jack Straw; Geoff Hoon, the Secretary of State for Defence; and

Adam Ingram, the Armed Forces Minister. In addition, five international lawyers working with non-governmental agencies outlined a case against Britain for submission to an international "alternative" court called the Permanent Peoples' Tribunal in Rome, and then the case will be brought to the prosecutor's office of the ICC in The Hague. It is now up to the ICC chief prosecutor Luis Moreno Ocampo to decide whether there is any substance to the suit. Were he to conclude that Prime Minister Blair and others should face legal proceedings, the British judicial authorities would be informed and given the option of taking over the case. Only if they refused to do so would the ICC start proceedings. However, as will be demonstrated in much greater detail in the subsequent chapter, the lack of empowerment and policing force could hinder any efforts of the Prosecutor to act even if the British judicial system fails to do so.

We have not yet explored the potential of the court to act along diplomatic lines; even without the ability to arrest, detain, and prosecute, a universal court's existence could produce an ability to constrain or control the most atrocious crimes against humanity via its legitimacy as an institution of social control.

Assuming the ICC to have universal jurisdiction could imply that the court is able to act as a constraint against the worst crimes against international society before they occur. At best, we could speculate that an empowered court's influence would manifest in a greater likelihood that diplomatic resolutions would be given more time to play out. In the case of Iraq, an ICC able to fully prosecute crimes of aggressions might have forestalled the U.S.'s rush to war and allowed Blix's weapon inspection teams adequate time to finish their investigations. The Court, to act as a constraint via a general deterrent, is an optimistic view of the future potential of the ICC, one that we will explore in Chapter VII.

Summary

In order to illustrate the significance, and limitations, of an International Criminal Court, this chapter raised a number of questions in its presentation of a hypothetical scenario outlining how the court would present a legal argument defining the actions of the United States and the United Kingdom vis-à-vis their 2003 invasion of Iraq as criminal. The nature and substance of these nations' violations of international law is clear. These are the very sorts of crimes the ICC was designed to prevent and to prosecute. We selected this case for scholastic, rhetorical, and even political reasons. It illustrates the purpose of the court, its scope, and the Achilles Heel at its core. However, this does not mean that we see the court as an empty gesture—in fact its very creation is a landmark in the evolution of inter-state relations and organization. It is the purpose of this book to explore how the court came about, how it is structured, and how international society can revise the court in order to make it better able to do what it was designed to do: control the most egregious violations of international law and world peace. Our next chapter will examine ways in which the potential of the

International Criminal Court can be enhanced. Within the current global situation, it is our contertion that the best hope for peace and for the protection of civilians worldwide is a strongly empowered, expanded, and highly active ICC.

Notes

1 However, we should note that this is typically how war crimes cases before the World Court of Justice in The Hague occur

2 In the aftermath of a military campaign, with one of the aggressor parties subdued and its leaders in custody, the court is able to bring charges

3 The Caroline Affair (1837-1842) began when Canadian authorities seized and burned the U S vessel, Caroline, that was on the U S shore of the Niagara River near Buffalo

Chapter VII

Enhancing the Potential of the International Criminal Court

The past chapters have examined the history and development of the Rome Statute, its structure and function, controversial issues of the Court, and finally the criminological relevance of the Court for state crime, terrorism, and transnational crimes. It seems only natural that any analysis should also include a section discussing policy implications. Consequentially, this next section, based on earlier critiques and analysis, lays out what we believe are policies that would enhance the potential of the court, thus strengthening it as a control apparatus for addressing state crime, terrorism, and transnational crimes. In doing so, we briefly revisit key issues such as jurisdiction, and limited empowerment and policing. We conclude by offering a brief overview of the Court, what it can and is currently doing, what it should do, and the need for an enhanced social control institution.

Jurisdictional Issues

The issue of jurisdiction has been discussed throughout this book as it represents the core of the Court's ability to act as an effective social control. Moreover, we explored how jurisdiction was, and continues to be, a contentious matter by states most at risk for international prosecution of war crimes, crimes against humanity, and genocide. Recall the Court's jurisdiction is limited to individuals, thus omitting states as actors and other organizations such as transnational corporations. Further, it is a treaty, consequentially requiring compliance from the onset, throughout the investigative stage, and turning over of defendants once subpoenaed. It has limited scope of crimes under its jurisdiction. Our position is that jurisdiction of the Court should be enhanced to a universal scope, recognize criminal liability of states and transnational organizations as well as individuals (beyond the scope of reparations), and crimes covered should include specific terminology defining aggression and adding terrorism (including state terrorism) within the scope of crimes covered. We now examine each of these more thoroughly.

Universal Jurisdiction

One of the most significant potential policies which would ensure the Court become a more legitimate and fully empowered institution of social control would be to grant it universal jurisdiction. Recalling from Chapter V, this could be achieved via several venues: (1) in seven years through Article 123 wherein the Statute could be enhanced; (2) it could attain the status of customary law (however, this would require general consensus and a tribunal, ICJ, UN, or the Court itself declaring such via prosecution of an individual (s) not covered such as the ICJ ruled); and (3) the least likely way for the Court to attain universal jurisdiction would be that all nation-states consented to the Court's jurisdiction without reservations or the opt-out clause previously discussed. However, as the criminological research on state crime has shown, states with the most at risk economically, politically, and ideologically, such as the U.S., are highly unlikely to allow themselves to be regulated by outside agencies (Mullins et al. 2004). This scenario also illuminates one of the weaknesses with Article 13 (b) wherein the Security Council can agree to extend temporary jurisdiction to the Court beyond the conditions of other Articles to reach individuals not covered under the Court's jurisdiction. Just as state compliance is unlikely by highly powered nation-states, the same states sit on, or have allies on, the Security Council, utilizing their veto power in accordance with their political, economic, and ideological interests. For example, it is highly unlikely that Israel or Sharon would have charges brought before the ICC as the U.S. would use its veto power; nor would the U.S. or Bush have a case brought against it for the Iraq invasion and occupation we explored in Chapter I as the U.S. has veto under Article 13 (b).

The potential of the Rome Statute reaching the level of customary law (*erga omnes*) is a realistic possibility according to precedence set by international law and the International Court of Justice. The International Court of Justice states:

> With respect to the other elements usually regarded as necessary before a conventional rule can be considered to have become a general rule of international law, it might be that, even without the passage of any considerable amount of time, a very widespread and representative participation in the convention might suffice of itself, provided it included that of states whose interests were especially affected (ICJ Continental Shelf Case, 1969)

Therefore, the Rome Statute in the future may be conceived as general customary law such as the Nuremberg Principles and reach a level of universal jurisdiction regardless of the wording or limitations of jurisdiction. The phrasing of the Treaty can then be altered under Article 123 of the Rome Statute. However, to make this a political reality, some entity within international society must attain a level of influence to rival that of the United States. As of this writing, we see the possibility that the European Union has such potential. While recent political setbacks temper our optimism (e.g., the failure of several member nations to ratify the EU constitution), the potential economic, political, and military power represented by this trans-national governmental body could balance the undue influence the U.S. wields in world affairs. We see it as essential that the ICC be supported by significantly empowered state or trans-state entities to bring political and economic pressures to bear upon the more powerful members of international society with a tendency to act with impunity vis-à-vis international law.

States as Actors

The concept of a state as an entity possessing individual rights and subject to criminal liability is not a new idea. As Henkin (1995: 111) points out: "At Nuremberg, sitting in judgment on the recent past, the Allied victors declared waging aggressive war to be a state crime (under both treaty and customary law) as well as an individual crime by those who represented and acted for the aggressor state." In 1976 the International Law Commission again discussed the notion of state criminal responsibility (Jorgensen 2000: 28). Moreover, several legal scholars have observed there is a connection between individual criminal responsibility and state criminal responsibility under international law (Kramer, Michalowski, and Rothe 2005). Cassese (2003: 19) suggests that most of the offenses proscribed under international law "for the perpetration of which it endeavours to punish the individuals that allegedly committed them" are considered by international law "as particularly serious violations by States"; consequentially, when a crimes is committed by an individual "not acting in a private capacity, a dual responsibility may follow: criminal liability of the individual, falling under international criminal law, and State responsibility, regulated by international rules on this matter."

Furthermore, during the process of negotiations of the Rome Statute in 1998, the French delegate introduced a proposal for the inclusion of organizations including states. Of the two drafts proposed, one Draft Statute contained an Article that would subject legal entities to the Court's jurisdiction if the crimes were committed on behalf of such legal persons or their agencies or representatives. In the end this was dismissed as contradictory to the principle of a complimentary system (Sadat 2002). Jorgensen (2000) also has called for the use of state criminal responsibility. We agree with her claim that there is a link between state and individual criminal responsibility. In terms of the criteria used to determine which acts are criminal she argues "all acts which constitute international crimes may in principle entail individual or state responsibility, or both, depending on the nature and circumstances of the breach, and that the two notions can complement each other" (Jorgensen 2000: 139). She concludes that "both history and more recent state practice show that state responsibility for international crimes is an emerging category of customary international law" (Jorgensen 2000: 279). In sum, "the emergent principle of criminal law is that states themselves can commit crimes, and they can and should be held criminally responsible for them" (Kramer, Michalowski, and Rothe 2005).

By inclusion of states as criminally responsible actors, we believe this would eliminate a major obstacle of non-liability currently evidenced in state criminological analysis. By including a state as criminally liable it would follow that, as acting Head of State, the individual(s) at the top of a political apparatus be held responsible. Thus, leaders cannot avoid responsibility through claims of ignorance, non-participation, hegemonic propagandized counter-claims, and plausible deniability to protect both its inner circle and military leaders by limiting prosecutions to the lowest levels of involvement (Schmitt 2005). Such additional prosecutorial possibilities will place a level of responsibility upon state leaders that should undercut existing criminogenic tendencies in the modern nation states. It will also heighten the energies funneled into the due diligence governments practice in the overt sight of their sub-units.

Moreover, for the ICC to generate much needed general and specific deterrence among criminal states, it must be able to focus its prosecution on the leaders of a given state and the state itself. A polity as an organization will not necessarily be deterred from criminal action if it can merely sacrifice individual agents to the court as it can sacrifice individual soldiers and units on a battlefield (Mullins et al. 2004). As acting Head of State, individuals would be held liable just as precedent was set at the Nuremberg Trials wherein Germany was considered criminally liable as was Hitler. Furthermore, Kauzlarich and Kramer's (1998) work emphasizes that the loci of state criminality is the state, not the individual. Structural and organizational conditions combine with individual predilections and positions to generate these offenses; punishment of individuals will not be able to deter the polities themselves from offending. One can sanction numerous bureaucrats, soldiers, and spies without eliminating a state's ability or motivation to engage in criminal behaviors. The most powerful motivational elements arise within the state itself, not within the state's agents (Mullins et al. 2004). Moreover, states as criminal actors would further ensure victim(s) compensation and a sense of justice for those victimized. It also would allow for sanctions to be set against the state versus utilizing the underpowered ICJ or trying to get the Security Council to grant such a sanction with existing veto votes.

Obviously, one cannot incarcerate a state. However, the ability to levy trade and other sanctions upon criminal states may act as further controls. Restriction of trade, imposition of tariffs, denial of loans from foreign powers or the International Monetary Fund, or insistence upon collection of outstanding debts are all tools which the ICC could use to exert social control. This requires that there exist political and economic bodies capable of and willing to engage in such sanctioning behaviors.

While sanctions are often criticized as ineffective, these claims are often made disingenuously as part of broader political rhetorics or they specificities of a case are inappropriately generalized. For example, one case which is frequently pointed to concerning the inability of economic sanctions to produce a desired result is Iraq under Saddam Hussein. Indeed, the UN imposed sanctions did little to reduce the Baathist party's control over the state. There were real effects of the trade embargoes—citizens suffered mass deprivation. Yet, they had little recourse save armed insurrection against the totalitarian régime they lived under. Most Iraqis were well aware of the consequences of such actions, as the memories of the failed uprising in the aftermath of the Kuwait invasion were still strong. Indeed, economic sanctions are potentially poor control mechanisms against military dictatorships and other totalitarian states (e.g., North Korea, what Putin is returning Russia to). Such actions do not influence the elite in control of these nations who all ready have a tendency toward ignoring the deprivations experienced by the general population. Yet, they may be highly effective against republics

While the Iraqis had no recourse to bring pressure to bear on their government to comply with UN demands and get the economic sanctions lifted, citizens of, for example, the U.S., do With national elections being held every two years, the populace has the ability to respond (and respond quickly) to replace a government acting counter to the populace's interests. While U.S. public sentiment is parochial at best (and childish at worst—recall the immature, anti-French sentiment in the run up to 2003 Iraq invasion), there is little tolerance among the middle class for personal deprivations. This self-interest strongly motivates voting behavior, especially within swing vote constituencies. This is simply part and parcel of the state's culture of hyper-capitalism and instant gratification. While critical sociologists and criminologists often identify this set of cultural constellations as criminogenic in nature, it may actually be an effective control, directly in line with Ross's (2000) arguments about the role of public opinion in the control of state crime, which we discussed in Chapter II.

Transnational Organizations

The idea of criminal liability of organizations is not new either. Within the scope of criminological research such claims have been made for several decades. Moreover, during the Rome Statute Prepatory Committee meetings the concept of organizations and states were added into one of the existing Drafts (see Chapter IV). As was also discussed, the recent Agreement by the Economic and Social Council (2003) to which the U.S. is a signatory specifically addresses the criminal liability of transnational organizations. Furthermore, it specifically mentions that these organizations (actors within the organization) fall under the purview of international law and the ICC. The 2003 Norms on the Responsibilities of Transnational Corporations and Other Business Enterprises with regard to Human Rights Agreement sets precedence for our policy suggestion that transnational organizations should fall under the purview of the ICC and be defined as such in the Statute.

Article 18 also of this Agreement also sets up criminal liability to which the ICC could potentially have jurisdiction. It states: "in connection with determining damages, in regard to criminal sanctions, and in all other respects, these Norms shall be applied by national courts and/or international tribunals, pursuant to national and international law" (E/CN.4/Sub.2/2003/12/Rev.2). Our contention is that the Court should consider cases involving transnational organizations that are violating the existing crimes covered. Clearly transnational organizations played a significant role in the case of the Democratic Republic of Congo currently under investigation at the ICC. As international corporate capitalism has expanded, the world seems to be increasingly composed of organizations that, for all intents and purposes, operate in the absence of any real formal social controls or constraints. While informal controls exist, they are typically constructed and implemented under the purview and in the interests of global elites that control the most powerful of these organizations. Therefore, we believe that along with individuals and nation-states, international corporate organizations need to have controls and constraints via the ICC.

Inclusion of Other Crimes

Terrorism

In Chapter I, we made a case that terrorism should be defined and included under the category of crimes covered by the ICC. Recall also from Chapters II and IV, that historical attempts to merge terrorism with an international criminal court did occur. Moreover, Chapter III explored how terrorism, coupled with drug trafficking, served as the impetus to re-begin work on developing an ICC. Furthermore, by conceptualizing and trying terrorist incidents as crimes against humanity, the ICC could provide an apolitical location to bring charges and determine guilt versus an *ad hoc* or a politically charged unilateral military tribunal. As we pointed out, the application of terrorism as a label is highly subjective and overtly political. Yet, we believe by defining the label and including it in the Court's jurisdiction, a potential apolitical venue exists. In recognizing the complexities and subjectivity of the term we briefly review attempts to define what constitutes the tactic of terrorism.

The terms *terrorists* and *terrorism* are entrenched in a definitional quagmire. The difficulty in defining—even conceptualizing—terrorism is the pejorative connotations it holds. It is subjective in terms of the social, political, ideological, and historical context. Furthermore, politicians and state leaders frequently try to define the term by asserting the primacy of their preferred ideological versions consistent with their interests. For example, the term *terrorism* has been defined in official U.S. documents as the "calculated use of violence or threat of violence to attain political, religious, or ideological goals. Terrorism is accomplished by means of intimidation, coercion, or instilling fear" (White House 2002). The United Nations states: "Terrorism is, in most cases, essentially a political act. It is meant to inflict dramatic and deadly injury on civilians and to create an atmosphere of fear, generally for a political or ideological (whether secular or religious) purpose" (United Nations Report of the Policy Working Group on the United Nations and Terrorism 2002).

Currently, there are nineteen global or regional treaties directly pertaining to the subject of international terrorism. However, a consistent or agreed upon definition eludes the legal, political, and academic literature. As stated in the 2004 United Nations Chronicle:

> Fighting terrorism has been a long-standing concern of the General Assembly Beginning in 1963, the United Nations has focused on building a legal framework to eliminate international terrorism however, despite this progress, one of the central challenges facing the Assembly has been the definition of terrorism itself Since 1996, the Assembly's Sixth (Legal) Committee has worked on drafting a comprehensive convention on international terrorism, which will include a definition of terrorism However, negotiations remain stalled due to disagreements between States on how to distinguish liberation movements from terrorist cells Thus, until States resolve the adage that "one man's terrorist is another man's freedom fighter," the debate over a universal definition of terrorism will continue (United Nations Chronicle 4/2004)

As difficult as it may be, the key to constraining and/or controlling acts of terrorism lie in resolving the definitional debate and allowing the ICC jurisdiction over individuals, states, and transnational organizations utilizing terrorist tactics that could be classified as crimes against humanity, war crimes, and acts of genocide. We believe agreement must start by with the acts that constitute terrorism while bearing in mind all existing international standards, norms, and treaties on human, political, and economic rights.

Aggression

Wars of aggression are the most destructive and destabilizing of all state crimes. It is for this reason that the Nuremberg Charter defined wars of aggression as "the supreme international crime." Moreover, the act of aggression has long been set as both customary law and legally defined by the UN Charter. The specific prohibition of aggressive war is found in Article 2(4) of the Charter which reads: "All members shall refrain in their international relations from the threat or use of force against the territorial integrity or political independence of any state, or [behave] in any other manner inconsistent with the purposes of the United Nations."

Recalling from Chapter IV, the International Law Commission and the UN General Assembly (1974) had previously defined aggression. The precedent definition was "the use of armed force by a State against the sovereignty, territorial integrity or political independence of another State, or in any other manner inconsistent with the United Nations" (quoted from Harris 1999: 579). Yet, the fact remains during the Rome Statute negotiations, at the insistence of the U.S. Ambassador, the definition was not carried over to the treaty; thus, as undefined it failed to be settled prior to the final moments when a vote was taken passing the Rome Statute (see Article 5 (2) for specific details). At this point, the crime of aggression cannot fall under the Court's jurisdiction until the original seven-year span is expired (from the signing of the Rome Statute) and additions can be made. Specifically, a new provision must now be adopted in accordance with Articles 121 and 123 defining the crime and setting out the conditions under which the Court shall exercise jurisdiction with respect to this crime.

Enhanced Empowerment

The subject of enhanced empowerment is indeed controversial, as it would entail further financial burden to the Court and supporting states as well as commitment to the training and hiring of a sub-agency within the Court's purview. However, we believe it is a necessary step to ensure compliance by states as well as an acting secondary source to ensure individuals are brought forth into the Court's jurisdiction. Furthermore this agency could act to retrieve documentation and evidence (just as domestic policing agencies do), serve and/or arrest suspects, and ensure safe travel to detention during court proceedings. The ICC must have the authority to subpoena state records, non-accused witnesses and other currently "protected" sets of information crucial to any prosecution. Even with a broader power to bring charges against individuals and organizations, this authority is meaningless without the power to obtain necessary supporting evidence and/or a court entity to act as the enforcement in attaining this evidence or suspects. Simply, there is no domestic court in existence that does not have an attached investigation/enforcement body.

While INTERPOL currently exits, we believe the enforcement agency of the Court should consist of independent agents, hired and trained for the specific duty of court enforcement. This also negates any argument against such an agency on the grounds of hegemonic or religious propaganda such as the development of a one-world government with an alleged militaristic force. Moreover, an enhanced enforcement entity would also address one of our critiques in the limitations of the Court's enforcement through subpoenas, state compliance in this process, or that of witnesses.

Taken as a whole, our suggestions are directed towards modifying existing Articles established in the Rome Statute in order to generate an international legal body that can produce significant reductions in state crime. The ICC must attain high levels of sanctioning and deterrent ability as well as substantial relational distance and legitimacy to fulfill its promise. Optimistically, we see the potential within the ICC to become a major instrument in the control and constraint of state crime and an institution providing much needed social justice on the international level.

Summary

We have explored the long and embittered endeavor of creating an international criminal court, the multiplicities of contradictions, political interests, and ideology involved in developing the Rome Statue, the more recent U.S. attempts to thwart its efficacy, and the Court's significance to criminological inquiry and state crime. We then offered what we believe are valid and necessary adoptions to the Statute and the Court for it to be an effective system of international control. We now revisit what the court can and is doing and then close with a brief summary of the policies we have suggested.

Currently, the ICC is a criminal court based on the concept of complimentary; consequentially, states may willingly participate or decline to be a party to, such as the United States. Beyond this, the jurisdiction of the Court is limited to acts on the territory of a state signatory or by nationals of a party state. The exception to this is when the United Nations Security Council recommends a case to the Prosecutor-granting temporary jurisdiction for the alleged acts. While it is necessary for a state to consent to participate in this institution, we must also remember that the Court currently only addresses crimes committed by specific individuals versus political entities or organizations. Moreover, the scope of crimes covered by the Court is limited to war crimes, crimes against humanity, and genocide. Once aggression is defined, it too shall fall under the Court's jurisdiction. The scope of crimes covered coupled with the limitations of individual liability does not allow the Court to address the hidden aspects of crime or crimes that could still be classified as crimes against humanity, war crimes, or genocide. Specifically, state terrorism, unilateral war mongering, or the hybrid of state-corporate crime are left unregulated and without controls or constraints.

Currently, if a state signatory does commit one of the crimes listed by the Court, the domestic judicial system (or military) has precedence for addressing or prosecuting those responsible. It is only when the aforementioned conditions have been met that the Court may intervene. Again, the exception is when a state fails to address the actions or does so in a manner that clearly indicates impunity.

We have also explored the limitations for attaining evidence and/or witnesses pertaining to cases, as the Court is limited to issuing subpoenas. Along these same lines, the Court is not structured with an enforcement agency. Again, this forces the Court to rely on state compliance and as the criminological theoretical frame has shown state self-regulation or compliance is highly unlikely when not in the states' own interests.

While this may seem rather pessimistic, let us again state that we do have hope that the Court can act in an apolitical way to reduce the worst atrocities of mankind. Currently, there are three cases under investigation by the Prosecutor and one additional case that has been referred and is pending decisions on further investigation.

Recalling from Chapter II, the case against The Democratic Republic of Congo has been closely analyzed and monitored by the Prosecutor's Office since July 2003, initially with a focus on crimes committed in the Ituri region. In September 2003 the Prosecutor informed the States Parties that he was ready to request authorization from the Pre-Trial Chamber to use its powers to start the investigation. In a letter in November 2003 the government of the DRC welcomed the involvement of the ICC and went one step further in March 2004 by referring their situation in the country to the Court.

The Chief Prosecutor also determined that there was a reasonable basis to open an investigation into the situation in Northern Uganda, following a self-referral by Uganda in December 2003. On 31 March 2005 the Prosecutor received its first referral from the United Nations Security Council on Darfur (Resolution 1593). A document archive from the International Commission of Inquiry on Darfur was also presented to the Prosecutor. The case is under full investigation by the Court. However, as we explored our concerns over the role of the Security Council in accepting or rejecting cases to the Prosecutor, it should be noted that the U.S. abstained from using its vote yea or nay and instead insisted upon the Council including, at the U.S. request, a provision that exempted persons of non-party states in the Sudan from ICC prosecution. Consequentially, persons from countries not party who were supporting the United Nations or African Union's efforts would not fall under the Court's jurisdiction even if involved in the atrocities. The resolution provided clear protection for United States persons: No United States person supporting operations in the Sudan would be subject to investigation or prosecution because of this resolution. That did not mean that there would be immunity for American citizens that acted in violation of the law. The United States would continue to discipline its own people when appropriate (Res. 1593: SC/8351).

Most recently, 1 July 2005 the Prosecutor received a referral concerning Central African Republic. As we explored in Chapter IV, this is the initial stage in accordance with the Rome Statute and the Rules of Procedure and Evidence, wherein the Prosecutor will carry out an analysis in order to determine whether to initiate an investigation.

We see these cases brought to the Court as an optimistic sign that the Court is being seen and utilized as a legitimate and fully capable institution of social control (again note the limitations for cases brought forth, enforcement, and crimes covered). However, we maintain that if the ICC is to fulfill its stated mission·

> Affirming that the most serious crimes of concern to the international community as a whole must not go unpunished and that their effective prosecution must be ensured by taking measures at the national level and by enhancing international cooperation Determined to put an end to impunity for the perpetrators of these crimes and thus to contribute to the prevention of such crimes

As currently structured and empowered, the ICC cannot fulfill its potentials or stated mission. Specifically, since nations must voluntarily come under the control of the court, the most powerful and potentially criminogenic states can avoid control simply by refusing participation. As the aforementioned policies have suggested, the Court must: (1) attain universal jurisdiction; (2) become fully empowered with its own enforcement agency; (3) expand the scope of individuals to include state and transnational entities; (4) add the much needed definition of crimes of aggression; and (5) add and define terrorism as an additional crime falling under the Court's purview. We see these modifications as necessary for the Court to attain a full level of legitimacy and as a full-time institution of social control. Moreover, as the world and global capitalistic interests become more intertwined, a fully empowered universal court is necessary to deter and respond to the most heinous crimes against humanity as a whole. While the term *international community* is touted as a realism of the international order, we must follow through with the emerging principles and values that go along with such an ideology.[1] This must include a fully enforced universal criminal court.

Notes

1 For more information regarding the history and promotion of the ideology behind an international community, see Rothe and Mullins 2005 www un org/Pubs/chronicle/2004/issue4/0404p27 html

Appendix A

Contradictions of International Society

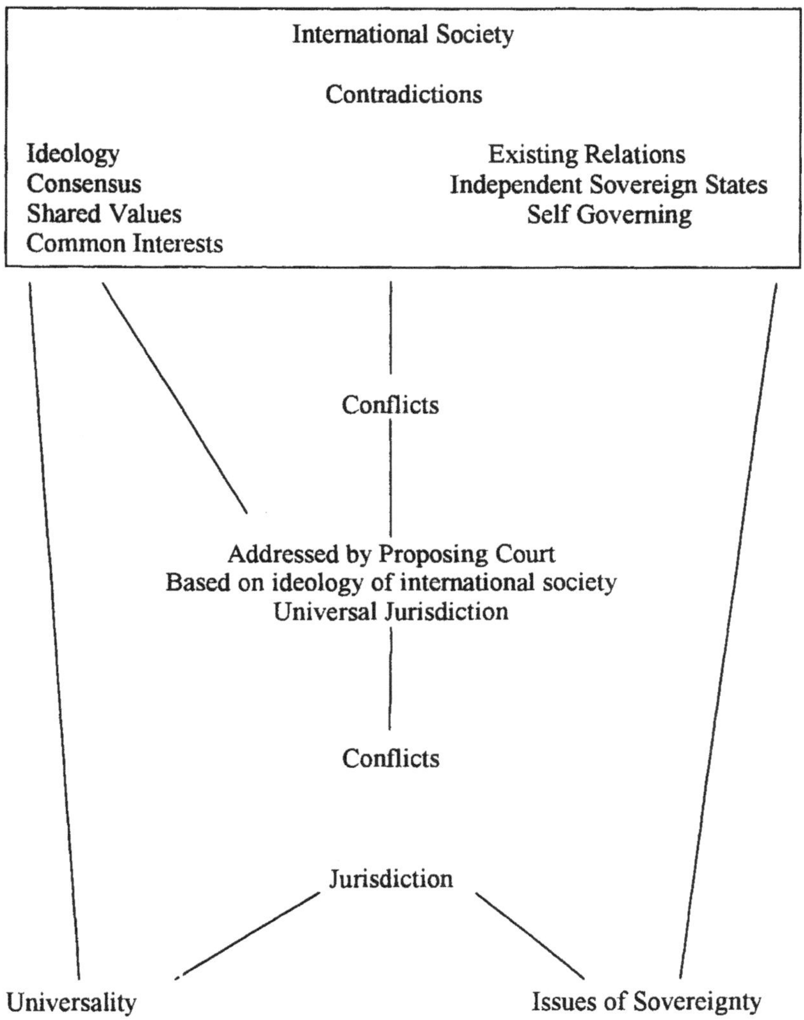
International Society
Contradictions
Ideology
Consensus
Shared Values
Common Interests
Existing Relations
Independent Sovereign States
Self Governing
Conflicts
Addressed by Proposing Court
Based on ideology of international society
Universal Jurisdiction
Conflicts
Jurisdiction
Universality
Issues of Sovereignty

Appendix B

Significant International Contingencies

Pre-League of Nations 1872-1918

Key Events:

Franco-Prussian War; 1914: Austria declared war on Serbia; Germany declared war on Russia; France intruded into Belgium; WWI ends in 1918.

Attempts to Create an International Criminal Court:

1872. Moynier of ICRC; Peace Society of United States; 1874 Emperor Alexander II convened Conference in Brussels; General Ulysses Grant wrote to the Universal Peace Union; 1895: the ICRC again attempted to establish support for Court in Geneva; Second Hague Conference of 1907.

League of Nations 1919-1944

Key Events:

IMT for Germany and allies formed; Geneva Conventions of 1925; Paris Pact of 1928; International Conventions on Amelioration of the Wounded; Geneva 1929; 1928: Resolution of the Sixth Pan-American Conference; 1933: Convention on the definiticn of Aggressor, London; 1933: Anti War Treaty of Non-

Aggression and Conciliation, Rio de Janeiro; Spanish Civil War; WWII; End of WWII.

Attempts to Create an International Criminal Court:

1919: M. Leon Bourgeois of France to propose ICC; Article 14 of the Charter for the League of Nations; 1920: Committee formed to create an ICC; 1926: ILA approved plan for an ICC; 1934: France submitted a memorandum for the establishment of an international penal court; 1936: The Repression of Terrorism Prevention and Treaty for an ICC; 1943: The London International Assembly Prepared a final Convention proposing and ICC be created by the newly emerging UNN; 1944: Dissolution of League of Nations.

United Nations 1945-1975

Key Events:

Nuremberg Trials; Japanese IMTs; Nuremberg Principles; Four Geneva Conventions; Korean War; Cold War begins; Arab League States versus Israel; Indonesia conflict; Kashmir conflict; World Court of Justice; 1948: Creation of International Law Commission; 1948: Universal Declaration of Human Rights; 1961: Amnesty International is formed; Bay of Pigs; Congo conflict; Suez Canal conflict; UN Emergency Force is formed; Cuban Missile Crisis occurs; Vietnam War; The Six Day War; Biafran War (Nigeria); Apollo Moon Landing; U.S. invades Cambodia and Laos; Apartheid; 1972: Vietnam War ends; 1974: Aggression is defined in international law; Soviet/Afghan War begins; Founding of Human Rights Watch; Convention on Elimination of all forms of Discrimination is created.

Attempts to Create an International Criminal Court:

1946: UN takes on task to develop an ICC; International Congress convened in Paris to form ICC; The Economic and Social Committee (ECOSOC) draft for an ICC; 1948: The General Assembly passed the proposal on and requested the International Law Commission to create an ICC; 1950: The General Assembly formed another Special Committee to draft a convention to establish an ICC; 1954: all efforts ceased during Cold War.

1975-2004

Key Events:

1974: December the definition of aggression made it to the UN General Assembly and was accepted; 1980s: U.S./Soviet hostilities cease; Soviet/Afghan War; Rwanda-genocide; Yugoslavia war crimes; U.S. covertly invades Nicaragua; Iran/Contra Affair; Convention Against Torture; Convention for Rights of Children; 1985: Resolution on Terrorism; End of Cold War; Gulf War; NATO Bosnia action; U.S. Embassy bombings and retaliatory strikes; Afghan War; U.S. invasion of Iraq.

Attempts to Create an International Criminal Court:

1974: The League Council of the UN renewed interest in an ICC; 1977: ILC suggested revising Draft for the ICC; 1981: ILC again requests ICC; 1989: Trinidad and Tobago request an ICC be formed to address Terrorism and drug-trafficking; 1989: GA officially requests ILC to examine potential of an ICC; 1989: International Institute of Higher Studies in Criminal Sciences in conjunction with the UN prepare a draft of an ICC; 1992: the ILC created a working group for creating an ICC; 1994: 2 drafts Statutes completed; 1995: Ad Hoc Committee was formed for an ICC; 1996: Prepatory Committee was formed; 1998: the Committee had finalized a draft statute to be considered at the 1998 Diplomatic Conference; 1998: The Rome Statute of the International Criminal Court was founded.

Appendix C

Rome Statute of the International Criminal Court

Text of the Rome Statute circulated as document A/CONF.183/9 of 17 July 1998 and corrected by procès-verbaux of 10 November 1998, 12 July 1999, 30 November 1999, 8 May 2000, 17 January 2001 and 16 January 2002. The Statute entered into force on 1 July 2002. Produced by the Public Information and Documentation Section of the ICC Maanweg 174, 2516 AB The Hague, The Netherlands

This Table of Contents is not part of the text of the Rome Statute adopted by the United Nations Diplomatic Conference of Plenipotentiaries on the Establishment of an International Criminal Court on 12 July 1998. It has been included in this publication for ease of reference.

Rome Statute of the International Criminal Court Table of Contents

Art.

PREAMBLE

PART 1. ESTABLISHMENT OF THE COURT

1 The Court
2. Relationship of the Court with the United Nations

3. Seat of the Court
4. Legal status and powers of the Court

PART 2. JURISDICTION, ADMISSIBILITY AND APPLICABLE LAW

5. Crimes within the jurisdiction of the Court
6. Genocide
7. Crimes against humanity
8. War Crimes
9. Elements of Crimes
10. Treaty does not limit developing rules of law
11. Jurisdiction ratione temporis
12. Preconditions to the exercise of jurisdiction
13. Exercise of jurisdiction
14. Referral of a situation by a State Party
15. Prosecutor
16. Deferral of investigation or prosecution
17. Issues of admissibility
18. Preliminary rulings regarding admissibility
19. Challenges to the jurisdiction of the Court or the admissibility of a case
20. *Ne bis in idem*
21 Applicable law

PART 3. GENERAL PRINCIPLES OF CRIMINAL LAW

22. *Nullum crimen sine lege*
23. *Nulla poena sine lege*
24. Non-retroactivity ratione personae
25. Individual criminal responsibility
26. Exclusion of jurisdiction over persons under eighteen
27. Irrelevance of official capacity
28. Responsibility of commanders and other superiors
29. Non-applicability of statute of limitations
30. Mental element
31. Grounds for excluding criminal responsibility
32. Mistake of fact or mistake of law
33. Superior orders and prescription of law

PART 4. COMPOSITION AND ADMINISTRATION OF THE COURT

34. Organs of the Court
35. Service of judges
36. Qualifications, nomination and election of judges
37. Judicial vacancies

38. The Presidency
39. Chambers
40. Independence of judges
41. Excusing and disqualification of judges
42. The Office of the Prosecutor
43. The Registry
44. Staff
45. Solemn undertaking
46. Removal from office
47. Disciplinary measures
48. Privileges and immunities
49. Salaries, allowances and expenses
50. Official and working languages
51. Rules of Procedure and Evidence
52. Regulations of the Court

PART 5. INVESTIGATION AND PROSECUTION

53. Initiation of an investigation
54. Duties and powers of the Prosecutor with respect to investigations
55. Rights of persons during an investigation
56. Role of the Pre-Trial Chamber in relation to a unique investigative opportunity
57. Functions and powers of the Pre-Trial Chamber
58. Issuance by the Pre-Trial Chamber of a warrant of arrest or a summons to appear
59. Arrest proceedings in the custodial State
60. Initial proceedings before the Court
61. Confirmation of the charges before trial

PART 6. THE TRIAL

62. Place of trial
63. Trial in the presence of the accused
64. Functions and powers of the Trial Chamber
65. Proceedings on an admission of guilt
66. Presumption of innocence
67. Rights of the accused
68. Protection of the victims and witnesses and their participation in the proceedings
69. Evidence
70. Offences against the administration of justice
71. Sanctions for misconduct before the Court
72. Protection of national security information
73. Third-party information or documents

74. Requirements for the decision
75. Reparations to victims
76. Sentencing

PART 7. PENALTIES

77. Applicable penalties
78. Determination of the sentence
79. Trust Fund
80. Non-prejudice to national application of penalties and national laws

PART 8. APPEAL AND REVISION

81. Appeal against decision of acquittal or conviction or against sentence
82. Appeal against other decisions
83. Proceedings on appeal
84. Revision of conviction or sentence
85. Compensation to an arrested or convicted person

PART 9. INTERNATIONAL COOPERATION AND JUDICIAL ASSISTANCE

86. General obligation to cooperate
87. Requests for cooperation: general provisions
88. Availability of procedures under national law
89. Surrender of persons to the Court
90. Competing requests
91. Contents of request for arrest and surrender
92. Provisional arrest
93. Other forms of cooperation
94. Postponement of execution of a request in respect of ongoing investigation or prosecution
95. Postponement of execution of a request in respect of an admissibility challenge
96. Contents of request for other forms of assistance under article 93
97. Consultations
98. Cooperation with respect to waiver of immunity and consent to surrender
99. Execution of request under articles 93 and 96
100. Costs
101. Rule of speciality
102. Use of terms

PART 10. ENFORCEMENT

103. Role of States in enforcement of sentences of imprisonment
104. Change in designation of State of enforcement

105. Enforcement of the sentence
106. Supervision of enforcement of sentences and conditions of imprisonment
107. Transfer of the person upon completion of sentence
108. Limitation on the prosecution or punishment of other offences
109. Enforcement of fines and forfeiture measures
110. Review by the Court concerning reduction of sentence
111. Escape

PART 11. ASSEMBLY OF STATES PARTIES

112. Assembly of States Parties

PART 12. FINANCING

113. Financial Regulations
114. Payment of expenses
115. Funds of the Court and of the Assembly of States Parties
116 Voluntary contributions
117. Assessment of contributions
118. Annual audit

PART 13. FINAL CLAUSES

119. Settlement of disputes
120. Reservations
121 Amendments
122. Amendments to provisions of an institutional nature
123. Review of the Statute
124. Transitional Provision
125. Signature, ratification, acceptance, approval or accession
126. Entry into force
127. Withdrawal
128. Authentic texts

ROME STATUTE OF THE INTERNATIONAL CRIMINAL COURT

PREAMBLE

The States Parties to this Statute,

Conscious that all peoples are united by common bonds, their cultures pieced together in a shared heritage, and concerned that this delicate mosaic may be shattered at any time,

Mindful that during this century millions of children, women and men have been victims of unimaginable atrocities that deeply shock the conscience of humanity,

Recognizing that such grave crimes threaten the peace, security and well-being of the world,

Affirming that the most serious crimes of concern to the international community as a whole must not go unpunished and that their effective prosecution must be ensured by taking measures at the national level and by enhancing international cooperation,

Determined to put an end to impunity for the perpetrators of these crimes and thus to contribute to the prevention of such crimes,

Recalling that it is the duty of every State to exercise its criminal jurisdiction over those responsible for international crimes,

Reaffirming the Purposes and Principles of the Charter of the United Nations, and in particular that all States shall refrain from the threat or use of force against the territorial integrity or political independence of any State, or in any other manner inconsistent with the Purposes of the United Nations,

Emphasizing in this connection that nothing in this Statute shall be taken as authorizing any State Party to intervene in an armed conflict or in the internal affairs of any State,

Determined to these ends and for the sake of present and future generations, to establish an independent permanent International Criminal Court in relationship with the United Nations system, with jurisdiction over the most serious crimes of concern to the international community as a whole,

Emphasizing that the International Criminal Court established under this Statute shall be complementary to national criminal jurisdictions,

Resolved to guarantee lasting respect for and the enforcement of international justice,

Have agreed as follows:

PART 1. ESTABLISHMENT OF THE COURT

Article 1
The Court

An International Criminal Court ("the Court") is hereby established. It shall be a permanent institution and shall have the power to exercise its jurisdiction over persons for the most serious crimes of international concern, as referred to in this Statute, and shall be complementary to national criminal jurisdictions. The jurisdiction and functioning of the Court shall be governed by the provisions of this Statute.

Article 2
Relationship of the Court with the United Nations

The Court shall be brought into relationship with the United Nations through an agreement to be approved by the Assembly of States Parties to this Statute and thereafter concluded by the President of the Court on its behalf.

Article 3
Seat of the Court

1. The seat of the Court shall be established at The Hague in the Netherlands ("the host State").
2. The Court shall enter into a headquarters agreement with the host State, to be approved by the Assembly of States Parties and thereafter concluded by the President of the Court on its behalf.
3. The Court may sit elsewhere, whenever it considers it desirable, as provided in this Statute.

Article 4
Legal status and powers of the Court

1. The Court shall have international legal personality. It shall also have such legal capacity as may be necessary for the exercise of its functions and the fulfillment of its purposes.
2. The Court may exercise its functions and powers, as provided in this Statute, on the territory of any State Party and, by special agreement, on the territory of any other State.

PART 2. JURISDICTION, ADMISSIBILITY AND APPLICABLE LAW

Article 5
Crimes within the jurisdiction of the Court

1. The jurisdiction of the Court shall be limited to the most serious crimes of concern to the international community as a whole. The Court has jurisdiction in accordance with this Statute with respect to the following crimes:
    (a) The crime of genocide;
    (b) Crimes against humanity;
    (c) War crimes;
    (d) The crime of aggression.
2. The Court shall exercise jurisdiction over the crime of aggression once a provision is adopted in accordance with articles 121 and 123 defining the crime and setting out the conditions under which the Court shall exercise jurisdiction with respect to this crime. Such a provision shall be consistent with the relevant provisions of the Charter of the United Nations.

Article 6
Genocide

For the purpose of this Statute, "genocide" means any of the following acts committed with intent to destroy, in whole or in part, a national, ethnical, racial or religious group, as such:

(a) Killing members of the group;

(b) Causing serious bodily or mental harm to members of the group;

(c) Deliberately inflicting on the group conditions of life calculated to bring about its physical destruction in whole or in part;

(d) Imposing measures intended to prevent births within the group;

(e) Forcibly transferring children of the group to another group.

Article 7
Crimes against humanity

1. For the purpose of this Statute, "crime against humanity" means any of the following acts when committed as part of a widespread or systematic attack directed against any civilian population, with knowledge of the attack:

(a) Murder;

(b) Extermination;

(c) Enslavement;

(d) Deportation or forcible transfer of population;

(e) Imprisonment or other severe deprivation of physical liberty in violation of fundamental rules of international law;

(f) Torture;

(g) Rape, sexual slavery, enforced prostitution, forced pregnancy, enforced sterilization, or any other form of sexual violence of comparable gravity;

(h) Persecution against any identifiable group or collectivity on political, racial, national, ethnic, cultural, religious, gender as defined in paragraph 3, or other grounds that are universally recognized as impermissible under international law, in connection with any act referred to in this paragraph or any crime within the jurisdiction of the Court;

(i) Enforced disappearance of persons;

(j) The crime of apartheid;

(k) Other inhumane acts of a similar character intentionally causing great suffering, or serious injury to body or to mental or physical health.

2. For the purpose of paragraph 1:

(a) "Attack directed against any civilian population" means a course of conduct involving the multiple commission of acts referred to in paragraph 1 against any civilian population, pursuant to or in furtherance of a State or organizational policy to commit such attack;

(b) "Extermination" includes the intentional infliction of conditions of life, inter alia the deprivation of access to food and medicine, calculated to bring about the destruction of part of a population;

(c) "Enslavement" means the exercise of any or all of the powers attaching to the right of ownership over a person and includes the exercise of such power in the course of trafficking in persons, in particular women and children;

(d) "Deportation or forcible transfer of population" means forced displacement of the persons concerned by expulsion or other coercive acts from the area in which they are lawfully present, without grounds permitted under international law;

(e) "Torture" means the intentional infliction of severe pain or suffering, whether physical or mental, upon a person in the custody or under the control of the accused; except that torture shall not include pain or suffering arising only from, inherent in or incidental to, lawful sanctions;

(f) "Forced pregnancy" means the unlawful confinement of a woman forcibly made pregnant, with the intent of affecting the ethnic composition of any population or carrying out other grave violations of international law. This definition shall not in any way be interpreted as affecting national laws relating to pregnancy;

(g) "Persecution" means the intentional and severe deprivation of fundamental rights contrary to international law by reason of the identity of the group or collectivity,

(h) "The crime of apartheid" means inhumane acts of a character similar to those referred to in paragraph 1, committed in the context of an institutionalized regime of systematic oppression and domination by one racial group over any other racial group or groups and committed with the intention of maintaining that regime;

(i) "Enforced disappearance of persons" means the arrest, detention or abduction of persons by, or with the authorization, support or acquiescence of, a State or a political organization, followed by a refusal to acknowledge that deprivation of freedom or to give information on the fate or whereabouts of those persons, with the intention of removing them from the protection of the law for a prolonged period of time.

3. For the purpose of this Statute, it is understood that the term "gender" refers to the two sexes, male and female, within the context of society. The term "gender" does not indicate any meaning different from the above.

Article 8
War crimes

1. The Court shall have jurisdiction in respect of war crimes in particular when committed as part of a plan or policy or as part of a large-scale commission of such crimes.

2. For the purpose of this Statute, "war crimes" means:

(a) Grave breaches of the Geneva Conventions of 12 August 1949, namely, any of the following acts against persons or property protected under the provisions of the relevant Geneva Convention:

(i) Wilful killing;
(ii) Torture or inhuman treatment, including biological experiments;
(iii) Wilfully causing great suffering, or serious injury to body or health;
(iv) Extensive destruction and appropriation of property, not justified by military necessity and carried out unlawfully and wantonly;
(v) Compelling a prisoner of war or other protected person to serve in the forces of a hostile Power;
(vi) Wilfully depriving a prisoner of war or other protected person of the rights of fair and regular trial;
(vii) Unlawful deportation or transfer or unlawful confinement;
(viii) Taking of hostages.

(b) Other serious violations of the laws and customs applicable in international armed conflict, within the established framework of international law, namely, any of the following acts:

(i) Intentionally directing attacks against the civilian population as such or against individual civilians not taking direct part in hostilities;
(ii) directing attacks against civilian objects, that is, objects which are not military objectives;
(iii) Intentionally directing attacks against personnel, installations, material, units or vehicles involved in a humanitarian assistance or peacekeeping mission in accordance with the Charter of the United Nations, as long as they are entitled to the protection given to civilians or civilian objects under the international law of armed conflict;
(iv) Intentionally launching an attack in the knowledge that such attack will cause incidental loss of life or injury to civilians or damage to civilian objects or widespread, long-term and severe damage to the natural environment which would be clearly excessive in relation to the concrete and direct overall military advantage anticipated;
(v) Attacking or bombarding, by whatever means, towns, villages, dwellings or buildings which are undefended and which are not military objectives;
(vi) Killing or wounding a combatant who, having laid down his arms or having no longer means of defence, has surrendered at discretion;
(vii) Making improper use of a flag of truce, of the flag or of the military insignia and uniform of the enemy or of the United Nations,

as well as of the distinctive emblems of the Geneva Conventions, resulting in death or serious personal injury;

(viii) The transfer, directly or indirectly, by the Occupying Power of parts of its own civilian population into the territory it occupies, or the deportation or transfer of all or parts of the population of the occupied territory within or outside this territory;

(ix) Intentionally directing attacks against buildings dedicated to religion, education, art, science or charitable purposes, historic monuments, hospitals and places where the sick and wounded are collected, provided they are not military objectives;

(x) Subjecting persons who are in the power of an adverse party to physical mutilation or to medical or scientific experiments of any kind which are neither justified by the medical, dental or hospital treatment of the person concerned nor carried out in his or her interest, and which cause death to or seriously endanger the health of such person or persons;

(xi) Killing or wounding treacherously individuals belonging to the hostile nation or army;

(xii) Declaring that no quarter will be given;

(xiii) Destroying or seizing the enemy's property unless such destruction or seizure be imperatively demanded by the necessities of war;

(xiv) Declaring abolished, suspended or inadmissible in a court of law the rights and actions of the nationals of the hostile party;

(xv) Compelling the nationals of the hostile party to take part in the operations of war directed against their own country, even if they were in the belligerent's service before the commencement of the war;

(xvi) Pillaging a town or place, even when taken by assault;

(xvii) Employing poison or poisoned weapons;

(xviii) Employing asphyxiating, poisonous or other gases, and all analogous liquids, materials or devices;

(xix) Employing bullets which expand or flatten easily in the human body, such as bullets with a hard envelope which does not entirely cover the core or is pierced with incisions;

(xx) Employing weapons, projectiles and material and methods of warfare which are of a nature to cause superfluous injury or unnecessary suffering or which are inherently indiscriminate in violation of the international law of armed conflict, provided that such weapons, projectiles and material and methods of warfare are the subject of a comprehensive prohibition and are included in an annex to this Statute, by an amendment in accordance with the relevant provisions set forth in articles 121 and 123;

(xxi) Committing outrages upon personal dignity, in particular humiliating and degrading treatment;

(xxii) Committing rape, sexual slavery, enforced prostitution, forced pregnancy, as defined in article 7, paragraph 2 (f), enforced sterilization, or any other form of sexual violence also constituting a grave breach of the Geneva Conventions;

(xxiii) Utilizing the presence of a civilian or other protected person to render certain points, areas or military forces immune from military operations;

(xxiv) Intentionally directing attacks against buildings, material, medical units and transport, and personnel using the distinctive emblems of the Geneva Conventions in conformity with international law;

(xxv) Intentionally using starvation of civilians as a method of warfare by depriving them of objects indispensable to their survival, including willfully impeding relief supplies as provided for under the Geneva Conventions;

(xxvi) Conscripting or enlisting children under the age of fifteen years into the national armed forces or using them to participate actively in hostilities.

(c) In the case of an armed conflict not of an international character, serious violations of article 3 common to the four Geneva Conventions of 12 August 1949, namely, any of the following acts committed against persons taking no active part in the hostilities, including members of armed forces who have laid down their arms and those placed hors de combat by sickness, wounds, detention or any other cause:

(i) Violence to life and person, in particular murder of all kinds, mutilation, cruel treatment and torture;

(ii) Committing outrages upon personal dignity, in particular humiliating and degrading treatment;

(iii) Taking of hostages;

(iv) The passing of sentences and the carrying out of executions without previous judgment pronounced by a regularly constituted court, affording all judicial guarantees which are generally recognized as indispensable.

(d) Paragraph 2 (c) applies to armed conflicts not of an international character and thus does not apply to situations of internal disturbances and tensions, such as riots, isolated and sporadic acts of violence or other acts of a similar nature

(e) Other serious violations of the laws and customs applicable in armed conflicts not of an international character, within the established framework of international law, namely, any of the following acts:

(i) Intentionally directing attacks against the civilian population as such or against individual civilians not taking direct part in hostilities;
(ii) Intentionally directing attacks against buildings, material, medical units and transport, and personnel using the distinctive emblems of the Geneva Conventions in conformity with international law;
(iii) Intentionally directing attacks against personnel, installations, material, units or vehicles involved in a humanitarian assistance or peacekeeping mission in accordance with the Charter of the United Nations, as long as they are entitled to the protection given to civilians or civilian objects under the international law of armed conflict;
(iv) Intentionally directing attacks against buildings dedicated to religion, education, art, science or charitable purposes, historic monuments, hospitals and places where the sick and wounded are collected, provided they are not military objectives;
(v) Pillaging a town or place, even when taken by assault;
(vi) Committing rape, sexual slavery, enforced prostitution, forced pregnancy, as defined in article 7, paragraph 2 (f), enforced sterilization, and any other form of sexual violence also constituting a serious violation of article 3 common to the four Geneva Conventions;
(vii) Conscripting or enlisting children under the age of fifteen years into armed forces or groups or using them to participate actively in hostilities;
(viii) Ordering the displacement of the civilian population for reasons related to the conflict, unless the security of the civilians involved or imperative military reasons so demand;
(ix) Killing or wounding treacherously a combatant adversary;
(x) Declaring that no quarter will be given;
(xi) Subjecting persons who are in the power of another party to the conflict to physical mutilation or to medical or scientific experiments of any kind which are neither justified by the medical, dental or hospital treatment of the person concerned nor carried out in his or her interest, and which cause death to or seriously endanger the health of such person or persons;
(xii) Destroying or seizing the property of an adversary unless such destruction or seizure be imperatively demanded by the necessities of the conflict;

(f) Paragraph 2 (e) applies to armed conflicts not of an international character and thus does not apply to situations of internal disturbances and tensions, such as riots, isolated and sporadic acts of violence or other acts of a similar nature. It applies to armed conflicts that take place in the territory of a State

when there is protracted armed conflict between governmental authorities and organized armed groups or between such groups.
3. Nothing in paragraph 2 (c) and (e) shall affect the responsibility of a Government to maintain or re-establish law and order in the State or to defend the unity and territorial integrity of the State, by all legitimate means.

Article 9
Elements of Crimes

1. Elements of Crimes shall assist the Court in the interpretation and application of articles 6, 7 and 8. They shall be adopted by a two-thirds majority of the members of the Assembly of States Parties.
2 Amendments to the Elements of Crimes may be proposed by:
(a) Any State Party;
(b) The judges acting by an absolute majority;
(c) The Prosecutor.
Such amendments shall be adopted by a two-thirds majority of the members of the Assembly of States Parties.
3. The Elements of Crimes and amendments thereto shall be consistent with this Statute.

Article 10

Nothing in this Part shall be interpreted as limiting or prejudicing in any way existing or developing rules of international law for purposes other than this Statute.

Article 11
Jurisdiction ratione temporis

1. The Court has jurisdiction only with respect to crimes committed after the entry into force of this Statute.
2. If a State becomes a Party to this Statute after its entry into force, the Court may exercise its jurisdiction only with respect to crimes committed after the entry into force of this Statute for that State, unless that State has made a declaration under article 12, paragraph 3.

Article 12
Preconditions to the exercise of jurisdiction

1. A State which becomes a Party to this Statute thereby accepts the jurisdiction of the Court with respect to the crimes referred to in article 5.

2. In the case of article 13, paragraph (a) or (c), the Court may exercise its jurisdiction if one or more of the following States are Parties to this Statute or have accepted the jurisdiction of the Court in accordance with paragraph 3:

(a) The State on the territory of which the conduct in question occurred or, if the crime was committed on board a vessel or aircraft, the State of registration of that vessel or aircraft;

(b) The State of which the person accused of the crime is a national.

3. If the acceptance of a State which is not a Party to this Statute is required under paragraph 2, that State may, by declaration lodged with the Registrar, accept the exercise of jurisdiction by the Court with respect to the crime in question. The accepting State shall cooperate with the Court without any delay or exception in accordance with Part 9.

Article 13
Exercise of jurisdiction

The Court may exercise its jurisdiction with respect to a crime referred to in article 5 in accordance with the provisions of this Statute if:

(a) A situation in which one or more of such crimes appears to have been committed is referred to the Prosecutor by a State Party in accordance with article 14;

(b) A situation in which one or more of such crimes appears to have been committed is referred to the Prosecutor by the Security Council acting under Chapter VII of the Charter of the United Nations; or

(c) The Prosecutor has initiated an investigation in respect of such a crime in accordance with article 15.

Article 14
Referral of a situation by a State Party

1. A State Party may refer to the Prosecutor a situation in which one or more crimes within the jurisdiction of the Court appear to have been committed requesting the Prosecutor to investigate the situation for the purpose of determining whether one or more specific persons should be charged with the commission of such crimes.

2. As far as possible, a referral shall specify the relevant circumstances and be accompanied by such supporting documentation as is available to the State referring the situation.

Article 15
Prosecutor

1. The Prosecutor may initiate investigations proprio motu on the basis of information on crimes within the jurisdiction of the Court.

2. The Prosecutor shall analyse the seriousness of the information received. For this purpose, he or she may seek additional information from States, organs of the United Nations, intergovernmental or non-governmental organizations, or other reliable sources that he or she deems appropriate, and may receive written or oral testimony at the seat of the Court.
3. If the Prosecutor concludes that there is a reasonable basis to proceed with an investigation, he or she shall submit to the Pre-Trial Chamber a request for authorization of an investigation, together with any supporting material collected. Victims may make representations to the Pre-Trial Chamber, in accordance with the Rules of Procedure and Evidence.
4. If the Pre-Trial Chamber, upon examination of the request and the supporting material, considers that there is a reasonable basis to proceed with an investigation, and that the case appears to fall within the jurisdiction of the Court, it shall authorize the commencement of the investigation, without prejudice to subsequent determinations by the Court with regard to the jurisdiction and admissibility of a case.
5. The refusal of the Pre-Trial Chamber to authorize the investigation shall not preclude the presentation of a subsequent request by the Prosecutor based on new facts or evidence regarding the same situation.
6. If, after the preliminary examination referred to in paragraphs 1 and 2, the Prosecutor concludes that the information provided does not constitute a reasonable basis for an investigation, he or she shall inform those who provided the information This shall not preclude the Prosecutor from considering further information submitted to him or her regarding the same situation in the light of new facts or evidence

Article 16
Deferral of investigation or prosecution

No investigation or prosecution may be commenced or proceeded with under this Statute for a period of 12 months after the Security Council, in a resolution adopted under Chapter VII of the Charter of the United Nations, has requested the Court to that effect; that request may be renewed by the Council under the same conditions.

Article 17
Issues of admissibility

1. Having regard to paragraph 10 of the Preamble and article 1, the Court shall determine that a case is inadmissible where

(a) The case is being investigated or prosecuted by a State which has jurisdiction over it, unless the State is unwilling or unable genuinely to carry out the investigation or prosecution;

(b) The case has been investigated by a State which has jurisdiction over it and the State has decided not to prosecute the person concerned, unless the decision resulted from the unwillingness or inability of the State genuinely to prosecute;

(c) The person concerned has already been tried for conduct which is the subject of the complaint, and a trial by the Court is not permitted under article 20, paragraph 3;

(d) The case is not of sufficient gravity to justify further action by the Court.

2. In order to determine unwillingness in a particular case, the Court shall consider, having regard to the principles of due process recognized by international law, whether one or more of the following exist, as applicable:

(a) The proceedings were or are being undertaken or the national decision was made for the purpose of shielding the person concerned from criminal responsibility for crimes within the jurisdiction of the Court referred to in article 5;

(b) There has been an unjustified delay in the proceedings which in the circumstances is inconsistent with an intent to bring the person concerned to justice;

(c) The proceedings were not or are not being conducted independently or impartially, and they were or are being conducted in a manner which, in the circumstances, is inconsistent with an intent to bring the person concerned to justice.

3. In order to determine inability in a particular case, the Court shall consider whether, due to a total or substantial collapse or unavailability of its national judicial system, the State is unable to obtain the accused or the necessary evidence and testimony or otherwise unable to carry out its proceedings.

Article 18
Preliminary rulings regarding admissibility

1. When a situation has been referred to the Court pursuant to article 13 (a) and the Prosecutor has determined that there would be a reasonable basis to commence an investigation, or the Prosecutor initiates an investigation pursuant to articles 13 (c) and 15, the Prosecutor shall notify all States Parties and those States which, taking into account the information available, would normally exercise jurisdiction over the crimes concerned. The Prosecutor may notify such States on a confidential basis and, where the Prosecutor believes it necessary to protect persons, prevent destruction of evidence or prevent the absconding of persons, may limit the scope of the information provided to States.

2 Within one month of receipt of that notification, a State may inform the Court that it is investigating or has investigated its nationals or others within its jurisdiction with respect to criminal acts which may constitute crimes referred to in article 5 and which relate to the information provided in the notification to

States. At the request of that State, the Prosecutor shall defer to the State's investigation of those persons unless the Pre-Trial Chamber, on the application of the Prosecutor, decides to authorize the investigation.
3. The Prosecutor's deferral to a State's investigation shall be open to review by the Prosecutor six months after the date of deferral or at any time when there has been a significant change of circumstances based on the State's unwillingness or inability genuinely to carry out the investigation.
4. The State concerned or the Prosecutor may appeal to the Appeals Chamber against a ruling of the Pre-Trial Chamber, in accordance with article 82. The appeal may be heard on an expedited basis.
5. When the Prosecutor has deferred an investigation in accordance with paragraph 2, the Prosecutor may request that the State concerned periodically inform the Prosecutor of the progress of its investigations and any subsequent prosecutions. States Parties shall respond to such requests without undue delay.
6. Pending a ruling by the Pre-Trial Chamber, or at any time when the Prosecutor has deferred an investigation under this article, the Prosecutor may, on an exceptional basis, seek authority from the Pre-Trial Chamber to pursue necessary investigative steps for the purpose of preserving evidence where there is a unique opportunity to obtain important evidence or there is a significant risk that such evidence may not be subsequently available.
7. A State which has challenged a ruling of the Pre-Trial Chamber under this article may challenge the admissibility of a case under article 19 on the grounds of additional significant facts or significant change of circumstances.

Article 19
Challenges to the jurisdiction of the Court or the admissibility of a case

1. The Court shall satisfy itself that it has jurisdiction in any case brought before it. The Court may, on its own motion, determine the admissibility of a case in accordance with article 17.
2. Challenges to the admissibility of a case on the grounds referred to in article 17 or challenges to the jurisdiction of the Court may be made by:

(a) An accused or a person for whom a warrant of arrest or a summons to appear has been issued under article 58;

(b) A State which has jurisdiction over a case, on the ground that it is investigating or prosecuting the case or has investigated or prosecuted; or

(c) A State from which acceptance of jurisdiction is required under article 12.

3. The Prosecutor may seek a ruling from the Court regarding a question of jurisdiction or admissibility. In proceedings with respect to jurisdiction or admissibility, those who have referred the situation under article 13, as well as victims, may also submit observations to the Court.
4. The admissibility of a case or the jurisdiction of the Court may be challenged only once by any person or State referred to in paragraph 2. The chal-

lenge shall take place prior to or at the commencement of the trial. In exceptional circumstances, the Court may grant leave for a challenge to be brought more than once or at a time later than the commencement of the trial. Challenges to the admissibility of a case, at the commencement of a trial, or subsequently with the leave of the Court, may be based only on article 17, paragraph 1 (c).

5. A State referred to in paragraph 2 (b) and (c) shall make a challenge at the earliest opportunity.

6. Prior to the confirmation of the charges, challenges to the admissibility of a case or challenges to the jurisdiction of the Court shall be referred to the Pre-Trial Chamber. After confirmation of the charges, they shall be referred to the Trial Chamber. Decisions with respect to jurisdiction or admissibility may be appealed to the Appeals Chamber in accordance with article 82.

7. If a challenge is made by a State referred to in paragraph 2 (b) or (c), the Prosecutor shall suspend the investigation until such time as the Court makes a determination in accordance with article 17.

8. Pending a ruling by the Court, the Prosecutor may seek authority from the Court:

(a) To pursue necessary investigative steps of the kind referred to in article 18, paragraph 6;

(b) To take a statement or testimony from a witness or complete the collection and examination of evidence which had begun prior to the making of the challenge; and

(c) In cooperation with the relevant States, to prevent the absconding of persons in respect of whom the Prosecutor has already requested a warrant of arrest under article 58.

9. The making of a challenge shall not affect the validity of any act performed by the Prosecutor or any order or warrant issued by the Court prior to the making of the challenge.

10. If the Court has decided that a case is inadmissible under article 17, the Prosecutor may submit a request for a review of the decision when he or she is fully satisfied that new facts have arisen which negate the basis on which the case had previously been found inadmissible under article 17.

11. If the Prosecutor, having regard to the matters referred to in article 17, defers an investigation, the Prosecutor may request that the relevant State make available to the Prosecutor information on the proceedings. That information shall, at the request of the State concerned, be confidential. If the Prosecutor thereafter decides to proceed with an investigation, he or she shall notify the State to which deferral of the proceedings has taken place.

Article 20
Ne bis in idem

1. Except as provided in this Statute, no person shall be tried before the Court with respect to conduct which formed the basis of crimes for which the person has been convicted or acquitted by the Court.
2. No person shall be tried by another court for a crime referred to in article 5 for which that person has already been convicted or acquitted by the Court.
3. No person who has been tried by another court for conduct also proscribed under article 6, 7 or 8 shall be tried by the Court with respect to the same conduct unless the proceedings in the other court:

(a) Were for the purpose of shielding the person concerned from criminal responsibility for crimes within the jurisdiction of the Court; or

(b) Otherwise were not conducted independently or impartially in accordance with the norms of due process recognized by international law and were conducted in a manner which, in the circumstances, was inconsistent with an intent to bring the person concerned to justice.

Article 21
Applicable law

1. The Court shall apply:

(a) In the first place, this Statute, Elements of Crimes and its Rules of Procedure and Evidence;

(b) In the second place, where appropriate, applicable treaties and the principles and rules of international law, including the established principles of the international law of armed conflict;

(c) Failing that, general principles of law derived by the Court from national laws of legal systems of the world including, as appropriate, the national laws of States that would normally exercise jurisdiction over the crime, provided that those principles are not inconsistent with this Statute and with international law and internationally recognized norms and standards.

2. The Court may apply principles and rules of law as interpreted in its previous decisions.
3. The application and interpretation of law pursuant to this article must be consistent with internationally recognized human rights, and be without any adverse distinction founded on grounds such as gender as defined in article 7, paragraph 3, age, race, colour, language, religion or belief, political or other opinion, national, ethnic or social origin, wealth, birth or other status.

PART 3. GENERAL PRINCIPLES OF CRIMINAL LAW

Article 22
Nullum crimen sine lege

1. A person shall not be criminally responsible under this Statute unless the conduct in question constitutes, at the time it takes place, a crime within the jurisdiction of the Court.
2. The definition of a crime shall be strictly construed and shall not be extended by analogy. In case of ambiguity, the definition shall be interpreted in favour of the person being investigated, prosecuted or convicted.
3. This article shall not affect the characterization of any conduct as criminal under international law independently of this Statute.

Article 23
Nulla poena sine lege

A person convicted by the Court may be punished only in accordance with this Statute

Article 24
Non-retroactivity ratione personae

1 No person shall be criminally responsible under this Statute for conduct prior to the entry into force of the Statute.
2. In the event of a change in the law applicable to a given case prior to a final judgement, the law more favourable to the person being investigated, prosecuted or convicted shall apply.

Article 25
Individual criminal responsibility

1. The Court shall have jurisdiction over natural persons pursuant to this Statute.
2. A person who commits a crime within the jurisdiction of the Court shall be individually responsible and liable for punishment in accordance with this Statute.
3. In accordance with this Statute, a person shall be criminally responsible and liable for punishment for a crime within the jurisdiction of the Court if that person:

(a) Commits such a crime, whether as an individual, jointly with another or through another person, regardless of whether that other person is criminally responsible;

(b) Orders, solicits or induces the commission of such a crime which in fact occurs or is attempted;

(c) For the purpose of facilitating the commission of such a crime, aids, abets or otherwise assists in its commission or its attempted commission, including providing the means for its commission;

(d) In any other way contributes to the commission or attempted commission of such a crime by a group of persons acting with a common purpose. Such contribution shall be intentional and shall either:

(i) Be made with the aim of furthering the criminal activity or criminal purpose of the group, where such activity or purpose involves the commission of a crime within the jurisdiction of the Court; or

(ii) Be made in the knowledge of the intention of the group to commit the crime;

(e) In respect of the crime of genocide, directly and publicly incites others to commit genocide;

(f) Attempts to commit such a crime by taking action that commences its execution by means of a substantial step, but the crime does not occur because of circumstances independent of the person's intentions. However, a person who abandons the effort to commit the crime or otherwise prevents the completion of the crime shall not be liable for punishment under this Statute for the attempt to commit that crime if that person completely and voluntarily gave up the criminal purpose.

4. No provision in this Statute relating to individual criminal responsibility shall affect the responsibility of States under international law.

Article 26
Exclusion of jurisdiction over persons under eighteen

The Court shall have no jurisdiction over any person who was under the age of 18 at the time of the alleged commission of a crime.

Article 27
Irrelevance of official capacity

1. This Statute shall apply equally to all persons without any distinction based on official capacity. In particular, official capacity as a Head of State or Government, a member of a Government or parliament, an elected representative or a government official shall in no case exempt a person from criminal responsibility under this Statute, nor shall it, in and of itself, constitute a ground for reduction of sentence.

2. Immunities or special procedural rules which may attach to the official capacity of a person, whether under national or international law, shall not bar the Court from exercising its jurisdiction over such a person.

Article 28
Responsibility of commanders and other superiors

In addition to other grounds of criminal responsibility under this Statute for crimes within the jurisdiction of the Court:

(a) A military commander or person effectively acting as a military commander shall be criminally responsible for crimes within the jurisdiction of the Court committed by forces under his or her effective command and control, or effective authority and control as the case may be, as a result of his or her failure to exercise control properly over such forces, where:

- (i) That military commander or person either knew or, owing to the circumstances at the time, should have known that the forces were committing or about to commit such crimes; and
- (ii) That military commander or person failed to take all necessary and reasonable measures within his or her power to prevent or repress their commission or to submit the matter to the competent authorities for investigation and prosecution.

(b) With respect to superior and subordinate relationships not described in paragraph (a), a superior shall be criminally responsible for crimes within the jurisdiction of the Court committed by subordinates under his or her effective authority and control, as a result of his or her failure to exercise control properly over such subordinates, where:

- (i) The superior either knew, or consciously disregarded information which clearly indicated, that the subordinates were committing or about to commit such crimes;
- (ii) The crimes concerned activities that were within the effective responsibility and control of the superior; and
- (iii) The superior failed to take all necessary and reasonable measures within his or her power to prevent or repress their commission or to submit the matter to the competent authorities for investigation and prosecution.

Article 29
Non-applicability of statute of limitations

The crimes within the jurisdiction of the Court shall not be subject to any statute of limitations

Article 30
Mental element

1. Unless otherwise provided, a person shall be criminally responsible and liable for punishment for a crime within the jurisdiction of the Court only if the material elements are committed with intent and knowledge.

2. For the purposes of this article, a person has intent where:

(a) In relation to conduct, that person means to engage in the conduct;

(b) In relation to a consequence, that person means to cause that consequence or is aware that it will occur in the ordinary course of events.

3. For the purposes of this article, "knowledge" means awareness that a circumstance exists or a consequence will occur in the ordinary course of events. "Know" and "knowingly" shall be construed accordingly.

Article 31
Grounds for excluding criminal responsibility

1. In addition to other grounds for excluding criminal responsibility provided for in this Statute, a person shall not be criminally responsible if, at the time of that person's conduct:

(a) The person suffers from a mental disease or defect that destroys that person's capacity to appreciate the unlawfulness or nature of his or her conduct, or capacity to control his or her conduct to conform to the requirements of law;

(b) The person is in a state of intoxication that destroys that person's capacity to appreciate the unlawfulness or nature of his or her conduct, or capacity to control his or her conduct to conform to the requirements of law, unless the person has become voluntarily intoxicated under such circumstances that the person knew, or disregarded the risk, that, as a result of the intoxication, he or she was likely to engage in conduct constituting a crime within the jurisdiction of the Court;

(c) The person acts reasonably to defend himself or herself or another person or, in the case of war crimes, property which is essential for the survival of the person or another person or property which is essential for accomplishing a military mission, against an imminent and unlawful use of force in a manner proportionate to the degree of danger to the person or the other person or property protected. The fact that the person was involved in a defensive operation conducted by forces shall not in itself constitute a ground for excluding criminal responsibility under this subparagraph;

(d) The conduct which is alleged to constitute a crime within the jurisdiction of the Court has been caused by duress resulting from a threat of imminent death or of continuing or imminent serious bodily harm against that person or another person, and the person acts necessarily and reasonably to avoid this threat, provided that the person does not intend to cause a greater harm than the one sought to be avoided. Such a threat may either be:

(i) Made by other persons; or

(ii) Constituted by other circumstances beyond that person's control.

2. The Court shall determine the applicability of the grounds for excluding criminal responsibility provided for in this Statute to the case before it.

3. At trial, the Court may consider a ground for excluding criminal responsibility other than those referred to in paragraph 1 where such a ground is derived

from applicable law as set forth in article 21. The procedures relating to the consideration of such a ground shall be provided for in the Rules of Procedure and Evidence.

Article 32
Mistake of fact or mistake of law

1. A mistake of fact shall be a ground for excluding criminal responsibility only if it negates the mental element required by the crime.
2. A mistake of law as to whether a particular type of conduct is a crime within the jurisdiction of the Court shall not be a ground for excluding criminal responsibility. A mistake of law may, however, be a ground for excluding criminal responsibility if it negates the mental element required by such a crime, or as provided for in article 33.

Article 33
Superior orders and prescription of law

1. The fact that a crime within the jurisdiction of the Court has been committed by a person pursuant to an order of a Government or of a superior, whether military or civilian, shall not relieve that person of criminal responsibility unless:

(a) The person was under a legal obligation to obey orders of the Government or the superior in question;

(b) The person did not know that the order was unlawful; and

(c) The order was not manifestly unlawful.

2. For the purposes of this article, orders to commit genocide or crimes against humanity are manifestly unlawful.

PART 4. COMPOSITION AND ADMINISTRATION OF THE COURT

Article 34
Organs of the Court

The Court shall be composed of the following organs:

(a) The Presidency;

(b) An Appeals Division, a Trial Division and a Pre-Trial Division;

(c) The Office of the Prosecutor;

(d) The Registry.

Article 35
Service of judges

1. All judges shall be elected as full-time members of the Court and shall be available to serve on that basis from the commencement of their terms of office.
2. The judges composing the Presidency shall serve on a full-time basis as soon as they are elected.
3. The Presidency may, on the basis of the workload of the Court and in consultation with its members, decide from time to time to what extent the remaining judges shall be required to serve on a full-time basis. Any such arrangement shall be without prejudice to the provisions of article 40.
4. The financial arrangements for judges not required to serve on a full-time basis shall be made in accordance with article 49.

Article 36
Qualifications, nomination and election of judges

1. Subject to the provisions of paragraph 2, there shall be 18 judges of the Court.
2. (a) The Presidency, acting on behalf of the Court, may propose an increase in the number of judges specified in paragraph 1, indicating the reasons why this is considered necessary and appropriate. The Registrar shall promptly circulate any such proposal to all States Parties.

(b) Any such proposal shall then be considered at a meeting of the Assembly of States Parties to be convened in accordance with article 112. The proposal shall be considered adopted if approved at the meeting by a vote of two thirds of the members of the Assembly of States Parties and shall enter into force at such time as decided by the Assembly of States Parties.

(c) (i) Once a proposal for an increase in the number of judges has been adopted under subparagraph (b), the election of the additional judges shall take place at the next session of the Assembly of States Parties in accordance with paragraphs 3 to 8, and article 37, paragraph 2;

(ii) Once a proposal for an increase in the number of judges has been adopted and brought into effect under subparagraphs (b) and (c) (i), it shall be open to the Presidency at any time thereafter, if the workload of the Court justifies it, to propose a reduction in the number of judges, provided that the number of judges shall not be reduced below that specified in paragraph 1. The proposal shall be dealt with in accordance with the procedure laid down in subparagraphs (a) and (b). In the event that the proposal is adopted, the number of judges shall be progressively decreased as the terms of office of serving judges expire, until the necessary number has been reached.

3. (a) The judges shall be chosen from among persons of high moral character, impartiality and integrity who possess the qualifications required in their respective States for appointment to the highest judicial offices.

(b) Every candidate for election to the Court shall:

(i) Have established competence in criminal law and procedure, and the necessary relevant experience, whether as judge, prosecutor, advocate or in other similar capacity, in criminal proceedings; or

(ii) Have established competence in relevant areas of international law such as international humanitarian law and the law of human rights, and extensive experience in a professional legal capacity which is of relevance to the judicial work of the Court;

(c) Every candidate for election to the Court shall have an excellent knowledge of and be fluent in at least one of the working languages of the Court.

4. (a) Nominations of candidates for election to the Court may be made by any State Party to this Statute, and shall be made either:

(i) By the procedure for the nomination of candidates for appointment to the highest judicial offices in the State in question; or

(ii) By the procedure provided for the nomination of candidates for the International Court of Justice in the Statute of that Court. Nominations shall be accompanied by a statement in the necessary detail specifying how the candidate fulfils the requirements of paragraph 3.

(b) Each State Party may put forward one candidate for any given election who need not necessarily be a national of that State Party but shall in any case be a national of a State Party.

(c) The Assembly of States Parties may decide to establish, if appropriate, an Advisory Committee on nominations. In that event, the Committee's composition and mandate shall be established by the Assembly of States Parties.

5. For the purposes of the election, there shall be two lists of candidates:

List A containing the names of candidates with the qualifications specified in paragraph 3 (b) (i); and

List B containing the names of candidates with the qualifications specified in paragraph 3 (b) (ii).

A candidate with sufficient qualifications for both lists may choose on which list to appear. At the first election to the Court, at least nine judges shall be elected from list A and at least five judges from list B. Subsequent elections shall be so organized as to maintain the equivalent proportion on the Court of judges qualified on the two lists.

6. (a) The judges shall be elected by secret ballot at a meeting of the Assembly of States Parties convened for that purpose under article 112. Subject to paragraph 7, the persons elected to the Court shall be the 18 candidates who obtain the highest number of votes and a two-thirds majority of the States Parties present and voting.

(b) In the event that a sufficient number of judges is not elected on the first ballot, successive ballots shall be held in accordance with the procedures laid down in subparagraph (a) until the remaining places have been filled.
7. No two judges may be nationals of the same State. A person who, for the purposes of membership of the Court, could be regarded as a national of more than one State shall be deemed to be a national of the State in which that person ordinarily exercises civil and political rights.
8. (a) The States Parties shall, in the selection of judges, take into account the need, within the membership of the Court, for:

(i) The representation of the principal legal systems of the world;
(ii) Equitable geographical representation; and
(iii) A fair representation of female and male judges.

(b) States Parties shall also take into account the need to include judges with legal expertise on specific issues, including, but not limited to, violence against women or children.
9. (a) Subject to subparagraph (b), judges shall hold office for a term of nine years and, subject to subparagraph (c) and to article 37, paragraph 2, shall not be eligible for re-election.

(b) At the first election, one third of the judges elected shall be selected by lot to serve for a term of three years; one third of the judges elected shall be selected by lot to serve for a term of six years; and the remainder shall serve for a term of nine years.

(c) A judge who is selected to serve for a term of three years under subparagraph (b) shall be eligible for re-election for a full term.
10. Notwithstanding paragraph 9, a judge assigned to a Trial or Appeals Chamber in accordance with article 39 shall continue in office to complete any trial or appeal the hearing of which has already commenced before that Chamber.

Article 37
Judicial vacancies

1. In the event of a vacancy, an election shall be held in accordance with article 36 to fill the vacancy.
2. A judge elected to fill a vacancy shall serve for the remainder of the predecessor's term and, if that period is three years or less, shall be eligible for re-election for a full term under article 36.

Article 38
The Presidency

1. The President and the First and Second Vice-Presidents shall be elected by an absolute majority of the judges. They shall each serve for a term of three years or until the end of their respective terms of office as judges, whichever expires earlier. They shall be eligible for reelection once.

2. The First Vice-President shall act in place of the President in the event that the President is unavailable or disqualified. The Second Vice-President shall act in place of the President in the event that both the President and the First Vice-President are unavailable or disqualified.
3. The President, together with the First and Second Vice-Presidents, shall constitute the Presidency, which shall be responsible for:

(a) The proper administration of the Court, with the exception of the Office of the Prosecutor; and

(b) The other functions conferred upon it in accordance with this Statute.

4. In discharging its responsibility under paragraph 3 (a), the Presidency shall coordinate with and seek the concurrence of the Prosecutor on all matters of mutual concern.

Article 39
Chambers

1. As soon as possible after the election of the judges, the Court shall organize itself into the divisions specified in article 34, paragraph (b). The Appeals Division shall be composed of the President and four other judges, the Trial Division of not less than six judges and the Pre-Trial Division of not less than six judges. The assignment of judges to divisions shall be based on the nature of the functions to be performed by each division and the qualifications and experience of the judges elected to the Court, in such a way that each division shall contain an appropriate combination of expertise in criminal law and procedure and in international law. The Trial and Pre-Trial Divisions shall be composed predominantly of judges with criminal trial experience.
2. (a) The judicial functions of the Court shall be carried out in each division by Chambers.

(b) (i) The Appeals Chamber shall be composed of all the judges of the Appeals Division;

(ii) The functions of the Trial Chamber shall be carried out by three judges of the Trial Division;

(iii) The functions of the Pre-Trial Chamber shall be carried out either by three judges of the Pre-Trial Division or by a single judge of that division in accordance with this Statute and the Rules of Procedure and Evidence;

(c) Nothing in this paragraph shall preclude the simultaneous constitution of more than one Trial Chamber or Pre-Trial Chamber when the efficient management of the Court's workload so requires.

3 (a) Judges assigned to the Trial and Pre-Trial Divisions shall serve in those divisions for a period of three years, and thereafter until the completion of any case the hearing of which has already commenced in the division concerned.

(b) Judges assigned to the Appeals Division shall serve in that division for their entire term of office.

4. Judges assigned to the Appeals Division shall serve only in that division. Nothing in this article shall, however, preclude the temporary attachment of judges from the Trial Division to the Pre-Trial Division or vice versa, if the Presidency considers that the efficient management of the Court's workload so requires, provided that under no circumstances shall a judge who has participated in the pre-trial phase of a case be eligible to sit on the Trial Chamber hearing that case.

Article 40
Independence of the judges

1. The judges shall be independent in the performance of their functions.
2. Judges shall not engage in any activity which is likely to interfere with their judicial functions or to affect confidence in their independence.
3. Judges required to serve on a full-time basis at the seat of the Court shall not engage in any other occupation of a professional nature.
4. Any question regarding the application of paragraphs 2 and 3 shall be decided by an absolute majority of the judges. Where any such question concerns an individual judge, that judge shall not take part in the decision.

Article 41
Excusing and disqualification of judges

1. The Presidency may, at the request of a judge, excuse that judge from the exercise of a function under this Statute, in accordance with the Rules of Procedure and Evidence.
2. (a) A judge shall not participate in any case in which his or her impartiality might reasonably be doubted on any ground. A judge shall be disqualified from a case in accordance with this paragraph if, inter alia, that judge has previously been involved in any capacity in that case before the Court or in a related criminal case at the national level involving the person being investigated or prosecuted. A judge shall also be disqualified on such other grounds as may be provided for in the Rules of Procedure and Evidence.

(b) The Prosecutor or the person being investigated or prosecuted may request the disqualification of a judge under this paragraph.

(c) Any question as to the disqualification of a judge shall be decided by an absolute majority of the judges. The challenged judge shall be entitled to present his or her comments on the matter, but shall not take part in the decision.

Article 42
The Office of the Prosecutor

1. The Office of the Prosecutor shall act independently as a separate organ of the Court. It shall be responsible for receiving referrals and any substantiated

information on crimes within the jurisdiction of the Court, for examining them and for conducting investigations and prosecutions before the Court. A member of the Office shall not seek or act on instructions from any external source.
2. The Office shall be headed by the Prosecutor. The Prosecutor shall have full authority over the management and administration of the Office, including the staff, facilities and other resources thereof. The Prosecutor shall be assisted by one or more Deputy Prosecutors, who shall be entitled to carry out any of the acts required of the Prosecutor under this Statute. The Prosecutor and the Deputy Prosecutors shall be of different nationalities. They shall serve on a full-time basis.
3. The Prosecutor and the Deputy Prosecutors shall be persons of high moral character, be highly competent in and have extensive practical experience in the prosecution or trial of criminal cases. They shall have an excellent knowledge of and be fluent in at least one of the working languages of the Court.
4. The Prosecutor shall be elected by secret ballot by an absolute majority of the members of the Assembly of States Parties. The Deputy Prosecutors shall be elected in the same way from a list of candidates provided by the Prosecutor. The Prosecutor shall nominate three candidates for each position of Deputy Prosecutor to be filled. Unless a shorter term is decided upon at the time of their election, the Prosecutor and the Deputy Prosecutors shall hold office for a term of nine years and shall not be eligible for re-election.
5. Neither the Prosecutor nor a Deputy Prosecutor shall engage in any activity which is likely to interfere with his or her prosecutorial functions or to affect confidence in his or her independence. They shall not engage in any other occupation of a professional nature.
6. The Presidency may excuse the Prosecutor or a Deputy Prosecutor, at his or her request, from acting in a particular case.
7. Neither the Prosecutor nor a Deputy Prosecutor shall participate in any matter in which their impartiality might reasonably be doubted on any ground. They shall be disqualified from a case in accordance with this paragraph if, inter alia, they have previously been involved in any capacity in that case before the Court or in a related criminal case at the national level involving the person being investigated or prosecuted.
8. Any question as to the disqualification of the Prosecutor or a Deputy Prosecutor shall be decided by the Appeals Chamber.

(a) The person being investigated or prosecuted may at any time request the disqualification of the Prosecutor or a Deputy Prosecutor on the grounds set out in this article;

(b) The Prosecutor or the Deputy Prosecutor, as appropriate, shall be entitled to present his or her comments on the matter;

9. The Prosecutor shall appoint advisers with legal expertise on specific issues, including, but not limited to, sexual and gender violence and violence against children.

Article 43
The Registry

1. The Registry shall be responsible for the non-judicial aspects of the administration and servicing of the Court, without prejudice to the functions and powers of the Prosecutor in accordance with article 42.
2. The Registry shall be headed by the Registrar, who shall be the principal administrative officer of the Court. The Registrar shall exercise his or her functions under the authority of the President of the Court.
3. The Registrar and the Deputy Registrar shall be persons of high moral character, be highly competent and have an excellent knowledge of and be fluent in at least one of the working languages of the Court.
4. The judges shall elect the Registrar by an absolute majority by secret ballot, taking into account any recommendation by the Assembly of States Parties. If the need arises and upon the recommendation of the Registrar, the judges shall elect, in the same manner, a Deputy Registrar.
5. The Registrar shall hold office for a term of five years, shall be eligible for re-election once and shall serve on a full-time basis. The Deputy Registrar shall hold office for a term of five years or such shorter term as may be decided upon by an absolute majority of the judges, and may be elected on the basis that the Deputy Registrar shall be called upon to serve as required.
6. The Registrar shall set up a Victims and Witnesses Unit within the Registry. This Unit shall provide, in consultation with the Office of the Prosecutor, protective measures and security arrangements, counselling and other appropriate assistance for witnesses, victims who appear before the Court, and others who are at risk on account of testimony given by such witnesses. The Unit shall include staff with expertise in trauma, including trauma related to crimes of sexual violence.

Article 44
Staff

1. The Prosecutor and the Registrar shall appoint such qualified staff as may be required to their respective offices. In the case of the Prosecutor, this shall include the appointment of investigators.
2. In the employment of staff, the Prosecutor and the Registrar shall ensure the highest standards of efficiency, competency and integrity, and shall have regard, mutatis mutandis, to the criteria set forth in article 36, paragraph 8.
3. The Registrar, with the agreement of the Presidency and the Prosecutor, shall propose Staff Regulations which include the terms and conditions upon which the staff of the Court shall be appointed, remunerated and dismissed. The Staff Regulations shall be approved by the Assembly of States Parties.
4. The Court may, in exceptional circumstances, employ the expertise of gratis personnel offered by States Parties, intergovernmental organizations or non-

governmental organizations to assist with the work of any of the organs of the Court. The Prosecutor may accept any such offer on behalf of the Office of the Prosecutor. Such gratis personnel shall be employed in accordance with guidelines to be established by the Assembly of States Parties.

Article 45
Solemn undertaking

Before taking up their respective duties under this Statute, the judges, the Prosecutor, the Deputy Prosecutors, the Registrar and the Deputy Registrar shall each make a solemn undertaking in open court to exercise his or her respective functions impartially and conscientiously.

Article 46
Removal from office

1. A judge, the Prosecutor, a Deputy Prosecutor, the Registrar or the Deputy Registrar shall be removed from office if a decision to this effect is made in accordance with paragraph 2, in cases where that person:

(a) Is found to have committed serious misconduct or a serious breach of his or her duties under this Statute, as provided for in the Rules of Procedure and Evidence; or

(b) Is unable to exercise the functions required by this Statute.

2. A decision as to the removal from office of a judge, the Prosecutor or a Deputy Prosecutor under paragraph 1 shall be made by the Assembly of States Parties, by secret ballot:

(a) In the case of a judge, by a two-thirds majority of the States Parties upon a recommendation adopted by a two-thirds majority of the other judges;

(b) In the case of the Prosecutor, by an absolute majority of the States Parties;

(c) In the case of a Deputy Prosecutor, by an absolute majority of the States Parties upon the recommendation of the Prosecutor.

3. A decision as to the removal from office of the Registrar or Deputy Registrar shall be made by an absolute majority of the judges.

4. A judge, Prosecutor, Deputy Prosecutor, Registrar or Deputy Registrar whose conduct or ability to exercise the functions of the office as required by this Statute is challenged under this article shall have full opportunity to present and receive evidence and to make submissions in accordance with the Rules of Procedure and Evidence. The person in question shall not otherwise participate in the consideration of the matter.

Article 47
Disciplinary measures

A judge, Prosecutor, Deputy Prosecutor, Registrar or Deputy Registrar who has committed misconduct of a less serious nature than that set out in article 46, paragraph 1, shall be subject to disciplinary measures, in accordance with the Rules of Procedure and Evidence.

Article 48
Privileges and immunities

1. The Court shall enjoy in the territory of each State Party such privileges and immunities as are necessary for the fulfilment of its purposes.
2. The judges, the Prosecutor, the Deputy Prosecutors and the Registrar shall, when engaged on or with respect to the business of the Court, enjoy the same privileges and immunities as are accorded to heads of diplomatic missions and shall, after the expiry of their terms of office, continue to be accorded immunity from legal process of every kind in respect of words spoken or written and acts performed by them in their official capacity.
3. The Deputy Registrar, the staff of the Office of the Prosecutor and the staff of the Registry shall enjoy the privileges and immunities and facilities necessary for the performance of their functions, in accordance with the agreement on the privileges and immunities of the Court.
4. Counsel, experts, witnesses or any other person required to be present at the seat of the Court shall be accorded such treatment as is necessary for the proper functioning of the Court, in accordance with the agreement on the privileges and immunities of the Court.
5. The privileges and immunities of:

(a) A judge or the Prosecutor may be waived by an absolute majority of the judges;

(b) The Registrar may be waived by the Presidency;

(c) The Deputy Prosecutors and staff of the Office of the Prosecutor may be waived by the Prosecutor;

(d) The Deputy Registrar and staff of the Registry may be waived by the Registrar.

Article 49
Salaries, allowances and expenses

The judges, the Prosecutor, the Deputy Prosecutors, the Registrar and the Deputy Registrar shall receive such salaries, allowances and expenses as may be decided upon by the Assembly of States Parties. These salaries and allowances shall not be reduced during their terms of office.

Article 50
Official and working languages

1. The official languages of the Court shall be Arabic, Chinese, English, French, Russian and Spanish. The judgements of the Court, as well as other decisions resolving fundamental issues before the Court, shall be published in the official languages. The Presidency shall, in accordance with the criteria established by the Rules of Procedure and Evidence, determine which decisions may be considered as resolving fundamental issues for the purposes of this paragraph.
2. The working languages of the Court shall be English and French. The Rules of Procedure and Evidence shall determine the cases in which other official languages may be used as working languages.
3. At the request of any party to a proceeding or a State allowed to intervene in a proceeding, the Court shall authorize a language other than English or French to be used by such a party or State, provided that the Court considers such authorization to be adequately justified.

Article 51
Rules of Procedure and Evidence

1. The Rules of Procedure and Evidence shall enter into force upon adoption by a two-thirds majority of the members of the Assembly of States Parties.
2 Amendments to the Rules of Procedure and Evidence may be proposed by:
(a) Any State Party;
(b) The judges acting by an absolute majority; or
(c) The Prosecutor.

Such amendments shall enter into force upon adoption by a two-thirds majority of the members of the Assembly of States Parties.
3. After the adoption of the Rules of Procedure and Evidence, in urgent cases where the Rules do not provide for a specific situation before the Court, the judges may, by a two-thirds majority, draw up provisional Rules to be applied until adopted, amended or rejected at the next ordinary or special session of the Assembly of States Parties.
4. The Rules of Procedure and Evidence, amendments thereto and any provisional Rule shall be consistent with this Statute. Amendments to the Rules of Procedure and Evidence as well as provisional Rules shall not be applied retroactively to the detriment of the person who is being investigated or prosecuted or who has been convicted.
5. In the event of conflict between the Statute and the Rules of Procedure and Evidence, the Statute shall prevail.

Article 52
Regulations of the Court

1. The judges shall, in accordance with this Statute and the Rules of Procedure and Evidence, adopt, by an absolute majority, the Regulations of the Court necessary for its routine functioning.
2. The Prosecutor and the Registrar shall be consulted in the elaboration of the Regulations and any amendments thereto.
3. The Regulations and any amendments thereto shall take effect upon adoption unless otherwise decided by the judges. Immediately upon adoption, they shall be circulated to States Parties for comments. If within six months there are no objections from a majority of States Parties, they shall remain in force.

PART 5. INVESTIGATION AND PROSECUTION

Article 53
Initiation of an investigation

1. The Prosecutor shall, having evaluated the information made available to him or her, initiate an investigation unless he or she determines that there is no reasonable basis to proceed under this Statute. In deciding whether to initiate an investigation, the Prosecutor shall consider whether:

(a) The information available to the Prosecutor provides a reasonable basis to believe that a crime within the jurisdiction of the Court has been or is being committed;

(b) The case is or would be admissible under article 17; and

(c) Taking into account the gravity of the crime and the interests of victims, there are nonetheless substantial reasons to believe that an investigation would not serve the interests of justice. If the Prosecutor determines that there is no reasonable basis to proceed and his or her determination is based solely on subparagraph (c) above, he or she shall inform the Pre-Trial Chamber.

2. If, upon investigation, the Prosecutor concludes that there is not a sufficient basis for a prosecution because:

(a) There is not a sufficient legal or factual basis to seek a warrant or summons under article 58;

(b) The case is inadmissible under article 17; or

(c) A prosecution is not in the interests of justice, taking into account all the circumstances, including the gravity of the crime, the interests of victims and the age or infirmity of the alleged perpetrator, and his or her role in the alleged crime; the Prosecutor shall inform the Pre-Trial Chamber and the State making a referral under article 14 or the Security Council in a case under article 13, paragraph (b), of his or her conclusion and the reasons for the conclusion.

3. (a) At the request of the State making a referral under article 14 or the Security Council under article 13, paragraph (b), the Pre-Trial Chamber may

review a decision of the Prosecutor under paragraph 1 or 2 not to proceed and may request the Prosecutor to reconsider that decision.

(b) In addition, the Pre-Trial Chamber may, on its own initiative, review a decision of the Prosecutor not to proceed if it is based solely on paragraph 1 (c) or 2 (c). In such a case, the decision of the Prosecutor shall be effective only if confirmed by the Pre-Trial Chamber.

4. The Prosecutor may, at any time, reconsider a decision whether to initiate an investigation or prosecution based on new facts or information.

Article 54
Duties and powers of the Prosecutor with respect to investigations

1. The Prosecutor shall:

(a) In order to establish the truth, extend the investigation to cover all facts and evidence relevant to an assessment of whether there is criminal responsibility under this Statute, and, in doing so, investigate incriminating and exonerating circumstances equally;

(b) Take appropriate measures to ensure the effective investigation and prosecution of crimes within the jurisdiction of the Court, and in doing so, respect the interests and personal circumstances of victims and witnesses, including age, gender as defined in article 7, paragraph 3, and health, and take into account the nature of the crime, in particular where it involves sexual violence, gender violence or violence against children; and

(c) Fully respect the rights of persons arising under this Statute.

2 The Prosecutor may conduct investigations on the territory of a State:

(a) In accordance with the provisions of Part 9; or

(b) As authorized by the Pre-Trial Chamber under article 57, paragraph 3 (d).

3. The Prosecutor may:

(a) Collect and examine evidence;

(b) Request the presence of and question persons being investigated, victims and witnesses;

(c) Seek the cooperation of any State or intergovernmental organization or arrangement in accordance with its respective competence and/or mandate;

(d) Enter into such arrangements or agreements, not inconsistent with this Statute, as may be necessary to facilitate the cooperation of a State, intergovernmental organization or person;

(e) Agree not to disclose, at any stage of the proceedings, documents or information that the Prosecutor obtains on the condition of confidentiality and solely for the purpose of generating new evidence, unless the provider of the information consents; and

(f) Take necessary measures, or request that necessary measures be taken, to ensure the confidentiality of information, the protection of any person or the preservation of evidence.

Article 55
Rights of persons during an investigation

1. In respect of an investigation under this Statute, a person:

(a) Shall not be compelled to incriminate himself or herself or to confess guilt;

(b) Shall not be subjected to any form of coercion, duress or threat, to torture or to any other form of cruel, inhuman or degrading treatment or punishment;

(c) Shall, if questioned in a language other than a language the person fully understands and speaks, have, free of any cost, the assistance of a competent interpreter and such translations as are necessary to meet the requirements of fairness; and

(d) Shall not be subjected to arbitrary arrest or detention, and shall not be deprived of his or her liberty except on such grounds and in accordance with such procedures as are established in this Statute.

2. Where there are grounds to believe that a person has committed a crime within the jurisdiction of the Court and that person is about to be questioned either by the Prosecutor, or by national authorities pursuant to a request made under Part 9, that person shall also have the following rights of which he or she shall be informed prior to being questioned:

(a) To be informed, prior to being questioned, that there are grounds to believe that he or she has committed a crime within the jurisdiction of the Court;

(b) To remain silent, without such silence being a consideration in the determination of guilt or innocence;

(c) To have legal assistance of the person's choosing, or, if the person does not have legal assistance, to have legal assistance assigned to him or her, in any case where the interests of justice so require, and without payment by the person in any such case if the person does not have sufficient means to pay for it; and

(d) To be questioned in the presence of counsel unless the person has voluntarily waived his or her right to counsel.

Article 56
Role of the Pre-Trial Chamber in relation to a unique investigative opportunity

1. (a) Where the Prosecutor considers an investigation to present a unique opportunity to take testimony or a statement from a witness or to examine, collect or test evidence, which may not be available subsequently for the purposes of a trial, the Prosecutor shall so inform the Pre-Trial Chamber.

(b) In that case, the Pre-Trial Chamber may, upon request of the Prosecutor, take such measures as may be necessary to ensure the efficiency and integrity of the proceedings and, in particular, to protect the rights of the defence.

(c) Unless the Pre-Trial Chamber orders otherwise, the Prosecutor shall provide the relevant information to the person who has been arrested or appeared in response to a summons in connection with the investigation referred to in subparagraph (a), in order that he or she may be heard on the matter.

2. The measures referred to in paragraph 1 (b) may include:

(a) Making recommendations or orders regarding procedures to be followed;

(b) Directing that a record be made of the proceedings;

(c) Appointing an expert to assist;

(d) Authorizing counsel for a person who has been arrested, or appeared before the Court in response to a summons, to participate, or where there has not yet been such an arrest or appearance or counsel has not been designated, appointing another counsel to attend and represent the interests of the defence;

(e) Naming one of its members or, if necessary, another available judge of the Pre-Trial or Trial Division to observe and make recommendations or orders regarding the collection and preservation of evidence and the questioning of persons;

(f) Taking such other action as may be necessary to collect or preserve evidence.

3. (a) Where the Prosecutor has not sought measures pursuant to this article but the Pre-Trial Chamber considers that such measures are required to preserve evidence that it deems would be essential for the defence at trial, it shall consult with the Prosecutor as to whether there is good reason for the Prosecutor's failure to request the measures. If upon consultation, the Pre-Trial Chamber concludes that the Prosecutor's failure to request such measures is unjustified, the Pre-Trial Chamber may take such measures on its own initiative.

(b) A decision of the Pre-Trial Chamber to act on its own initiative under this paragraph may be appealed by the Prosecutor. The appeal shall be heard on an expedited basis.

4. The admissibility of evidence preserved or collected for trial pursuant to this article, or the record thereof, shall be governed at trial by article 69, and given such weight as determined by the Trial Chamber.

Article 57
Functions and powers of the Pre-Trial Chamber

1. Unless otherwise provided in this Statute, the Pre-Trial Chamber shall exercise its functions in accordance with the provisions of this article.

2. (a) Orders or rulings of the Pre-Trial Chamber issued under articles 15, 18, 19, 54, paragraph 2, 61, paragraph 7, and 72 must be concurred in by a majority of its judges.

(b) In all other cases, a single judge of the Pre-Trial Chamber may exercise the functions provided for in this Statute, unless otherwise provided for in the Rules of Procedure and Evidence or by a majority of the Pre-Trial Chamber.

3. In addition to its other functions under this Statute, the Pre-Trial Chamber may:

(a) At the request of the Prosecutor, issue such orders and warrants as may be required for the purposes of an investigation;

(b) Upon the request of a person who has been arrested or has appeared pursuant to a summons under article 58, issue such orders, including measures such as those described in article 56, or seek such cooperation pursuant to Part 9 as may be necessary to assist the person in the preparation of his or her defence;
Rome Statute of the International Criminal Court 39

(c) Where necessary, provide for the protection and privacy of victims and witnesses, the preservation of evidence, the protection of persons who have been arrested or appeared in response to a summons, and the protection of national security information.

(d) Authorize the Prosecutor to take specific investigative steps within the territory of a State Party without having secured the cooperation of that State under Part 9 if, whenever possible having regard to the views of the State concerned, the Pre-Trial Chamber has determined in that case that the State is clearly unable to execute a request for cooperation due to the unavailability of any authority or any component of its judicial system competent to execute the request for cooperation under Part 9;

(e) Where a warrant of arrest or a summons has been issued under article 58, and having due regard to the strength of the evidence and the rights of the parties concerned, as provided for in this Statute and the Rules of Procedure and Evidence, seek the cooperation of States pursuant to article 93, paragraph 1 (k), to take protective measures for the purpose of forfeiture, in particular for the ultimate benefit of victims.

Article 58
Issuance by the Pre-Trial Chamber of a warrant of arrest or a summons to appear

1. At any time after the initiation of an investigation, the Pre-Trial Chamber shall, on the application of the Prosecutor, issue a warrant of arrest of a person if, having examined the application and the evidence or other information submitted by the Prosecutor, it is satisfied that:

(a) There are reasonable grounds to believe that the person has committed a crime within the jurisdiction of the Court; and

(b) The arrest of the person appears necessary:

(i) To ensure the person's appearance at trial;

(ii) To ensure that the person does not obstruct or endanger the investigation or the court proceedings; or

(iii) Where applicable, to prevent the person from continuing with the commission of that crime or a related crime which is within the jurisdiction of the Court and which arises out of the same circumstances.

2. The application of the Prosecutor shall contain:

(a) The name of the person and any other relevant identifying information;

(b) A specific reference to the crimes within the jurisdiction of the Court which the person is alleged to have committed;

(c) A concise statement of the facts which are alleged to constitute those crimes;

(d) A summary of the evidence and any other information which establish reasonable grounds to believe that the person committed those crimes; and

(e) The reason why the Prosecutor believes that the arrest of the person is necessary.

3. The warrant of arrest shall contain:

(a) The name of the person and any other relevant identifying information;

(b) A specific reference to the crimes within the jurisdiction of the Court for which the person's arrest is sought; and

(c) A concise statement of the facts which are alleged to constitute those crimes.

4. The warrant of arrest shall remain in effect until otherwise ordered by the Court.

5. On the basis of the warrant of arrest, the Court may request the provisional arrest or the arrest and surrender of the person under Part 9.

6. The Prosecutor may request the Pre-Trial Chamber to amend the warrant of arrest by modifying or adding to the crimes specified therein. The Pre-Trial Chamber shall so amend the warrant if it is satisfied that there are reasonable grounds to believe that the person committed the modified or additional crimes.

7. As an alternative to seeking a warrant of arrest, the Prosecutor may submit an application requesting that the Pre-Trial Chamber issue a summons for the person to appear. If the Pre-Trial Chamber is satisfied that there are reasonable grounds to believe that the person committed the crime alleged and that a summons is sufficient to ensure the person's appearance, it shall issue the summons, with or without conditions restricting liberty (other than detention) if provided for by national law, for the person to appear. The summons shall contain:

(a) The name of the person and any other relevant identifying information;

(b) The specified date on which the person is to appear;

(c) A specific reference to the crimes within the jurisdiction of the Court which the person is alleged to have committed; and

(d) A concise statement of the facts which are alleged to constitute the crime. The summons shall be served on the person.

Article 59
Arrest proceedings in the custodial State

1. A State Party which has received a request for provisional arrest or for arrest and surrender shall immediately take steps to arrest the person in question in accordance with its laws and the provisions of Part 9.

2. A person arrested shall be brought promptly before the competent judicial authority in the custodial State which shall determine, in accordance with the law of that State, that:

(a) The warrant applies to that person;

(b) The person has been arrested in accordance with the proper process; and

(c) The person's rights have been respected.

3. The person arrested shall have the right to apply to the competent authority in the custodial State for interim release pending surrender.

4. In reaching a decision on any such application, the competent authority in the custodial State shall consider whether, given the gravity of the alleged crimes, there are urgent and exceptional circumstances to justify interim release and whether necessary safeguards exist to ensure that the custodial State can fulfil its duty to surrender the person to the Court. It shall not be open to the competent authority of the custodial State to consider whether the warrant of arrest was properly issued in accordance with article 58, paragraph 1 (a) and (b).

5. The Pre-Trial Chamber shall be notified of any request for interim release and shall make recommendations to the competent authority in the custodial State The competent authority in the custodial State shall give full consideration to such recommendations, including any recommendations on measures to prevent the escape of the person, before rendering its decision.

6. If the person is granted interim release, the Pre-Trial Chamber may request periodic reports on the status of the interim release.

7. Once ordered to be surrendered by the custodial State, the person shall be delivered to the Court as soon as possible.

Article 60
Initial proceedings before the Court

1. Upon the surrender of the person to the Court, or the person's appearance before the Court voluntarily or pursuant to a summons, the Pre-Trial Chamber shall satisfy itself that the person has been informed of the crimes which he or she is alleged to have committed, and of his or her rights under this Statute, including the right to apply for interim release pending trial.

2. A person subject to a warrant of arrest may apply for interim release pending trial. If the Pre-Trial Chamber is satisfied that the conditions set forth in article 58, paragraph 1, are met, the person shall continue to be detained. If it is not so satisfied, the Pre-Trial Chamber shall release the person, with or without conditions.

3. The Pre-Trial Chamber shall periodically review its ruling on the release or detention of the person, and may do so at any time on the request of the Prosecutor or the person. Upon such review, it may modify its ruling as to detention, release or conditions of release, if it is satisfied that changed circumstances so require.

4. The Pre-Trial Chamber shall ensure that a person is not detained for an unreasonable period prior to trial due to inexcusable delay by the Prosecutor. If such delay occurs, the Court shall consider releasing the person, with or without conditions.
5. If necessary, the Pre-Trial Chamber may issue a warrant of arrest to secure the presence of a person who has been released.

Article 61
Confirmation of the charges before trial

1. Subject to the provisions of paragraph 2, within a reasonable time after the person's surrender or voluntary appearance before the Court, the Pre-Trial Chamber shall hold a hearing to confirm the charges on which the Prosecutor intends to seek trial. The hearing shall be held in the presence of the Prosecutor and the person charged, as well as his or her counsel.
2. The Pre-Trial Chamber may, upon request of the Prosecutor or on its own motion, hold a hearing in the absence of the person charged to confirm the charges on which the Prosecutor intends to seek trial when the person has:

(a) Waived his or her right to be present; or

(b) Fled or cannot be found and all reasonable steps have been taken to secure his or her appearance before the Court and to inform the person of the charges and that a hearing to confirm those charges will be held. In that case, the person shall be represented by counsel where the Pre-Trial Chamber determines that it is in the interests of justice.

3. Within a reasonable time before the hearing, the person shall:

(a) Be provided with a copy of the document containing the charges on which the Prosecutor intends to bring the person to trial; and

(b) Be informed of the evidence on which the Prosecutor intends to rely at the hearing. The Pre-Trial Chamber may issue orders regarding the disclosure of information for the purposes of the hearing.

4. Before the hearing, the Prosecutor may continue the investigation and may amend or withdraw any charges. The person shall be given reasonable notice before the hearing of any amendment to or withdrawal of charges. In case of a withdrawal of charges, the Prosecutor shall notify the Pre-Trial Chamber of the reasons for the withdrawal.
5. At the hearing, the Prosecutor shall support each charge with sufficient evidence to establish substantial grounds to believe that the person committed the crime charged. The Prosecutor may rely on documentary or summary evidence and need not call the witnesses expected to testify at the trial.
6. At the hearing, the person may.

(a) Object to the charges;

(b) Challenge the evidence presented by the Prosecutor; and

(c) Present evidence.

7. The Pre-Trial Chamber shall, on the basis of the hearing, determine whether there is sufficient evidence to establish substantial grounds to believe that the person committed each of the crimes charged. Based on its determination, the Pre-Trial Chamber shall:

(a) Confirm those charges in relation to which it has determined that there is sufficient evidence, and commit the person to a Trial Chamber for trial on the charges as confirmed;

(b) Decline to confirm those charges in relation to which it has determined that there is insufficient evidence;

(c) Adjourn the hearing and request the Prosecutor to consider:

(i) Providing further evidence or conducting further investigation with respect to a particular charge; or

(ii) Amending a charge because the evidence submitted appears to establish a different crime within the jurisdiction of the Court.

8. Where the Pre-Trial Chamber declines to confirm a charge, the Prosecutor shall not be precluded from subsequently requesting its confirmation if the request is supported by additional evidence.

9. After the charges are confirmed and before the trial has begun, the Prosecutor may, with the permission of the Pre-Trial Chamber and after notice to the accused, amend the charges. If the Prosecutor seeks to add additional charges or to substitute more serious charges, a hearing under this article to confirm those charges must be held. After commencement of the trial, the Prosecutor may, with the permission of the Trial Chamber, withdraw the charges.

10. Any warrant previously issued shall cease to have effect with respect to any charges which have not been confirmed by the Pre-Trial Chamber or which have been withdrawn by the Prosecutor.

11. Once the charges have been confirmed in accordance with this article, the Presidency shall constitute a Trial Chamber which, subject to paragraph 9 and to article 64, paragraph 4, shall be responsible for the conduct of subsequent proceedings and may exercise any function of the Pre-Trial Chamber that is relevant and capable of application in those proceedings.

PART 6. THE TRIAL

Article 62
Place of trial

Unless otherwise decided, the place of the trial shall be the seat of the Court.

Article 63
Trial in the presence of the accused

1. The accused shall be present during the trial.

2. If the accused, being present before the Court, continues to disrupt the trial, the Trial Chamber may remove the accused and shall make provision for him or her to observe the trial and instruct counsel from outside the courtroom, through the use of communications technology, if required. Such measures shall be taken only in exceptional circumstances after other reasonable alternatives have proved inadequate, and only for such duration as is strictly required.

Article 64
Functions and powers of the Trial Chamber

1. The functions and powers of the Trial Chamber set out in this article shall be exercised in accordance with this Statute and the Rules of Procedure and Evidence.
2. The Trial Chamber shall ensure that a trial is fair and expeditious and is conducted with full respect for the rights of the accused and due regard for the protection of victims and witnesses.
3. Upon assignment of a case for trial in accordance with this Statute, the Trial Chamber assigned to deal with the case shall:

(a) Confer with the parties and adopt such procedures as are necessary to facilitate the fair and expeditious conduct of the proceedings;

(b) Determine the language or languages to be used at trial; and

(c) Subject to any other relevant provisions of this Statute, provide for disclosure of documents or information not previously disclosed, sufficiently in advance of the commencement of the trial to enable adequate preparation for trial

4. The Trial Chamber may, if necessary for its effective and fair functioning, refer preliminary issues to the Pre-Trial Chamber or, if necessary, to another available judge of the Pre-Trial Division.
5. Upon notice to the parties, the Trial Chamber may, as appropriate, direct that there be joinder or severance in respect of charges against more than one accused.
6. In performing its functions prior to trial or during the course of a trial, the Trial Chamber may, as necessary:

(a) Exercise any functions of the Pre-Trial Chamber referred to in article 61, paragraph 11;

(b) Require the attendance and testimony of witnesses and production of documents and other evidence by obtaining, if necessary, the assistance of States as provided in this Statute;

(c) Provide for the protection of confidential information;

(d) Order the production of evidence in addition to that already collected prior to the trial or presented during the trial by the parties;

(e) Provide for the protection of the accused, witnesses and victims; and

(f) Rule on any other relevant matters.

7. The trial shall be held in public. The Trial Chamber may, however, determine that special circumstances require that certain proceedings be in closed session for the purposes set forth in article 68, or to protect confidential or sensitive information to be given in evidence.
8. (a) At the commencement of the trial, the Trial Chamber shall have read to the accused the charges previously confirmed by the Pre-Trial Chamber. The Trial Chamber shall satisfy itself that the accused understands the nature of the charges. It shall afford him or her the opportunity to make an admission of guilt in accordance with article 65 or to plead not guilty.
(b) At the trial, the presiding judge may give directions for the conduct of proceedings, including to ensure that they are conducted in a fair and impartial manner. Subject to any Rome Statute of the International Criminal Court 45 directions of the presiding judge, the parties may submit evidence in accordance with the provisions of this Statute.
9. The Trial Chamber shall have, inter alia, the power on application of a party or on its own motion to:
(a) Rule on the admissibility or relevance of evidence; and
(b) Take all necessary steps to maintain order in the course of a hearing.
10. The Trial Chamber shall ensure that a complete record of the trial, which accurately reflects the proceedings, is made and that it is maintained and preserved by the Registrar.

Article 65
Proceedings on an admission of guilt

1. Where the accused makes an admission of guilt pursuant to article 64, paragraph 8 (a), the Trial Chamber shall determine whether:
(a) The accused understands the nature and consequences of the admission of guilt;
(b) The admission is voluntarily made by the accused after sufficient consultation with defence counsel; and
(c) The admission of guilt is supported by the facts of the case that are contained in:
(i) The charges brought by the Prosecutor and admitted by the accused;
(ii) Any materials presented by the Prosecutor which supplement the charges and which the accused accepts; and
(iii) Any other evidence, such as the testimony of witnesses, presented by the Prosecutor or the accused.
2. Where the Trial Chamber is satisfied that the matters referred to in paragraph 1 are established, it shall consider the admission of guilt, together with any additional evidence presented, as establishing all the essential facts that are required to prove the crime to which the admission of guilt relates, and may convict the accused of that crime.

3. Where the Trial Chamber is not satisfied that the matters referred to in paragraph 1 are established, it shall consider the admission of guilt as not having been made, in which case it shall order that the trial be continued under the ordinary trial procedures provided by this Statute and may remit the case to another Trial Chamber.
4. Where the Trial Chamber is of the opinion that a more complete presentation of the facts of the case is required in the interests of justice, in particular the interests of the victims, the Trial Chamber may:

(a) Request the Prosecutor to present additional evidence, including the testimony of witnesses; or

(b) Order that the trial be continued under the ordinary trial procedures provided by this Statute, in which case it shall consider the admission of guilt as not having been made and may remit the case to another Trial Chamber.

5. Any discussions between the Prosecutor and the defence regarding modification of the charges, the admission of guilt or the penalty to be imposed shall not be binding on the Court.

Article 66
Presumption of innocence

1. Everyone shall be presumed innocent until proved guilty before the Court in accordance with the applicable law.
2 The onus is on the Prosecutor to prove the guilt of the accused.
3. In order to convict the accused, the Court must be convinced of the guilt of the accused beyond reasonable doubt.

Article 67
Rights of the accused

1. In the determination of any charge, the accused shall be entitled to a public hearing, having regard to the provisions of this Statute, to a fair hearing conducted impartially, and to the following minimum guarantees, in full equality:

(a) To be informed promptly and in detail of the nature, cause and content of the charge, in a language which the accused fully understands and speaks;

(b) To have adequate time and facilities for the preparation of the defence and to communicate freely with counsel of the accused's choosing in confidence;

(c) To be tried without undue delay;

(d) Subject to article 63, paragraph 2, to be present at the trial, to conduct the defence in person or through legal assistance of the accused's choosing, to be informed, if the accused does not have legal assistance, of this right and to have legal assistance assigned by the Court in any case where the interests of justice so require, and without payment if the accused lacks sufficient means to pay for it;

(e) To examine, or have examined, the witnesses against him or her and to obtain the attendance and examination of witnesses on his or her behalf under the same conditions as witnesses against him or her. The accused shall also be entitled to raise defences and to present other evidence admissible under this Statute;

(f) To have, free of any cost, the assistance of a competent interpreter and such translations as are necessary to meet the requirements of fairness, if any of the proceedings of or documents presented to the Court are not in a language which the accused fully understands and speaks;

(g) Not to be compelled to testify or to confess guilt and to remain silent, without such silence being a consideration in the determination of guilt or innocence;

(h) To make an unsworn oral or written statement in his or her defence; and

(i) Not to have imposed on him or her any reversal of the burden of proof or any onus of rebuttal.

2. In addition to any other disclosure provided for in this Statute, the Prosecutor shall, as soon as practicable, disclose to the defence evidence in the Prosecutor's possession or control which he or she believes shows or tends to show the innocence of the accused, or to mitigate the guilt of the accused, or which may affect the credibility of prosecution evidence. In case of doubt as to the application of this paragraph, the Court shall decide.

Article 68
Protection of the victims and witnesses and their participation in the proceedings

1. The Court shall take appropriate measures to protect the safety, physical and psychological well-being, dignity and privacy of victims and witnesses. In so doing, the Court shall have regard to all relevant factors, including age, gender as defined in article 7, paragraph 3, and health, and the nature of the crime, in particular, but not limited to, where the crime involves sexual or gender violence or violence against children. The Prosecutor shall take such measures particularly during the investigation and prosecution of such crimes. These measures shall not be prejudicial to or inconsistent with the rights of the accused and a fair and impartial trial.

2. As an exception to the principle of public hearings provided for in article 67, the Chambers of the Court may, to protect victims and witnesses or an accused, conduct any part of the proceedings in camera or allow the presentation of evidence by electronic or other special means. In particular, such measures shall be implemented in the case of a victim of sexual violence or a child who is a victim or a witness, unless otherwise ordered by the Court, having regard to all the circumstances, particularly the views of the victim or witness.

3. Where the personal interests of the victims are affected, the Court shall permit their views and concerns to be presented and considered at stages of the proceedings determined to be appropriate by the Court and in a manner which is not prejudicial to or inconsistent with the rights of the accused and a fair and impartial trial. Such views and concerns may be presented by the legal representatives of the victims where the Court considers it appropriate, in accordance with the Rules of Procedure and Evidence.
4. The Victims and Witnesses Unit may advise the Prosecutor and the Court on appropriate protective measures, security arrangements, counselling and assistance as referred to in article 43, paragraph 6.
5. Where the disclosure of evidence or information pursuant to this Statute may lead to the grave endangerment of the security of a witness or his or her family, the Prosecutor may, for the purposes of any proceedings conducted prior to the commencement of the trial, withhold such evidence or information and instead submit a summary thereof. Such measures shall be exercised in a manner which is not prejudicial to or inconsistent with the rights of the accused and a fair and impartial trial.
6. A State may make an application for necessary measures to be taken in respect of the protection of its servants or agents and the protection of confidential or sensitive information.

Article 69
Evidence

1. Before testifying, each witness shall, in accordance with the Rules of Procedure and Evidence, give an undertaking as to the truthfulness of the evidence to be given by that witness
2. The testimony of a witness at trial shall be given in person, except to the extent provided by the measures set forth in article 68 or in the Rules of Procedure and Evidence. The Court may also permit the giving of viva voce (oral) or recorded testimony of a witness by means of video or audio technology, as well as the introduction of documents or written transcripts, subject to this Statute and in accordance with the Rules of Procedure and Evidence. These measures shall not be prejudicial to or inconsistent with the rights of the accused.
3. The parties may submit evidence relevant to the case, in accordance with article 64. The Court shall have the authority to request the submission of all evidence that it considers necessary for the determination of the truth.
4. The Court may rule on the relevance or admissibility of any evidence, taking into account, inter alia, the probative value of the evidence and any prejudice that such evidence may cause to a fair trial or to a fair evaluation of the testimony of a witness, in accordance with the Rules of Procedure and Evidence.
5. The Court shall respect and observe privileges on confidentiality as provided for in the Rules of Procedure and Evidence.

6. The Court shall not require proof of facts of common knowledge but may take judicial notice of them.
7. Evidence obtained by means of a violation of this Statute or internationally recognized human rights shall not be admissible if:

(a) The violation casts substantial doubt on the reliability of the evidence; or

(b) The admission of the evidence would be antithetical to and would seriously damage the integrity of the proceedings.

8. When deciding on the relevance or admissibility of evidence collected by a State, the Court shall not rule on the application of the State's national law.

Article 70
Offences against the administration of justice

1. The Court shall have jurisdiction over the following offences against its administration of justice when committed intentionally:

(a) Giving false testimony when under an obligation pursuant to article 69, paragraph 1, to tell the truth;

(b) Presenting evidence that the party knows is false or forged;

(c) Corruptly influencing a witness, obstructing or interfering with the attendance or testimony of a witness, retaliating against a witness for giving testimony or destroying, tampering with or interfering with the collection of evidence;

(d) Impeding, intimidating or corruptly influencing an official of the Court for the purpose of forcing or persuading the official not to perform, or to perform improperly, his or her duties;

(e) Retaliating against an official of the Court on account of duties performed by that or another official;

(f) Soliciting or accepting a bribe as an official of the Court in connection with his or her official duties.

2. The principles and procedures governing the Court's exercise of jurisdiction over offences under this article shall be those provided for in the Rules of Procedure and Evidence. The conditions for providing international cooperation to the Court with respect to its proceedings under this article shall be governed by the domestic laws of the requested State.
3. In the event of conviction, the Court may impose a term of imprisonment not exceeding five years, or a fine in accordance with the Rules of Procedure and Evidence, or both.
4. (a) Each State Party shall extend its criminal laws penalizing offences against the integrity of its own investigative or judicial process to offences against the administration of justice referred to in this article, committed on its territory, or by one of its nationals;

(b) Upon request by the Court, whenever it deems it proper, the State Party shall submit the case to its competent authorities for the purpose of prosecution.

Those authorities shall treat such cases with diligence and devote sufficient resources to enable them to be conducted effectively.

Article 71
Sanctions for misconduct before the Court

1. The Court may sanction persons present before it who commit misconduct, including disruption of its proceedings or deliberate refusal to comply with its directions, by administrative measures other than imprisonment, such as temporary or permanent removal from the courtroom, a fine or other similar measures provided for in the Rules of Procedure and Evidence.
2. The procedures governing the imposition of the measures set forth in paragraph 1 shall be those provided for in the Rules of Procedure and Evidence.

Article 72
Protection of national security information

1. This article applies in any case where the disclosure of the information or documents of a State would, in the opinion of that State, prejudice its national security interests. Such cases include those falling within the scope of article 56, paragraphs 2 and 3, article 61, paragraph 3, article 64, paragraph 3, article 67, paragraph 2, article 68, paragraph 6, article 87, paragraph 6 and article 93, as well as cases arising at any other stage of the proceedings where such disclosure may be at issue.
2. This article shall also apply when a person who has been requested to give information or evidence has refused to do so or has referred the matter to the State on the ground that disclosure would prejudice the national security interests of a State and the State concerned confirms that it is of the opinion that disclosure would prejudice its national security interests.
3. Nothing in this article shall prejudice the requirements of confidentiality applicable under article 54, paragraph 3 (e) and (f), or the application of article 73.
4. If a State learns that information or documents of the State are being, or are likely to be, disclosed at any stage of the proceedings, and it is of the opinion that disclosure would prejudice its national security interests, that State shall have the right to intervene in order to obtain resolution of the issue in accordance with this article.
5. If, in the opinion of a State, disclosure of information would prejudice its national security interests, all reasonable steps will be taken by the State, acting in conjunction with the Prosecutor, the defence or the Pre-Trial Chamber or Trial Chamber, as the case may be, to seek to resolve the matter by cooperative means. Such steps may include:

(a) Modification or clarification of the request;

(b) A determination by the Court regarding the relevance of the information or evidence sought, or a determination as to whether the evidence, though relevant, could be or has been obtained from a source other than the requested State;

(c) Obtaining the information or evidence from a different source or in a different form; or

(d) Agreement on conditions under which the assistance could be provided including, among other things, providing summaries or redactions, limitations on disclosure, use of in camera or ex parte proceedings, or other protective measures permissible under the Statute and the Rules of Procedure and Evidence.

6. Once all reasonable steps have been taken to resolve the matter through cooperative means, and if the State considers that there are no means or conditions under which the information or documents could be provided or disclosed without prejudice to its national security interests, it shall so notify the Prosecutor or the Court of the specific reasons for its decision, unless a specific description of the reasons would itself necessarily result in such prejudice to the State's national security interests.

7. Thereafter, if the Court determines that the evidence is relevant and necessary for the establishment of the guilt or innocence of the accused, the Court may undertake the following actions:

(a) Where disclosure of the information or document is sought pursuant to a request for cooperation under Part 9 or the circumstances described in paragraph 2, and the State has invoked the ground for refusal referred to in article 93, paragraph 4:

- (i) The Court may, before making any conclusion referred to in subparagraph 7 (a) (ii), request further consultations for the purpose of considering the State's representations, which may include, as appropriate, hearings in camera and ex parte;
- (ii) If the Court concludes that, by invoking the ground for refusal under article 93, paragraph 4, in the circumstances of the case, the requested State is not acting in accordance with its obligations under this Statute, the Court may refer the matter in accordance with article 87, paragraph 7, specifying the reasons for its conclusion; and
- (iii) The Court may make such inference in the trial of the accused as to the existence or non-existence of a fact, as may be appropriate in the circumstances; or

(b) In all other circumstances:

- (i) Order disclosure; or
- (ii) To the extent it does not order disclosure, make such inference in the trial of the accused as to the existence or non-existence of a fact, as may be appropriate in the circumstances

Article 73
Third-party information or documents

If a State Party is requested by the Court to provide a document or information in its custody, possession or control, which was disclosed to it in confidence by a State, intergovernmental organization or international organization, it shall seek the consent of the originator to disclose that document or information. If the originator is a State Party, it shall either consent to disclosure of the information or document or undertake to resolve the issue of disclosure with the Court, subject to the provisions of article 72. If the originator is not a State Party and refuses to consent to disclosure, the requested State shall inform the Court that it is unable to provide the document or information because of a pre-existing obligation of confidentiality to the originator

Article 74
Requirements for the decision

1. All the judges of the Trial Chamber shall be present at each stage of the trial and throughout their deliberations. The Presidency may, on a case-by-case basis, designate, as available, one or more alternate judges to be present at each stage of the trial and to replace a member of the Trial Chamber if that member is unable to continue attending.
2. The Trial Chamber's decision shall be based on its evaluation of the evidence and the entire proceedings. The decision shall not exceed the facts and circumstances described in the charges and any amendments to the charges. The Court may base its decision only on evidence submitted and discussed before it at the trial.
3. The judges shall attempt to achieve unanimity in their decision, failing which the decision shall be taken by a majority of the judges.
4. The deliberations of the Trial Chamber shall remain secret.
5. The decision shall be in writing and shall contain a full and reasoned statement of the Trial Chamber's findings on the evidence and conclusions. The Trial Chamber shall issue one decision. When there is no unanimity, the Trial Chamber's decision shall contain the views of the majority and the minority. The decision or a summary thereof shall be delivered in open court.

Article 75
Reparations to victims

1. The Court shall establish principles relating to reparations to, or in respect of, victims, including restitution, compensation and rehabilitation. On this basis, in its decision the Court may, either upon request or on its own motion in exceptional circumstances, determine the scope and extent of any damage, loss and

injury to, or in respect of, victims and will state the principles on which it is acting.

2. The Court may make an order directly against a convicted person specifying appropriate reparations to, or in respect of, victims, including restitution, compensation and rehabilitation. Where appropriate, the Court may order that the award for reparations be made through the Trust Fund provided for in article 79.

3. Before making an order under this article, the Court may invite and shall take account of representations from or on behalf of the convicted person, victims, other interested persons or interested States.

4. In exercising its power under this article, the Court may, after a person is convicted of a crime within the jurisdiction of the Court, determine whether, in order to give effect to an order which it may make under this article, it is necessary to seek measures under article 93, paragraph 1.

5. A State Party shall give effect to a decision under this article as if the provisions of article 109 were applicable to this article.

6. Nothing in this article shall be interpreted as prejudicing the rights of victims under national or international law.

Article 76
Sentencing

1. In the event of a conviction, the Trial Chamber shall consider the appropriate sentence to be imposed and shall take into account the evidence presented and submissions made during the trial that are relevant to the sentence.

2. Except where article 65 applies and before the completion of the trial, the Trial Chamber may on its own motion and shall, at the request of the Prosecutor or the accused, hold a further hearing to hear any additional evidence or submissions relevant to the sentence, in accordance with the Rules of Procedure and Evidence.

3. Where paragraph 2 applies, any representations under article 75 shall be heard during the further hearing referred to in paragraph 2 and, if necessary, during any additional hearing.

4. The sentence shall be pronounced in public and, wherever possible, in the presence of the accused.

PART 7. PENALTIES

Article 77
Applicable penalties

1. Subject to article 110, the Court may impose one of the following penalties on a person convicted of a crime referred to in article 5 of this Statute:

(a) Imprisonment for a specified number of years, which may not exceed a maximum of 30 years; or

(b) A term of life imprisonment when justified by the extreme gravity of the crime and the individual circumstances of the convicted person.

2. In addition to imprisonment, the Court may order:

(a) A fine under the criteria provided for in the Rules of Procedure and Evidence;

(b) A forfeiture of proceeds, property and assets derived directly or indirectly from that crime, without prejudice to the rights of bona fide third parties.

Article 78
Determination of the sentence

1. In determining the sentence, the Court shall, in accordance with the Rules of Procedure and Evidence, take into account such factors as the gravity of the crime and the individual circumstances of the convicted person.
2. In imposing a sentence of imprisonment, the Court shall deduct the time, if any, previously spent in detention in accordance with an order of the Court. The Court may deduct any time otherwise spent in detention in connection with conduct underlying the crime.
3. When a person has been convicted of more than one crime, the Court shall pronounce a sentence for each crime and a joint sentence specifying the total period of imprisonment. This period shall be no less than the highest individual sentence pronounced and shall not exceed 30 years imprisonment or a sentence of life imprisonment in conformity with article 77, paragraph 1 (b).

Article 79
Trust Fund

1. A Trust Fund shall be established by decision of the Assembly of States Parties for the benefit of victims of crimes within the jurisdiction of the Court, and of the families of such victims.
2. The Court may order money and other property collected through fines or forfeiture to be transferred, by order of the Court, to the Trust Fund.
3. The Trust Fund shall be managed according to criteria to be determined by the Assembly of States Parties.

Article 80
Non-prejudice to national application
of penalties and national laws

Nothing in this Part affects the application by States of penalties prescribed by their national law, nor the law of States which do not provide for penalties prescribed in this Part.

PART 8. APPEAL AND REVISION

Article 81
Appeal against decision of acquittal or conviction or against sentence

1. A decision under article 74 may be appealed in accordance with the Rules of Procedure and Evidence as follows:

(a) The Prosecutor may make an appeal on any of the following grounds:
- (i) Procedural error,
- (ii) Error of fact, or
- (iii) Error of law;

(b) The convicted person, or the Prosecutor on that person's behalf, may make an appeal on any of the following grounds:
- (i) Procedural error,
- (ii) Error of fact,
- (iii) Error of law, or
- (iv) Any other ground that affects the fairness or reliability of the proceedings or decision.

2. (a) A sentence may be appealed, in accordance with the Rules of Procedure and Evidence, by the Prosecutor or the convicted person on the ground of disproportion between the crime and the sentence;

(b) If on an appeal against sentence the Court considers that there are grounds on which the conviction might be set aside, wholly or in part, it may invite the Prosecutor and the convicted person to submit grounds under article 81, paragraph 1 (a) or (b), and may render a decision on conviction in accordance with article 83;

(c) The same procedure applies when the Court, on an appeal against conviction only, considers that there are grounds to reduce the sentence under paragraph 2 (a).

3. (a) Unless the Trial Chamber orders otherwise, a convicted person shall remain in custody pending an appeal;

(b) When a convicted person's time in custody exceeds the sentence of imprisonment imposed, that person shall be released, except that if the Prosecutor is also appealing, the release may be subject to the conditions under subparagraph (c) below;

(c) In case of an acquittal, the accused shall be released immediately, subject to the following.
- (i) Under exceptional circumstances, and having regard, inter alia, to the concrete risk of flight, the seriousness of the offence charged and the probability of success on appeal, the Trial Chamber, at the request of the Prosecutor, may maintain the detention of the person pending appeal;

(ii) A decision by the Trial Chamber under subparagraph (c) (i) may be appealed in accordance with the Rules of Procedure and Evidence.

4. Subject to the provisions of paragraph 3 (a) and (b), execution of the decision or sentence shall be suspended during the period allowed for appeal and for the duration of the appeal proceedings.

Article 82
Appeal against other decisions

1. Either party may appeal any of the following decisions in accordance with the Rules of Procedure and Evidence:

(a) A decision with respect to jurisdiction or admissibility;

(b) A decision granting or denying release of the person being investigated or prosecuted;

(c) A decision of the Pre-Trial Chamber to act on its own initiative under article 56, paragraph 3;

(d) A decision that involves an issue that would significantly affect the fair and expeditious conduct of the proceedings or the outcome of the trial, and for which, in the opinion of the Pre-Trial or Trial Chamber, an immediate resolution by the Appeals Chamber may materially advance the proceedings.

2. A decision of the Pre-Trial Chamber under article 57, paragraph 3 (d), may be appealed against by the State concerned or by the Prosecutor, with the leave of the Pre-Trial Chamber The appeal shall be heard on an expedited basis.

3. An appeal shall not of itself have suspensive effect unless the Appeals Chamber so orders, upon request, in accordance with the Rules of Procedure and Evidence.

4. A legal representative of the victims, the convicted person or a bona fide owner of property adversely affected by an order under article 75 may appeal against the order for reparations, as provided in the Rules of Procedure and Evidence.

Article 83
Proceedings on appeal

1. For the purposes of proceedings under article 81 and this article, the Appeals Chamber shall have all the powers of the Trial Chamber.

2. If the Appeals Chamber finds that the proceedings appealed from were unfair in a way that affected the reliability of the decision or sentence, or that the decision or sentence appealed from was materially affected by error of fact or law or procedural error, it may:

(a) Reverse or amend the decision or sentence; or

(b) Order a new trial before a different Trial Chamber.

For these purposes, the Appeals Chamber may remand a factual issue to the original Trial Chamber for it to determine the issue and to report back accordingly, or may itself call evidence to determine the issue. When the decision or sentence has been appealed only by the person convicted, or the Prosecutor on that person's behalf, it cannot be amended to his or her detriment.

3. If in an appeal against sentence the Appeals Chamber finds that the sentence is disproportionate to the crime, it may vary the sentence in accordance with Part 7.

4. The judgment of the Appeals Chamber shall be taken by a majority of the judges and shall be delivered in open court. The judgment shall state the reasons on which it is based. When there is no unanimity, the judgment of the Appeals Chamber shall contain the views of the majority and the minority, but a judge may deliver a separate or dissenting opinion on a question of law.

5. The Appeals Chamber may deliver its judgment in the absence of the person acquitted or convicted.

Article 84
Revision of conviction or sentence

1. The convicted person or, after death, spouses, children, parents or one person alive at the time of the accused's death who has been given express written instructions from the accused to bring such a claim, or the Prosecutor on the person's behalf, may apply to the Appeals Chamber to revise the final judgment of conviction or sentence on the grounds that:

(a) New evidence has been discovered that:

(i) Was not available at the time of trial, and such unavailability was not wholly or partially attributable to the party making application; and

(ii) Is sufficiently important that had it been proved at trial it would have been likely to have resulted in a different verdict;

(b) It has been newly discovered that decisive evidence, taken into account at trial and upon which the conviction depends, was false, forged or falsified;

(c) One or more of the judges who participated in conviction or confirmation of the charges has committed, in that case, an act of serious misconduct or serious breach of duty of sufficient gravity to justify the removal of that judge or those judges from office under article 46.

2. The Appeals Chamber shall reject the application if it considers it to be unfounded. If it determines that the application is meritorious, it may, as appropriate:

(a) Reconvene the original Trial Chamber;

(b) Constitute a new Trial Chamber; or

(c) Retain jurisdiction over the matter, with a view to, after hearing the parties in the manner set forth in the Rules of Procedure and Evidence, arriving at a determination on whether the judgment should be revised.

Article 85
Compensation to an arrested or convicted person

1. Anyone who has been the victim of unlawful arrest or detention shall have an enforceable right to compensation.
2. When a person has by a final decision been convicted of a criminal offence, and when subsequently his or her conviction has been reversed on the ground that a new or newly discovered fact shows conclusively that there has been a miscarriage of justice, the person who has suffered punishment as a result of such conviction shall be compensated according to law, unless it is proved that the non-disclosure of the unknown fact in time is wholly or partly attributable to him or her.
3 In exceptional circumstances, where the Court finds conclusive facts showing that there has been a grave and manifest miscarriage of justice, it may in its discretion award compensation, according to the criteria provided in the Rules of Procedure and Evidence, to a person who has been released from detention following a final decision of acquittal or a termination of the proceedings for that reason.

PART 9. INTERNATIONAL COOPERATION AND JUDICIAL ASSISTANCE

Article 86
General obligation to cooperate

States Parties shall, in accordance with the provisions of this Statute, cooperate fully with the Court in its investigation and prosecution of crimes within the jurisdiction of the Court.

Article 87
Requests for cooperation: general provisions

1. (a) The Court shall have the authority to make requests to States Parties for cooperation. The requests shall be transmitted through the diplomatic channel or any other appropriate channel as may be designated by each State Party upon ratification, acceptance, approval or accession. Subsequent changes to the designation shall be made by each State Party in accordance with the Rules of Procedure and Evidence.

(b) When appropriate, without prejudice to the provisions of subparagraph (a), requests may also be transmitted through the International Criminal Police Organization or any appropriate regional organization.

2. Requests for cooperation and any documents supporting the request shall either be in or be accompanied by a translation into an official language of the

requested State or one of the working languages of the Court, in accordance with the choice made by that State upon ratification, acceptance, approval or accession. Subsequent changes to this choice shall be made in accordance with the Rules of Procedure and Evidence.

3. The requested State shall keep confidential a request for cooperation and any documents supporting the request, except to the extent that the disclosure is necessary for execution of the request.

4. In relation to any request for assistance presented under this Part, the Court may take such measures, including measures related to the protection of information, as may be necessary to ensure the safety or physical or psychological well-being of any victims, potential witnesses and their families. The Court may request that any information that is made available under this Part shall be provided and handled in a manner that protects the safety and physical or psychological well-being of any victims, potential witnesses and their families.

5. (a) The Court may invite any State not party to this Statute to provide assistance under this Part on the basis of an ad hoc arrangement, an agreement with such State or any other appropriate basis.

(b) Where a State not party to this Statute, which has entered into an ad hoc arrangement or an agreement with the Court, fails to cooperate with requests pursuant to any such arrangement or agreement, the Court may so inform the Assembly of States Parties or, where the Security Council referred the matter to the Court, the Security Council.

6. The Court may ask any intergovernmental organization to provide information or documents. The Court may also ask for other forms of cooperation and assistance which may be agreed upon with such an organization and which are in accordance with its competence or mandate.

7. Where a State Party fails to comply with a request to cooperate by the Court contrary to the provisions of this Statute, thereby preventing the Court from exercising its functions and powers under this Statute, the Court may make a finding to that effect and refer the matter to the Assembly of States Parties or, where the Security Council referred the matter to the Court, to the Security Council.

Article 88
Availability of procedures under national law

States Parties shall ensure that there are procedures available under their national law for all of the forms of cooperation which are specified under this Part.

Article 89
Surrender of persons to the Court

1. The Court may transmit a request for the arrest and surrender of a person, together with the material supporting the request outlined in article 91, to any State on the territory of which that person may be found and shall request the cooperation of that State in the arrest and surrender of such a person. States Parties shall, in accordance with the provisions of this Part and the procedure under their national law, comply with requests for arrest and surrender.

2. Where the person sought for surrender brings a challenge before a national court on the basis of the principle of ne bis in idem as provided in article 20, the requested State shall immediately consult with the Court to determine if there has been a relevant ruling on admissibility. If the case is admissible, the requested State shall proceed with the execution of the request. If an admissibility ruling is pending, the requested State may postpone the execution of the request for surrender of the person until the Court makes a determination on admissibility.

3. (a) A State Party shall authorize, in accordance with its national procedural law, transportation through its territory of a person being surrendered to the Court by another State, except where transit through that State would impede or delay the surrender.

(b) A request by the Court for transit shall be transmitted in accordance with article 87. The request for transit shall contain:

(i) A description of the person being transported;

(ii) A brief statement of the facts of the case and their legal characterization; and

(iii) The warrant for arrest and surrender;

(c) A person being transported shall be detained in custody during the period of transit;

(d) No authorization is required if the person is transported by air and no landing is scheduled on the territory of the transit State;

(e) If an unscheduled landing occurs on the territory of the transit State, that State may require a request for transit from the Court as provided for in subparagraph (b). The transit State shall detain the person being transported until the request for transit is received and the transit is effected, provided that detention for purposes of this subparagraph may not be extended beyond 96 hours from the unscheduled landing unless the request is received within that time.

4. If the person sought is being proceeded against or is serving a sentence in the requested State for a crime different from that for which surrender to the Court is sought, the requested State, after making its decision to grant the request, shall consult with the Court.

Article 90
Competing requests

1. A State Party which receives a request from the Court for the surrender of a person under article 89 shall, if it also receives a request from any other State for the extradition of the same person for the same conduct which forms the basis of the crime for which the Court seeks the person's surrender, notify the Court and the requesting State of that fact.

2. Where the requesting State is a State Party, the requested State shall give priority to the request from the Court if:

(a) The Court has, pursuant to article 18 or 19, made a determination that the case in respect of which surrender is sought is admissible and that determination takes into account the investigation or prosecution conducted by the requesting State in respect of its request for extradition; or

(b) The Court makes the determination described in subparagraph (a) pursuant to the requested State's notification under paragraph 1.

3. Where a determination under paragraph 2 (a) has not been made, the requested State may, at its discretion, pending the determination of the Court under paragraph 2 (b), proceed to deal with the request for extradition from the requesting State but shall not extradite the person until the Court has determined that the case is inadmissible. The Court's determination shall be made on an expedited basis.

4. If the requesting State is a State not Party to this Statute the requested State, if it is not under an international obligation to extradite the person to the requesting State, shall give priority to the request for surrender from the Court, if the Court has determined that the case is admissible.

5. Where a case under paragraph 4 has not been determined to be admissible by the Court, the requested State may, at its discretion, proceed to deal with the request for extradition from the requesting State.

6. In cases where paragraph 4 applies except that the requested State is under an existing international obligation to extradite the person to the requesting State not Party to this Statute, the requested State shall determine whether to surrender the person to the Court or extradite the person to the requesting State. In making its decision, the requested State shall consider all the relevant factors, including but not limited to:

(a) The respective dates of the requests;

(b) The interests of the requesting State including, where relevant, whether the crime was committed in its territory and the nationality of the victims and of the person sought; and

(c) The possibility of subsequent surrender between the Court and the requesting State.

7. Where a State Party which receives a request from the Court for the surrender of a person also receives a request from any State for the extradition of the

same person for conduct other than that which constitutes the crime for which the Court seeks the person's surrender:

(a) The requested State shall, if it is not under an existing international obligation to extradite the person to the requesting State, give priority to the request from the Court;

(b) The requested State shall, if it is under an existing international obligation to extradite the person to the requesting State, determine whether to surrender the person to the Court or to extradite the person to the requesting State. In making its decision, the requested State shall consider all the relevant factors, including but not limited to those set out in paragraph 6, but shall give special consideration to the relative nature and gravity of the conduct in question.

8. Where pursuant to a notification under this article, the Court has determined a case to be inadmissible, and subsequently extradition to the requesting State is refused, the requested State shall notify the Court of this decision.

Article 91
Contents of request for arrest and surrender

1. A request for arrest and surrender shall be made in writing. In urgent cases, a request may be made by any medium capable of delivering a written record, provided that the request shall be confirmed through the channel provided for in article 87, paragraph 1 (a).

2. In the case of a request for the arrest and surrender of a person for whom a warrant of arrest has been issued by the Pre-Trial Chamber under article 58, the request shall contain or be supported by:

(a) Information describing the person sought, sufficient to identify the person, and information as to that person's probable location;

(b) A copy of the warrant of arrest; and

(c) Such documents, statements or information as may be necessary to meet the requirements for the surrender process in the requested State, except that those requirements should not be more burdensome than those applicable to requests for extradition pursuant to treaties or arrangements between the requested State and other States and should, if possible, be less burdensome, taking into account the distinct nature of the Court.

3. In the case of a request for the arrest and surrender of a person already convicted, the request shall contain or be supported by:

(a) A copy of any warrant of arrest for that person;

(b) A copy of the judgement of conviction;

(c) Information to demonstrate that the person sought is the one referred to in the judgement of conviction; and

(d) If the person sought has been sentenced, a copy of the sentence imposed and, in the case of a sentence for imprisonment, a statement of any time already served and the time remaining to be served.

4. Upon the request of the Court, a State Party shall consult with the Court, either generally or with respect to a specific matter, regarding any requirements under its national law that may apply under paragraph 2 (c). During the consultations, the State Party shall advise the Court of the specific requirements of its national law.

Article 92
Provisional arrest

1. In urgent cases, the Court may request the provisional arrest of the person sought, pending presentation of the request for surrender and the documents supporting the request as specified in article 91.
2. The request for provisional arrest shall be made by any medium capable of delivering a written record and shall contain:

(a) Information describing the person sought, sufficient to identify the person, and information as to that person's probable location;

(b) A concise statement of the crimes for which the person's arrest is sought and of the facts which are alleged to constitute those crimes, including, where possible, the date and location of the crime;

(c) A statement of the existence of a warrant of arrest or a judgement of conviction against the person sought; and

(d) A statement that a request for surrender of the person sought will follow.

3 A person who is provisionally arrested may be released from custody if the requested State has not received the request for surrender and the documents supporting the request as specified in article 91 within the time limits specified in the Rules of Procedure and Evidence. However, the person may consent to surrender before the expiration of this period if permitted by the law of the requested State. In such a case, the requested State shall proceed to surrender the person to the Court as soon as possible.
4. The fact that the person sought has been released from custody pursuant to paragraph 3 shall not prejudice the subsequent arrest and surrender of that person if the request for surrender and the documents supporting the request are delivered at a later date.

Article 93
Other forms of cooperation

1. States Parties shall, in accordance with the provisions of this Part and under procedures of national law, comply with requests by the Court to provide the following assistance in relation to investigations or prosecutions:

(a) The identification and whereabouts of persons or the location of items;

(b) The taking of evidence, including testimony under oath, and the production of evidence, including expert opinions and reports necessary to the Court;

(c) The questioning of any person being investigated or prosecuted;

(d) The service of documents, including judicial documents;

(e) Facilitating the voluntary appearance of persons as witnesses or experts before the Court;

(f) The temporary transfer of persons as provided in paragraph 7;

(g) The examination of places or sites, including the exhumation and examination of gravesites;

(h) The execution of searches and seizures;

(i) The provision of records and documents, including official records and documents;

(j) The protection of victims and witnesses and the preservation of evidence;

(k) The identification, tracing and freezing or seizure of proceeds, property and assets and instrumentalities of crimes for the purpose of eventual forfeiture, without prejudice to the rights of bona fide third parties; and

(l) Any other type of assistance which is not prohibited by the law of the requested State, with a view to facilitating the investigation and prosecution of crimes within the jurisdiction of the Court.

2. The Court shall have the authority to provide an assurance to a witness or an expert appearing before the Court that he or she will not be prosecuted, detained or subjected to any restriction of personal freedom by the Court in respect of any act or omission that preceded the departure of that person from the requested State.

3. Where execution of a particular measure of assistance detailed in a request presented under paragraph 1, is prohibited in the requested State on the basis of an existing fundamental legal principle of general application, the requested State shall promptly consult with the Court to try to resolve the matter. In the consultations, consideration should be given to whether the assistance can be rendered in another manner or subject to conditions. If after consultations the matter cannot be resolved, the Court shall modify the request as necessary.

4. In accordance with article 72, a State Party may deny a request for assistance, in whole or in part, only if the request concerns the production of any documents or disclosure of evidence which elates to its national security.

5. Before denying a request for assistance under paragraph 1 (l), the requested State shall consider whether the assistance can be provided subject to specified conditions, or whether the assistance can be provided at a later date or in an alternative manner, provided that if the Court or the Prosecutor accepts the assistance subject to conditions, the Court or the Prosecutor shall abide by them.

6. If a request for assistance is denied, the requested State Party shall promptly inform the Court or the Prosecutor of the reasons for such denial.

7. (a) The Court may request the temporary transfer of a person in custody for purposes of identification or for obtaining testimony or other assistance. The person may be transferred if the following conditions are fulfilled:

   (i) The person freely gives his or her informed consent to the transfer; and

   (ii) The requested State agrees to the transfer, subject to such conditions as that State and the Court may agree.

(b) The person being transferred shall remain in custody. When the purposes of the transfer have been fulfilled, the Court shall return the person without delay to the requested State.

8. (a) The Court shall ensure the confidentiality of documents and information, except as required for the investigation and proceedings described in the request.

(b) The requested State may, when necessary, transmit documents or information to the Prosecutor on a confidential basis. The Prosecutor may then use them solely for the purpose of generating new evidence.

(c) The requested State may, on its own motion or at the request of the Prosecutor, subsequently consent to the disclosure of such documents or information. They may then be used as evidence pursuant to the provisions of Parts 5 and 6 and in accordance with the Rules of Procedure and Evidence.

9. (a) (i) In the event that a State Party receives competing requests, other than for surrender or extradition, from the Court and from another State pursuant to an international obligation, the State Party shall endeavour, in consultation with the Court and the other State, to meet both requests, if necessary by postponing or attaching conditions to one or the other request.

   (ii) Failing that, competing requests shall be resolved in accordance with the principles established in article 90.

(b) Where, however, the request from the Court concerns information, property or persons which are subject to the control of a third State or an international organization by virtue of an international agreement, the requested States shall so inform the Court and the Court shall direct its request to the third State or international organization.

10. (a) The Court may, upon request, cooperate with and provide assistance to a State Party conducting an investigation into or trial in respect of conduct which constitutes a crime within the jurisdiction of the Court or which constitutes a serious crime under the national law of the requesting State.

(b) (i) The assistance provided under subparagraph (a) shall include, inter alia:

   a. The transmission of statements, documents or other types of evidence obtained in the course of an investigation or a trial conducted by the Court; and

   b. The questioning of any person detained by order of the Court,

(ii) In the case of assistance under subparagraph (b) (i) a:
a. If the documents or other types of evidence have been obtained with the assistance of a State, such transmission shall require the consent of that State;
b. If the statements, documents or other types of evidence have been provided by a witness or expert, such transmission shall be subject to the provisions of article 68.

(c) The Court may, under the conditions set out in this paragraph, grant a request for assistance under this paragraph from a State which is not a Party to this Statute.

Article 94
Postponement of execution of a request in respect of ongoing investigation or prosecution

1. If the immediate execution of a request would interfere with an ongoing investigation or prosecution of a case different from that to which the request relates, the requested State may postpone the execution of the request for a period of time agreed upon with the Court. However, the postponement shall be no longer than is necessary to complete the relevant investigation or prosecution in the requested State. Before making a decision to postpone, the requested State should consider whether the assistance may be immediately provided subject to certain conditions.
2. If a decision to postpone is taken pursuant to paragraph 1, the Prosecutor may, however, seek measures to preserve evidence, pursuant to article 93, paragraph 1 (j).

Article 95
Postponement of execution of a request in respect of an admissibility challenge

Where there is an admissibility challenge under consideration by the Court pursuant to article 18 or 19, the requested State may postpone the execution of a request under this Part pending a determination by the Court, unless the Court has specifically ordered that the Prosecutor may pursue the collection of such evidence pursuant to article 18 or 19

Article 96
Contents of request for other forms of assistance under article 93

1. A request for other forms of assistance referred to in article 93 shall be made in writing. In urgent cases, a request may be made by any medium capable

of delivering a written record, provided that the request shall be confirmed through the channel provided for in article 87, paragraph 1 (a).

2. The request shall, as applicable, contain or be supported by the following:

(a) A concise statement of the purpose of the request and the assistance sought, including the legal basis and the grounds for the request;

(b) As much detailed information as possible about the location or identification of any person or place that must be found or identified in order for the assistance sought to be provided;

(c) A concise statement of the essential facts underlying the request;

(d) The reasons for and details of any procedure or requirement to be followed;

(e) Such information as may be required under the law of the requested State in order to execute the request; and

(f) Any other information relevant in order for the assistance sought to be provided.

3. Upon the request of the Court, a State Party shall consult with the Court, either generally or with respect to a specific matter, regarding any requirements under its national law that may apply under paragraph 2 (e). During the consultations, the State Party shall advise the Court of the specific requirements of its national law.

4. The provisions of this article shall, where applicable, also apply in respect of a request for assistance made to the Court.

Article 97
Consultations

Where a State Party receives a request under this Part in relation to which it identifies problems which may impede or prevent the execution of the request, that State shall consult with the Court without delay in order to resolve the matter. Such problems may include, inter alia:

(a) Insufficient information to execute the request;

(b) In the case of a request for surrender, the fact that despite best efforts, the person sought cannot be located or that the investigation conducted has determined that the person in the requested State is clearly not the person named in the warrant; or

(c) The fact that execution of the request in its current form would require the requested State to breach a pre-existing treaty obligation undertaken with respect to another State.

Article 98
Cooperation with respect to waiver of immunity and consent to surrender

1. The Court may not proceed with a request for surrender or assistance which would require the requested State to act inconsistently with its obligations under international law with respect to the State or diplomatic immunity of a person or property of a third State, unless the Court can first obtain the cooperation of that third State for the waiver of the immunity.
2. The Court may not proceed with a request for surrender which would require the requested State to act inconsistently with its obligations under international agreements pursuant to which the consent of a sending State is required to surrender a person of that State to the Court, unless the Court can first obtain the cooperation of the sending State for the giving of consent for the surrender.

Article 99
Execution of requests under articles 93 and 96

1. Requests for assistance shall be executed in accordance with the relevant procedure under the law of the requested State and, unless prohibited by such law, in the manner specified in the request, including following any procedure outlined therein or permitting persons specified in the request to be present at and assist in the execution process.
2. In the case of an urgent request, the documents or evidence produced in response shall, at the request of the Court, be sent urgently.
3. Replies from the requested State shall be transmitted in their original language and form.
4. Without prejudice to other articles in this Part, where it is necessary for the successful execution of a request which can be executed without any compulsory measures, including specifically the interview of or taking evidence from a person on a voluntary basis, including doing so without the presence of the authorities of the requested State Party if it is essential for the request to be executed, and the examination without modification of a public site or other public place, the Prosecutor may execute such request directly on the territory of a State as follows:

(a) When the State Party requested is a State on the territory of which the crime is alleged to have been committed, and there has been a determination of admissibility pursuant to article 18 or 19, the Prosecutor may directly execute such request following all possible consultations with the requested State Party;

(b) In other cases, the Prosecutor may execute such request following consultations with the requested State Party and subject to any reasonable conditions or concerns raised by that State Party. Where the requested State Party identifies problems with the execution of a request pursuant to this subparagraph it shall, without delay, consult with the Court to resolve the matter.

5. Provisions allowing a person heard or examined by the Court under article 72 to invoke restrictions designed to prevent disclosure of confidential information connected with national security shall also apply to the execution of requests for assistance under this article.

Article 100
Costs

1. The ordinary costs for execution of requests in the territory of the requested State shall be borne by that State, except for the following, which shall be borne by the Court:

(a) Costs associated with the travel and security of witnesses and experts or the transfer under article 93 of persons in custody;

(b) Costs of translation, interpretation and transcription;

(c) Travel and subsistence costs of the judges, the Prosecutor, the Deputy Prosecutors, the Registrar, the Deputy Registrar and staff of any organ of the Court;

(d) Costs of any expert opinion or report requested by the Court;

(e) Costs associated with the transport of a person being surrendered to the Court by a custodial State; and

(f) Following consultations, any extraordinary costs that may result from the execution of a request.

2. The provisions of paragraph 1 shall, as appropriate, apply to requests from States Parties to the Court. In that case, the Court shall bear the ordinary costs of execution.

Article 101
Rule of speciality

1. A person surrendered to the Court under this Statute shall not be proceeded against, punished or detained for any conduct committed prior to surrender, other than the conduct or course of conduct which forms the basis of the crimes for which that person has been surrendered.

2. The Court may request a waiver of the requirements of paragraph 1 from the State which surrendered the person to the Court and, if necessary, the Court shall provide additional information in accordance with article 91. States Parties shall have the authority to provide a waiver to the Court and should endeavour to do so.

Article 102
Use of terms

For the purposes of this Statute:

(a) "surrender" means the delivering up of a person by a State to the Court, pursuant to this Statute.

(b) "extradition" means the delivering up of a person by one State to another as provided by treaty, convention or national legislation.

PART 10. ENFORCEMENT

Article 103
Role of States in enforcement of sentences of imprisonment

1. (a) A sentence of imprisonment shall be served in a State designated by the Court from a list of States which have indicated to the Court their willingness to accept sentenced persons.

(b) At the time of declaring its willingness to accept sentenced persons, a State may attach conditions to its acceptance as agreed by the Court and in accordance with this Part.

(c) A State designated in a particular case shall promptly inform the Court whether it accepts the Court's designation.

2. (a) The State of enforcement shall notify the Court of any circumstances, including the exercise of any conditions agreed under paragraph 1, which could materially affect the terms or extent of the imprisonment. The Court shall be given at least 45 days' notice of any such known or foreseeable circumstances. During this period, the State of enforcement shall take no action that might prejudice its obligations under article 110.

(b) Where the Court cannot agree to the circumstances referred to in subparagraph (a), it shall notify the State of enforcement and proceed in accordance with article 104, paragraph 1.

3. In exercising its discretion to make a designation under paragraph 1, the Court shall take into account the following:

(a) The principle that States Parties should share the responsibility for enforcing sentences of imprisonment, in accordance with principles of equitable distribution, as provided in the Rules of Procedure and Evidence;

(b) The application of widely accepted international treaty standards governing the treatment of prisoners;

(c) The views of the sentenced person;

(d) The nationality of the sentenced person;

(e) Such other factors regarding the circumstances of the crime or the person sentenced, or the effective enforcement of the sentence, as may be appropriate in designating the State of enforcement.

4. If no State is designated under paragraph 1, the sentence of imprisonment shall be served in a prison facility made available by the host State, in accordance with the conditions set out in the headquarters agreement referred to in article 3, paragraph 2. In such a case, the costs arising out of the enforcement of a sentence of imprisonment shall be borne by the Court.

Article 104
Change in designation of State of enforcement

1. The Court may, at any time, decide to transfer a sentenced person to a prison of another State.
2. A sentenced person may, at any time, apply to the Court to be transferred from the State of enforcement.

Article 105
Enforcement of the sentence

1. Subject to conditions which a State may have specified in accordance with article 103, paragraph 1 (b), the sentence of imprisonment shall be binding on the States Parties, which shall in no case modify it.
2. The Court alone shall have the right to decide any application for appeal and revision. The State of enforcement shall not impede the making of any such application by a sentenced person.

Article 106
Supervision of enforcement of sentences and conditions of imprisonment

1. The enforcement of a sentence of imprisonment shall be subject to the supervision of the Court and shall be consistent with widely accepted international treaty standards governing treatment of prisoners.
2. The conditions of imprisonment shall be governed by the law of the State of enforcement and shall be consistent with widely accepted international treaty standards governing treatment of prisoners; in no case shall such conditions be more or less favourable than those available to prisoners convicted of similar offences in the State of enforcement.
3. Communications between a sentenced person and the Court shall be unimpeded and confidential.

Article 107
Transfer of the person upon completion of sentence

1. Following completion of the sentence, a person who is not a national of the State of enforcement may, in accordance with the law of the State of enforce-

ment, be transferred to a State which is obliged to receive him or her, or to another State which agrees to receive him or her, taking into account any wishes of the person to be transferred to that State, unless the State of enforcement authorizes the person to remain in its territory.
2. If no State bears the costs arising out of transferring the person to another State pursuant to paragraph 1, such costs shall be borne by the Court.
3. Subject to the provisions of article 108, the State of enforcement may also, in accordance with its national law, extradite or otherwise surrender the person to a State which has requested the extradition or surrender of the person for purposes of trial or enforcement of a sentence.

Article 108
Limitation on the prosecution or punishment of other offences

1. A sentenced person in the custody of the State of enforcement shall not be subject to prosecution or punishment or to extradition to a third State for any conduct engaged in prior to that person's delivery to the State of enforcement, unless such prosecution, punishment or extradition has been approved by the Court at the request of the State of enforcement.
2. The Court shall decide the matter after having heard the views of the sentenced person.
3. Paragraph 1 shall cease to apply if the sentenced person remains voluntarily for more than 30 days in the territory of the State of enforcement after having served the full sentence imposed by the Court, or returns to the territory of that State after having left it.

Article 109
Enforcement of fines and forfeiture measures

1. States Parties shall give effect to fines or forfeitures ordered by the Court under Part 7, without prejudice to the rights of bona fide third parties, and in accordance with the procedure of their national law.
2. If a State Party is unable to give effect to an order for forfeiture, it shall take measures to recover the value of the proceeds, property or assets ordered by the Court to be forfeited, without prejudice to the rights of bona fide third parties.
3. Property, or the proceeds of the sale of real property or, where appropriate, the sale of other property, which is obtained by a State Party as a result of its enforcement of a judgment of the Court shall be transferred to the Court.

Article 110
Review by the Court concerning reduction of sentence

1. The State of enforcement shall not release the person before expiry of the sentence pronounced by the Court.

2. The Court alone shall have the right to decide any reduction of sentence, and shall rule on the matter after having heard the person.
3. When the person has served two thirds of the sentence, or 25 years in the case of life imprisonment, the Court shall review the sentence to determine whether it should be reduced. Such a review shall not be conducted before that time.
4. In its review under paragraph 3, the Court may reduce the sentence if it finds that one or more of the following factors are present:

(a) The early and continuing willingness of the person to cooperate with the Court in its investigations and prosecutions;

(b) The voluntary assistance of the person in enabling the enforcement of the judgments and orders of the Court in other cases, and in particular providing assistance in locating assets subject to orders of fine, forfeiture or reparation which may be used for the benefit of victims; or

(c) Other factors establishing a clear and significant change of circumstances sufficient to justify the reduction of sentence, as provided in the Rules of Procedure and Evidence.

5. If the Court determines in its initial review under paragraph 3 that it is not appropriate to reduce the sentence, it shall thereafter review the question of reduction of sentence at such intervals and applying such criteria as provided for in the Rules of Procedure and Evidence.

Article 111
Escape

If a convicted person escapes from custody and flees the State of enforcement, that State may, after consultation with the Court, request the person's surrender from the State in which the person is located pursuant to existing bilateral or multilateral arrangements, or may request that the Court seek the person's surrender, in accordance with Part 9. It may direct that the person be delivered to the State in which he or she was serving the sentence or to another State designated by the Court.

PART 11. ASSEMBLY OF STATES PARTIES

Article 112
Assembly of States Parties

1. An Assembly of States Parties to this Statute is hereby established. Each State Party shall have one representative in the Assembly who may be accompanied by alternates and advisers. Other States which have signed this Statute or the Final Act may be observers in the Assembly.
2. The Assembly shall:

(a) Consider and adopt, as appropriate, recommendations of the Preparatory Commission;

(b) Provide management oversight to the Presidency, the Prosecutor and the Registrar regarding the administration of the Court;

(c) Consider the reports and activities of the Bureau established under paragraph 3 and take appropriate action in regard thereto;

(d) Consider and decide the budget for the Court;

(e) Decide whether to alter, in accordance with article 36, the number of judges;

(f) Consider pursuant to article 87, paragraphs 5 and 7, any question relating to noncooperation;

(g) Perform any other function consistent with this Statute or the Rules of Procedure and Evidence.

3. (a) The Assembly shall have a Bureau consisting of a President, two Vice-Presidents and 18 members elected by the Assembly for three-year terms.

(b) The Bureau shall have a representative character, taking into account, in particular, equitable geographical distribution and the adequate representation of the principal legal systems of the world.

(c) The Bureau shall meet as often as necessary, but at least once a year. It shall assist the Assembly in the discharge of its responsibilities.

4. The Assembly may establish such subsidiary bodies as may be necessary, including an independent oversight mechanism for inspection, evaluation and investigation of the Court, in order to enhance its efficiency and economy.

5. The President of the Court, the Prosecutor and the Registrar or their representatives may participate, as appropriate, in meetings of the Assembly and of the Bureau.

6. The Assembly shall meet at the seat of the Court or at the Headquarters of the United Nations once a year and, when circumstances so require, hold special sessions. Except as otherwise specified in this Statute, special sessions shall be convened by the Bureau on its own initiative or at the request of one third of the States Parties.

7. Each State Party shall have one vote. Every effort shall be made to reach decisions by consensus in the Assembly and in the Bureau. If consensus cannot be reached, except as otherwise provided in the Statute:

(a) Decisions on matters of substance must be approved by a two-thirds majority of those present and voting provided that an absolute majority of States Parties constitutes the quorum for voting;

(b) Decisions on matters of procedure shall be taken by a simple majority of States Parties present and voting.

8. A State Party which is in arrears in the payment of its financial contributions towards the costs of the Court shall have no vote in the Assembly and in the Bureau if the amount of its arrears equals or exceeds the amount of the contributions due from it for the preceding two full years. The Assembly may, nevertheless, permit such a State Party to vote in the Assembly and in the Bureau if

it is satisfied that the failure to pay is due to conditions beyond the control of the State Party.

9. The Assembly shall adopt its own rules of procedure.

10. The official and working languages of the Assembly shall be those of the General Assembly of the United Nations.

PART 12. FINANCING

Article 113
Financial Regulations

Except as otherwise specifically provided, all financial matters related to the Court and the meetings of the Assembly of States Parties, including its Bureau and subsidiary bodies, shall be governed by this Statute and the Financial Regulations and Rules adopted by the Assembly of States Parties.

Article 114
Payment of expenses

Expenses of the Court and the Assembly of States Parties, including its Bureau and subsidiary bodies, shall be paid from the funds of the Court.

Article 115
Funds of the Court and of the Assembly of States Parties

The expenses of the Court and the Assembly of States Parties, including its Bureau and subsidiary bodies, as provided for in the budget decided by the Assembly of States Parties, shall be provided by the following sources:

(a) Assessed contributions made by States Parties;

(b) Funds provided by the United Nations, subject to the approval of the General Assembly, in particular in relation to the expenses incurred due to referrals by the Security Council.

Article 116
Voluntary contributions

Without prejudice to article 115, the Court may receive and utilize, as additional funds, voluntary contributions from Governments, international organizations, individuals, corporations and other entities, in accordance with relevant criteria adopted by the Assembly of States Parties.

Article 117
Assessment of contributions

The contributions of States Parties shall be assessed in accordance with an agreed scale of assessment, based on the scale adopted by the United Nations for its regular budget and adjusted in accordance with the principles on which that scale is based.

Article 118
Annual audit

The records, books and accounts of the Court, including its annual financial statements, shall be audited annually by an independent auditor.

PART 13. FINAL CLAUSES

Article 119
Settlement of disputes

1. Any dispute concerning the judicial functions of the Court shall be settled by the decision of the Court.
2. Any other dispute between two or more States Parties relating to the interpretation or application of this Statute which is not settled through negotiations within three months of their commencement shall be referred to the Assembly of States Parties. The Assembly may itself seek to settle the dispute or may make recommendations on further means of settlement of the dispute, including referral to the International Court of Justice in conformity with the Statute of that Court.

Article 120
Reservations

No reservations may be made to this Statute.

Article 121
Amendments

1. After the expiry of seven years from the entry into force of this Statute, any State Party may propose amendments thereto. The text of any proposed amendment shall be submitted to the Secretary-General of the United Nations, who shall promptly circulate it to all States Parties.
2. No sooner than three months from the date of notification, the Assembly of States Parties, at its next meeting, shall, by a majority of those present and voting, decide whether to take up the proposal. The Assembly may deal with the

proposal directly or convene a Review Conference if the issue involved so warrants.
3. The adoption of an amendment at a meeting of the Assembly of States Parties or at a Review Conference on which consensus cannot be reached shall require a two-thirds majority of States Parties.
4. Except as provided in paragraph 5, an amendment shall enter into force for all States Parties one year after instruments of ratification or acceptance have been deposited with the Secretary-General of the United Nations by seven-eighths of them.
5. Any amendment to articles 5, 6, 7 and 8 of this Statute shall enter into force for those States Parties which have accepted the amendment one year after the deposit of their instruments of ratification or acceptance. In respect of a State Party which has not accepted the amendment, the Court shall not exercise its jurisdiction regarding a crime covered by the amendment when committed by that State Party's nationals or on its territory.
6. If an amendment has been accepted by seven-eighths of States Parties in accordance with paragraph 4, any State Party which has not accepted the amendment may withdraw from this Statute with immediate effect, notwithstanding article 127, paragraph 1, but subject to article 127, paragraph 2, by giving notice no later than one year after the entry into force of such amendment.
7. The Secretary-General of the United Nations shall circulate to all States Parties any amendment adopted at a meeting of the Assembly of States Parties or at a Review Conference.

Article 122
Amendments to provisions of an institutional nature

1. Amendments to provisions of this Statute which are of an exclusively institutional nature, namely, article 35, article 36, paragraphs 8 and 9, article 37, article 38, article 39, paragraphs 1 (first two sentences), 2 and 4, article 42, paragraphs 4 to 9, article 43, paragraphs 2 and 3, and articles 44, 46, 47 and 49, may be proposed at any time, notwithstanding article 121, paragraph 1, by any State Party. The text of any proposed amendment shall be submitted to the Secretary-General of the United Nations or such other person designated by the Assembly of States Parties who shall promptly circulate it to all States Parties and to others participating in the Assembly.
2. Amendments under this article on which consensus cannot be reached shall be adopted by the Assembly of States Parties or by a Review Conference, by a two-thirds majority of States Parties. Such amendments shall enter into force for all States Parties six months after their adoption by the Assembly or, as the case may be, by the Conference.

Article 123
Review of the Statute

1. Seven years after the entry into force of this Statute the Secretary-General of the United Nations shall convene a Review Conference to consider any amendments to this Statute. Such review may include, but is not limited to, the list of crimes contained in article 5. The Conference shall be open to those participating in the Assembly of States Parties and on the same conditions.
2. At any time thereafter, at the request of a State Party and for the purposes set out in paragraph 1, the Secretary-General of the United Nations shall, upon approval by a majority of States Parties, convene a Review Conference.
3. The provisions of article 121, paragraphs 3 to 7, shall apply to the adoption and entry into force of any amendment to the Statute considered at a Review Conference.

Article 124
Transitional Provision

Notwithstanding article 12, paragraphs 1 and 2, a State, on becoming a party to this Statute, may declare that, for a period of seven years after the entry into force of this Statute for the State concerned, it does not accept the jurisdiction of the Court with respect to the category of crimes referred to in article 8 when a crime is alleged to have been committed by its nationals or on its territory. A declaration under this article may be withdrawn at any time. The provisions of this article shall be reviewed at the Review Conference convened in accordance with article 123, paragraph 1.

Article 125
Signature, ratification, acceptance, approval or accession

1. This Statute shall be open for signature by all States in Rome, at the headquarters of the Food and Agriculture Organization of the United Nations, on 17 July 1998. Thereafter, it shall remain open for signature in Rome at the Ministry of Foreign Affairs of Italy until 17 October 1998. After that date, the Statute shall remain open for signature in New York, at United Nations Headquarters, until 31 December 2000.
2. This Statute is subject to ratification, acceptance or approval by signatory States. Instruments of ratification, acceptance or approval shall be deposited with the Secretary-General of the United Nations.
3. This Statute shall be open to accession by all States. Instruments of accession shall be deposited with the Secretary-General of the United Nations.

Article 126
Entry into force

1. This Statute shall enter into force on the first day of the month after the 60th day following the date of the deposit of the 60th instrument of ratification, acceptance, approval or accession with the Secretary-General of the United Nations.
2. For each State ratifying, accepting, approving or acceding to this Statute after the deposit of the 60th instrument of ratification, acceptance, approval or accession, the Statute shall enter into force on the first day of the month after the 60th day following the deposit by such State of its instrument of ratification, acceptance, approval or accession.

Article 127
Withdrawal

1. A State Party may, by written notification addressed to the Secretary-General of the United Nations, withdraw from this Statute. The withdrawal shall take effect one year after the date of receipt of the notification, unless the notification specifies a later date.
2. A State shall not be discharged, by reason of its withdrawal, from the obligations arising from this Statute while it was a Party to the Statute, including any financial obligations which may have accrued. Its withdrawal shall not affect any cooperation with the Court in connection with criminal investigations and proceedings in relation to which the withdrawing State had a duty to cooperate and which were commenced prior to the date on which the withdrawal became effective, nor shall it prejudice in any way the continued consideration of any matter which was already under consideration by the Court prior to the date on which the withdrawal became effective

Article 128
Authentic texts

The original of this Statute, of which the Arabic, Chinese, English, French, Russian and Spanish texts are equally authentic, shall be deposited with the Secretary-General of the United Nations, who shall send certified copies thereof to all States.

IN WITNESS WHEREOF, the undersigned, being duly authorized thereto by their respective Governments, have signed this Statute

DONE at Rome, this 17th day of July 1998.

Appendix D

Bilateral Immunity Agreements U.S. 98(2) as of December 2004

1. Afghanistan: State Party to the Rome Statute—signed U.S. 98 (2) September 20, 2002; President GW Bush issued an indefinite waiver for Afghanistan from the ASPA on September 23, 2003.
2. Albania: State Party to the Rome Statute—signed and ratified U.S. 98(2) June 19, 2003; President GW Bush issued an indefinite waiver for Albania from the ASPA on July 29, 2003.
3. Antigua and Barbuda: State Party to the Rome Statute—signed and ratified U.S. 98 (2) September 30, 2003; President GW Bush issued an indefinite waiver from the ASPA on July 29, 2003.
4. Azerbaijan: Not party to the Rome Statute—signed U.S. 98(2) February 26, 2003 understood as reciprocal for both states.
5. Bahrain: State Party to the Rome Statute—signed U.S. 98 (2) February 6, 2003; Exempt from ASPA as non-NATO ally.
6. Bangladesh: State Party to the Rome Statute—signed U.S. 98(2) August 17, 2003 understood as reciprocal for both states.
7. Belize: State Party to the Rome Statute—signed U.S. 98(2)—date unknown. Belize was declared ineligible to receive military aid according to the ASPA on December 30, 2003.
8. Bhutan: Not party to the Rome Statute—signed and ratified U.S. 98(2) August 12, 2004 as reciprocal for both states.
9. Bolivia: State Party to the Rome Statute—signed and ratified U.S. 98(2) on May 19, 2003; July 1, 2003 President GW Bush issued a waiver from ASPA until January 2004.

10. Bosnia-Herzegovina: State Party to the Rome Statute—signed and ratified U.S. 98 (2) June 6, 2003; July 29, 2003 President GW Bush issued an indefinite waiver from the ASPA.
11. Botswana: State Party to the Rome Statute—signed U.S. 98(2) June 30, 2003; November 1, 2003 President GW Bush issued an indefinite waiver from the ASPA.
12. Brunel: Not a party to the Rome Statute—signed U.S. 98(2)—date unknown.
13. Burkina Faso: Signed the Rome Statue—signed U.S. 98(2) May 25, 2005; May 25, 2004 President GW Bush issued temporary waiver from ASPA for the duration of the SOFA.
14. Cambodia: State Party to the Rome Statute—signed U.S. 98(2) June 27, 2003; June 27, 2003 the U.S. gave Cambodia a 3 million dollar grant.
15. Central African Republic: State Party to the Rome Statute—signed U.S. 98 (2) April 6, 2004: July 1, 2003 the Central African Republic was declared ineligible for military assistance: April 6, 2004 President Bush issued a temporary waiver from ASPA for the duration of the SOFA.
16. Chad: Signed the Rome State—signed U.S. 98(2) July 21, 2003.
17. Colombia: State Party to the Rome Statute—signed and put in force U.S. 98(2) September 16, 2003; October 6, 2003 President GW Bush issued an indefinite waiver from ASPA.
18. Congo-Brazzaville: Signed Rome Statute—signed U.S. 98(2) August 2004; August 4, 2004 President GW Bush issued a Determination (2004-41) granting waiver from ASPA.
19. Cóte d'Ivoire: Signed the Rome Statute—signed U.S. 98(2) June 30, 2003.
20. Democratic of Congo: State Party to the Rome Statute—signed U.S. 98(2) March 18, 2003; September 24, 2003 President GW Bush issued an indefinite waiver from ASPA.
21. Dijbouti: State Party to the Rome Statute—signed U.S. 98(2) January 24, 2003; July 29, 2003 President GW Bush issued an indefinite waiver from ASPA.
22. Dominicia: State Party to the Rome Statute—signed U.S. 98(2) May 25, 2004; July 1, 2003 Dominica was declared ineligible for military assistance. May 25, 2004 President GW Bush issued a waiver from ASPA.
23. Dominic Republic: Signed the Rome Statute—signed U.S. 98(2) September 13, 2002.
24. East Timor: State Party to the Rome Statute—signed and approved U.S. 98(2) October 2003. July 29, 2003 President GW Bush issued an indefinite waiver from ASPA.
25. Egypt: Signed the Rome Statute—signed U.S. 98(2) March 5, 2003.

26. El Salvador: Not a party to the Rome Statute—signed U.S. 98(2) October 25, 2002.
27. Eritrea: Signed the Rome Statute—signed U.S. 98(2) July 8, 2004.
28. Ethiopia: Not a party to the Rome Statute—signed U.S. 98(2) October 8, 2004 as reciprocal.
29. Fiji: State Party to the Rome Statute—signed U.S. 98(2) November 2003 as non-reciprocal; July 1, 2003 Fiji was declared ineligible for military assistance; December 30, 2003 President GW Bush issued a permanent waiver from the ASPA.
30. Gabon: State Party to the Rome Statute—signed U.S. 98(2) April 15, 2003; July 1, 2003 President GW Bush issued a waiver from ASPA for duration of SOFA.
31 Gambia: State Party to the Rome Statute—signed U.S. 98(2) February 10, 2003; July 1, 2003 President GW Bush issued a waiver from ASPA for the duration of the SOFA.
32. Georgia: State Party to the Rome Statue—signed and ratified U.S. 98(2) May 7, 2003 as reciprocal; September 24, 2003 President GW Bush issued an indefinite waiver from ASPA.
33. Ghana: State Party to the Rome Statute—signed and ratified U.S. 98(2) October 30, 2003; July 29, 2003 President GW Bush issued an indefinite waiver from ASPA.
34. Guinea: Signed the Rome Statute—signed U.S. 98(2) April 6, 2004; September 25, 2003 President GW Bush issued a 6 month waiver from the ASPA.
35. Guyana: Signed the Rome Statute—signed and ratified U.S. 98(2) May 17, 2004.
36. Haiti: Signed the Rome Statute—signed U.S. 98(2) June 14, 2004.
37. Honduras: State Party to the Rome Statute—signed and ratified U.S. 98(2) May 30, 2003; September 24, 2003 President GW Bush issued an indefinite waiver from the ASPA.
38. India: Not a party to the Rome Statute—signed U.S. 98(2) December 26, 2002 as reciprocal.
39. Israel: Not a party to the Rome Statute—signed U.S. 98(2) August 4, 2002 as reciprocal: Exempt from all ASPA as major non-Nato ALLY.
40. Kazakhstan: Not a party to the Rome Statute—signed and approved U.S. 98(2) September 2003.
41. Kyrgyzstan: Signed the Rome Statute—signed U.S. 98(2) September 28, 2004.
42. Laos: Not a party to the Rome Statute—signed U.S. 98(2) October 24, 2003.

43. Liberia: Signed the Rome Statute—signed U.S. 98(2) October 8, 2003.
44. Macedonia FYR: State Party to the Rome Statute—signed and ratified U.S. 98(2) October 26, 2003; December 30, 2003 President GW Bush issued an indefinite waiver from ASPA.
45. Madagascar: Signed the Rome Statute—signed U.S. 98(2) April 23, 2003.
46. Malawi: State Party to the Rome Statute—signed U.S. 98(2) September 20, 2003; July 1, 2003 Malawi was declared ineligible to receive military assistance; November 1, 2003 President GW Bush issued an indefinite waiver from ASPA.
47. Maldives: Not a party to the Rome Statute—signed U.S. 98(2) April 9, 2003.
48. Marshall Islands: State Party to the Rome Statute—signed U.S. 98(2) September 10, 2002.
49. Mauritania: Not a party to the Rome Statute—signed and ratified U.S. 98(2) September 17, 2002 as reciprocal.
50. Mauritius: State Party to the Rome Statute—signed U.S. 98(2) June 25, 2003; July 29, 2003 President GW Bush issued an indefinite waiver from ASPA.
51. Micronesia: Not a party to the Rome Statute—signed U.S. 98(2) September 24, 2002.
52. Mongolia: State Party to the Rome Statute—signed U.S. 98(2) unknown date; July 1, 2003 President GW Bush issued an indefinite waiver from the ASPA.
53. Morocco: Signed the Rome Statue—secretly signed U.S. 98(2) unknown date.
54. Mozambique: Signed the Rome Statute—secretly signed U.S. 98(2) July 2003.
55. Naura: State Party to the Rome Statute—signed U.S. 98(2) February 26, 2003 as reciprocal.
56. Nepal: Not a party to the Rome Statute—signed U.S. 98(2) December 31, 2002 as reciprocal.
57. Nicaragua: Not a party to the Rome Statute—signed and ratified U.S. 98(2) July 9, 2003 as reciprocal.
58. Nigeria: State Party to the Rome Statute—signed and ratified U.S. 98(2) October 8, 2003; November 1, 2003 President GW Bush issued an indefinite waiver form the ASPA.
59. Pakistan: Not a party to the Rome Statute—signed U.S. 98(2) July 21, 2003 as reciprocal.
60. Palau: Not a party to the Rome Statute—signed U.S. 98(2) September 13, 2002.

61. Panama: State Party to the Rome Statute—signed U.S. 98(2) June 24, 2003; December 30, 2003 President GW Bush issued an indefinite waiver from the ASPA.
62. Papua New Guinea: Not a party to the Rome Statute—signed U.S. 98(2) September 30, 2004.
63. Philippines: Signed the Rome Statute—signed U.S. 98(2) May 14, 2003 as reciprocal; exempt from ASPA as major non-NATO ally.
64. Romania: State Party to the Rome Statue—signed U.S. 98(2) August 1, 2002; July 1, 2003 President GW Bush issued a waiver until November 1, 2003 and was later extended until May 1 on the basis of "national interest."
65. Rwanda: Not a party to the Rome Statute—signed U.S. 98(2) March 4, 2003 as reciprocal.
66. Senegal: State Party to the Rome Statute—signed U.S. 98(2) June 21, 2003: July 1, 2003 President GW Bush issued a waiver from ASPA for the duration of the SOFA.
67. Seychelles: Signed the Rome Statute—signed U.S. 98(2) in secret June 2003.
68. Sierra Leone: State Party to the Rome Statute—signed and ratified U.S. 98(2) May 6, 2003 as reciprocal; July 1, 2003 President GW Bush issued a waiver from ASPA for the duration of the SOFA.
69. Solomon Islands: Signed the Rome Statute—signed U.S. 98(2) September 20, 2003.
70. Sri Lanka: Not a party to the Rome Statute—signed U.S. 98(2) November 22, 2002 as reciprocal.
71. Tajikistan: State Party to the Rome Statute—signed and ratified U.S. 98(2) October 9, 2003 as reciprocal; July 1, 2003 President GW Bush issued a waiver for the ASPA for the duration of the SOFA.
72. Thailand: Signed the Rome Statute—signed the U.S. 98(2) June 3, 2003.
73. Togo: Not a party to the Rome Statute—signed U.S. 98(2) June 13, 2003
74. Tonga: Not a party to the Rome Statute—signed U.S. 98(2) March 21, 2003.
75. Tunisia: Not a party to the Rome Statue—allegedly signed in secret—no documentation available.
76. Tuvalu: Not a Party to the Rome Statue—signed U.S. 98(2) January 30, 2003.
77. Uganda: State Party to the Rome Statute—signed U.S. 98(2) June 12, 2003 as reciprocal; November 1, 2003 President GW Bush issued an indefinite waiver from ASPA.

***Immunity agreements by states as recorded by the Coalition for the International Criminal Court December 31, 2004.

Appendix E

Integrated Theoretical Model

International Level	Motivation	Opportunity	Constraints	Controls
	Political Interests	International Relations	International Reaction	International Law
	Economic Interests	Economic Supremacy	Political Pressure	International Sanctions
	Resources	Military Supremacy	Public Opinion	Economic Institutions
	Ideological Interests	Complimentary Legal System	NGO/Social Movement	
			Oversight Agencies	
State/Structural Level				
	Culture of Competition	Availability Illegal Means	International Reactions	Legal Sanctions
	Economic Pressure	Access to Resources	Political Pressure	Domestic Law
	Political Goals	Classified Materials	Media Scrutiny	
	Ideological Goals	Media Censorship	Public Opinion	
		State Propaganda	Social Movements	
		Role Specialization	Obstacles	
			Blocked Goals	
Organizational Level				
	Corporate Culture	Subculture of Resistance	Culture of Compliance	Codes of Conduct
	Organizational Goals	Defective SOP	Internal Constraints	Internal Controls
	Operative Goals	Illegal Means	Communication Process	
	Sub-unit Goals	Role Specialization	Reward Structure	
	Managerial Pressure	Task Segregation	Safety and Quality Processes	
	Reward Structure	Instrumental Rationality		
		Normalization of Deviance		
Interactional Level				
	Socialization	Rationalization	Personal Morality	Obedience to Authority
	Social Meaning	Techniques of Neutralization	Religion	Legitimacy of Law
	Individual Goals	Group Think	Socialization	
	Individual Ideology	Separation Consequences	Employment Security	
	Competitiveness	Diffusion of Responsibility		
	Individualism	Definition Situation		
	Material Success	Perceived Illegal Means		
	Driven Goal Success			

References

Allman, T D (2004) *Rogue State: America At War With The World* New York Nation Books

Amnesty International (2002) www amnesty org

Amnesty International (2004) Iraq One year on the human rights situation remains dire. March 18 www amnesty org/lubrary/Index/ ENGMDE140062004

Senator Ashcroft (1998 8) In Hearing Before the Subcommittee on Foreign Relations United States Senate One Hundred Fifth Congress, 2nd Session, 7/23/1998. Is A UN International Criminal Court In The U S National Interest? Washington U S Government Printing Office S HRG 105-724

Aulette J and R Michalowski (1993) "Fire in Hamlet A Case Study of State-Corporate Crime " Pp 171-206 In K Tunnel Ed *Political Crime in Contemporary America* New York Garland

Austin, J (1867) In Friedmann, W (1967) *Legal Theory* New York· Columbia University Press

Avalon Project (5/2002) http //www yale edu/lawweb/avalon/lawofwar/lawwar htm

Barak G (1991) *Crimes by the Capitalist State: An Introduction to State Criminality* Albany State University of New York Press

Bassiouni, M (1999) *International Criminal Law* 2nd Ed Vol I Ardsley, NY Transnational Publishers

——— (1999) *International Criminal Law* Mechanisms 2nd Ed Vol II Ardsley, NY Transnational Publishers

——— (1999) *International Criminal Law: Enforcement* 2nd Ed Vol III Ardsley, NY Transnational Publishers

——— (1998) *The Statute of the International Criminal Court* Ardsley, NY Transnational Publishers, Inc

——— (1997) "From Versailles to Rwanda in Seventy-Five Years The Need To Establish a Permanent International Criminal Court " *Harvard Human Rights Journal.* Vol 10. 11-62

——— (1975) *International Terrorism and Political Crimes.* Springfield, IL Charles C Thomas Publisher

Bassiouni, M and Veda Nanda (1973) *A Treatise on International Criminal Law. Vol. I Crimes and Punishment* Springfield, IL Charles C Thomas Publisher

Berg, B (1998) *Qualitative Research Methods for the Social Sciences* 3rd Ed Boston Allyn and Bacon

Black, D (1976) *The Behaviour of Law* New York Academic Press
——— (1998) *The Behavior of Law.* London Academic Press
Blix, H (2004), *Disarming Iraq* New York· Pantheon Books
Boyle, Francis (2004) *Destroying World Order: U.S. Imperialism in the Middle East Before and After September 11* Atlanta Clarity Press
Brown, B (1960) *The Natural Law Reader* New York Oceano Publications Inc
Brubaker, Roger 2004 "Nationalism Reframed Nationhood and the National Question in the New Europe." *The New Social Theory Reader.* Eds Seidman S and Alexander J 2004 London-New York Routledge Publishing Pp 231-244
Buncombe, A (2003) "U S Admits it used Napalm bombs in Iraq," The Independent (August 10)
Bursik, R J, Jr, & Grasmick, H G (1993) Economic deprivation and neighborhood crime rates, 1960-1980 *Law and Society Review* 27, 263-268 Pp 276-80
Carty, A (1991) Critical International Law Recent Trends in the Theory of International Law *European Journal of International Law.* Vol 2 1 66-96 www ejil org/journal/ Vo2/No1/index html
Cassesse, A (2002) *The Rome Statute of the International Criminal Court: A Commentary.* Vol I New York Oxford Press
——— (2002) *The Rome Statute of the International Criminal Court: A Commentary.* Vol II. New York Oxford Press
——— (2002) *The Rome Statute of the International Criminal Court: A Commentary.* Vol III Materials New York Oxford Press
——— (1998) On the Current Trend towards Criminal Prosecution and Punishment of Breaches of International Humanitarian Law. *European Journal of International Law.* Vol 9 1 2-19 http //www ejil org/ journal/Vol9/No1/index html
Chambliss, W (1993) *Making Law: The State, The Law, and Structural Contradictions.* Bloomington and Indianapolis Indiana University Press
——— (1989) "State Organized Crime" *Criminology* 27(2) 183-208
——— (1995) "Commentary by William J Chambliss" *Society of Social Problems Newsletter* 26 1 9
Chambliss, W and M Zatz (1993) *Making Law: The State, the Law, and Structural Contradictions.* Bloomington Indiana University Press
Chancellor Kent (1882 August) In Association for the Reform and Codification of the Law of Nations Pp 169-171 Report of the Tenth Annual Conference Liverpool, London William Clowes and Sons, Limited 1883
Charlesworth, H (2003) "Is International Law Relevant to the War in Iraq and its Aftermath?" *Telstra Address,* (October 29) Canberra, Australia National Press Club
Chomsky, N (2003) *Hegemony Or Survival: America's Quest For Global Dominance* New York Metropolitan Books
Cirincione, J, J Matthews, G Perkovich, and A Orton (2004) *WMD in Iraq: Evidence and Implications* Washington, D C Carnegie Endowment for International Peace
Clarke, R (2004) *Against All Enemies: Inside America's War on Terror.* New York· Free Press, CBS News
——— (2004) "Plans For Iraq Attack Began On 9/11," Washington, Sept 4, 2002 cbsnews com/stories/2002/09/04/september11/main520830 shtml
Coalition for the International Criminal Court (2002). International Criminal Court Homepage www ICCNOW org/html/country.html
Coalition for The International Criminal Court (2002) Assembly of States Parties Special Edition ICC Update New York ICC Press

Cohn, M (2004) "Torturing Hearts and Minds," *Truthout.* truthout org/docs04/ 050404A shtml

Colvin, Mark, Francis T Cullen, and Thomas Vander Ven. (2002). "Coercion, Social Support, and Crime An Emerging Theoretical Consensus." *Criminology* 40: 19-42

Cooper, A , John English, and Ramesh Thakur (2002) *Enhancing Global Governance: Towards A New Diplomacy* United Nations University Press

Corn, D (2003) *The Lies Of George W. Bush: Mastering the Politics of Deception.* New York Crown Publishers

Cullen, F and R Agnew. (2003). *Criminological Theory: Past to Present* California Roxbury Publishing Company

Danilenko, G (1991). "International Jus Cogens Issues of Law Making " *European Journal of International Law.* Vol 2·1 42-66 http //www ejil org/journal/Vol2/ No1/ index html

Danner, Mark (2004) *Torture And Truth* New York New York Review Books

——— "The Secret Way to War " *The New York Review* LII, Number 10, June 9, 2005 70-74

Deller, N , Arjun Makhijani, and John Burroughs (2003) *Rule of Power or Rule of Law? An Assessment of U.S. Policies and Actions Regarding Security-Related Treaties.* New York Apex Press

Dorrien, G (2004) *Imperial Designs: Neoconservatism and the New Pax Americana* New York Routledge

Dreyfuss, R and Vest, J (2004) "The Lie Factory," *Mother Jones*, January-February 34-41

Durkheim E (1933) *The Division of Labor In Society.* Trans G Simpson New York The Free Press

Eisendrath, C and Goodman, M (2004) *Bush League Diplomacy: How The Neoconservatives Are Putting The World At Risk.* Amherst, New York Prometheus Books

Falk, Richard (2004) *The Declining World Order: America's Imperial Geopolitics* New York Routledge

——— (2003) "What Future for the UN Charter System of War Prevention?" *American Journal of International Law*, 97/3. 590-598

Ferencz, B (1980) *An International Criminal Court, a Step Toward Peace: a Documentary Analysis. Vol I: Half Century of Hope.* New York Oceana Publications, Inc

——— (1980) *An International Criminal Court, a Step Toward Peace: a Documentary Analysis. Vol. II: The Beginning of Wisdom.* New York Oceana Publications, Inc

Franck, T (2003) "What Happens Now? The United Nations After Iraq," *American Journal of International Law,* 97/3 607-620

Friedrichs, D (1992) "State Crime or Governmental Crime Making Sense of the Conceptual Confusion " Pp 53-80 in Jeff Ross Ed *Controlling State Crime.* New York Garland

——— (1996) *Trusted criminals: White Collar Crime in Contemporary Society* Belmont, CA Wadsworth

——— (1996) Governmental Crime, Hitler and White Collar Crime A Problematic Relationship *Caribbean Journal of Criminology and Social Psychology*, 1 pp 44-63

——— (1998) *State Crime· Volumes I and II.* Aldershot, UK Ashgate/Dartsmouth

——— (2004) "White-Collar Crime in a Globalized World " Presentation at Western Michigan University, March 2004

Friedrichs, D O and J Friedrichs. (2002) "The World Bank and Crimes of Globalization A Case Study " *Social Justice* 29 (1-2) 1-12
Friedmann, W (1967) *Legal Theory* New York. Columbia University Press
Gardner, R (2003) "Neither Bush nor the Jurisprudes," *American Journal of International Law*, 97/3 585-590
Gellman, B (2004) "Iraq's Arsenal Was Only On Paper " *Washington Post*, January 7 A01
Senator Grams (1998) In Hearing Before the Subcommittee on Foreign Relations United States Senate One Hundred Fifth Congress, 2nd Session, Pp. 1 July 23, 1998 "Is A UN International Criminal Court In The U.S National Interest?" U S Government Printing Office, Washington S HRG 105-724
Green, P and T Ward (2000) "State Crime, Human Rights, and the Limits of Criminology " *Social Justice* 27 (1) 101
——— (2004) *State Crime: Governments, Violence and Corruption* London Pluto Press
Greenberg, K J and Joshua L Dratel, eds (2005). *The Torture Papers: The Road to Abu Ghraib* New York Cambridge University Press
Hampson, F (2002) *Madness in the Multitude.* New York Oxford Press
Harris, W (1954) *Tyranny on Trial* Dallas Southern Methodist University Press
Hartung, W (2004) *How Much Are You Making on the War Daddy? A Quick and Dirty Guide to War Profiteering in the Bush Administration* New York Nation Books
Senator Helms (1998) In Hearing Before the Subcommittee on Foreign Relations United States Senate One Hundred Fifth Congress, 2nd Session, Pp 2-3 July 23, 1998 "Is A UN International Criminal Court In The U.S National Interest?" U S Government Printing Office, Washington S HRG 105-724
Senator and Chairman Helms (2000) In Hearing Before the Committee on Foreign Relations United States Senate One Hundred Sixth Congress, 2nd Session, Pp 1 June 14, 2000 The International Criminal Court Protecting American Servicemen And Officials From The Threat Of International Prosecution U S Government Printing Office, Washington 67-980 CC S. HRG 106-769.
Henkin, L (1995) *International Law: Politics and Values* Dordrecht, The Netherlands Martinus Nijhoff
Hersh, S (2004). *Chain Of Command: The Road from 9-11 to Abu Ghraib* New York HarperCollins
——— (2004) "Torture at Abu Ghraib " *The New Yorker.* May 10
Hiro, D (2004) *Secrets And Lies: Operation 'Iraqi Freedom' And After* New York. Nation Books
Hudson, M (1943) *The Permanent Court of International Justice: 1920-1942.* New York The Macmillan Company.
——— (1938) "The Proposed International Criminal Court " *American Journal of International Law.* V 32AM 549-550
Human Rights Watch (2003) *Off Target: the Conduct of the War and Civilian Casualties in Iraq* New York Human Rights Watch
Innes, J (2003) "U S and UK Action in Post-War Iraq May Be Illegal," *The Scotsman*, May 22
International Humanitarian Law Database (2002) http //www icrc org/ihl
International Criminal Court Monitor (2002) http //www iccnow org

International Court of Justice (1969) In M Morris, (1999). "High Crimes and Misconceptions " In D Shelton, (2000) *International Crimes, Peace, and Human Rights: The Role of the International Criminal Court.* P 270 Transnational Publishers, Inc

Jackson, R (1946) *Case Against The Nazi War Criminals.* New York Alfred A Knopf Inc

Jehl, D and E Schmitt (2004). "Dogs and Other Harsh Tactics Linked to Military Intelligence," *New York Times* May 22, a 1

Jorgensen, N (2000). *The Responsibility of States for International Crimes.* Oxford Oxford University Press

Kauzlarich, D , C Mullins, and R A Matthews (2001, 2003) "A Complicity Continuum of State Crime " *Contemporary Justice Review* 6 (3) 241-254

Kauzlarich, D , and D O Friedrichs (2002-2003) "Crimes of the State " Pp 109-120 in M D Schwartz and S Hatty (Eds) *Controversial Issues in Criminology: Critical Criminology* Cincinnati Anderson

Kauzlarich, D , and R C Kramer (1993) "State-Corporate Crime in the U S Nuclear Weapons Production Complex " *The Journal of Human Justice,* 5(1) 1-26

——— (1995) "The Nuclear Terrorist State" *Peace Review* 7 (December) 333-337

——— (1998) *Crimes of the American Nuclear State: At Home and Abroad* Boston Northeastern University Press

Kauzlarich D , R C Kramer, and B Smith (1992) "Toward the Study of Governmental Crime Nuclear Weapons, Foreign Intervention, and International Law " *Humanity and Society,* 16 (4) 543-563

Kegley, C (1995) *Controversies in Realism and International Neoliberal Theory* New York St Martins Press

Klein, N (2003) "Bring Halliburton Home " *The Nation.* November 24 10

Koskeniemi, M (2003) "Heirarchy in International Law " *European Journal of International Law* http·//www ejil org/journal/Vol8/No4/ art2 html

Kramer, R (1982) "Corporate Crime An Organizational Perspective " Pp 75-94 In Wickman and Tom Daily, Eds *White Collar and Economic Crime* Lexington, KY Lexington Books

——— (1990a) "State-Corporate Crime " Presented at the North Central Sociological Association and the Southern Sociological Association

——— (1990b) "State-corporate Crime A Case Study of the Space Shuttle Challenger Explosion " Presented at the Edwin Sutherland Conference on White Collar Crime 50 Years of Research and Beyond, Indiana University

——— (1990c) "The Concept of State-Corporate Crime " Presented at the Society for the Study of Social Problems, Washington, D C

——— (1992) "The Space Shuttle Challenger Explosion A Case Study of State-Corporate Crime " Pp 212-241 in K Schlegel and D Weisburd (Eds) *White Collar Crime Reconsidered.* Boston Northeastern University Press

——— (1995) "Exploring State Criminality The Invasion of Panama " *Journal of Criminal Justice and Popular Culture.* 3(2) 43-52

Kramer, R and D Kauzlarich (1999). "The International Court of Justice Opinion on theIllegality of the Threat and Use of Nuclear Weapons Implication for Criminology " *Contemporary Justice Review,* 4-2 395-413

Kramer, R and R Michalowski (2006) *State-Corporate Crime: Wrongdoing At The Intersection Of Business And Government.* Ron Kramer and Raymond J Michalowski (Eds) Piscataway, NJ Rutgers University Press

——— (2005) "War, Aggression, and State Crime A Criminological Analysis of the Invasion and Occupation of Iraq." *British Journal of Criminology* 45 (No 4, June) 446-469

Kramer, R and R Michalowski (1990) "Toward an Integrated Theory of State-corporate Crime' Presented at the American Society of Criminology Baltimore, MD

Kramer, R, R Michalowski, and D Kauzlarich (2002) "The Origins and Developmentof the Concept and Theory of State-Corporate Crime" *Crime and Delinquency* 48 (2) 263-282

Kramer, R, R Michalowski, and D Rothe (2005) "The Supreme International Crime How the U S War in Iraq Threatens the Rule of Law" *Social Justice* 32 2

Krugman, P (2004) "What Went Wrong?" New York Times, April 23

Legal Information Institute (2003) Cornell University www law cornell edu/topic/international

Lynch, M and R Michalowski (2000) *The New Primer in Radical Criminology: Critical perspectives on Crime, Power, and Identity* New York Criminal Justice Press

Mahajan, R (2003) *Full Spectrum Dominance: U.S. Power In Iraq And Beyond* New York Seven Stories Press

Mandel, Michael (2004) *How America Gets Away With Murder: Illegal Wars, Collateral Damage and Crimes Against Humanity* London Pluto Press

Mate, A (2004) "Pillage Is Forbidden Why the Privatization of Iraq Is Illegal" *The Nation*, November 24 http //thenation com/doc mhtml?I= 20031124&s=pillage

Meintjies, G (1999) "Domestic Amnesties and International Accountability" in Shelton, D (2000) *International Crimes, Peace, and Human Rights: The Role of the International Criminal Court.* P 83 Ardsley, NY Transnational Publishers, Inc

Merton, Robert (1938) "Social structure and anomie" *American Sociological Review* 3 (6) 672-682

Michalowski, R and K Bitten (2004) "Transnational Environmental Crime," in P Reichel, ed, *Handbook of Transnational Crime.* Beverly Hills, CA Sage

Michalowski, R and Ronald Kramer (1987) "The Space Between the Laws The Problem of Corporate Crime in a Transnational Context" *Social Problems* 34 pp 34-53

Miller, R S (2003) *Collateral Damage From U.S. Depleted Uranium Munitions In Iraq* Winter Springs, Florida ZOR Foundation Inc

Moynier, G (1872) *Note sur la creation dune Institution Judiciare international Propre a Prevenir et a reprimer les infractions a la Convention de-Geneva*, Comite international De La Croix Rouge Bulletin International des Societies de Secours aux militaries Blesses No 11, 4/1872

Mullins, C W, David Kauzlarich, and Dawn Rothe (2002) "The International Criminal Court and the Control of State Crime Problems and Prospects" Presented at American Society of Criminology, Chicago November, 2002

——— (2004) "The International Criminal Court and the Control of State Crime: Problems and Prospects" *Critical Criminology: An International Journal* 12 3

Normand, R (2003) *Tearing Up the Rules: The Illegality of Invading Iraq* Brooklyn, NY· The Center for Economic and Social Rights

Packer, G (2004) "Letter from Baghdad War After War, What Washington Doesn't See" *The New Yorker*, November 24 58-85

Paternoster, Raymond, and Sally Simpson (1992) "A Rational Choice Theory of Corporate Crime" *Crimes of Privilege—Readings in White-Collar Crime.* Ed Neal Shover and John Paul Wright New York Oxford Press. 2001 194-210

Paternoster, R and Piquero, A (1995) "Reconceptualizing Deterrence An Empirical Test of Personal and Vicarious Experiences " *Journal of Research in Crime.*

Perrow, Charles (1984) *Normal Accidents: Living with High-Risk Technologies* New York Basic Books Reprinted in 1999. Princeton, NJ Princeton University Press

———. "Risky Systems. The Habit of Courting Disaster " *The Nation*, 242, October 11, 1986, 347-356

Pitt, W R (2002) *War On Iraq.* New York Context Books

Piquero, A. and Paternoster, R (1998). "An Application of Stafford and Warr's Reconceptualization of Deterrence to Drinking and Driving " *Journal of Research in Crime and Delinquency*, 35, 1, 5-41

Pollack, K (2004) "Spies, Lies, And Weapons What Went Wrong." *The Atlantic Monthly*, January/February. 78-92

Prados, J (2004) *Hoodwinked: The Documents That Reveal How Bush Sold Us A War* New York The New Press

Ragin, C and Howard Becker (1992) *What is a Case? Exploring the Foundations of Social Inquiry* Cambridge Cambridge University Press

Rai, M (2002) *War Plan Iraq: Ten Reasons Against War On Iraq.* London· Verso

——— (2003) *Regime Unchanged: Why The War On Iraq Changed Nothing* London Pluto Press

Rampton, S and J Stauber (2003) *Weapons of Mass Deception: The Uses of Propaganda in Bush's War on Iraq* New York Jeremy P Tarcher/Penguin

Ratner, M (2002) "The United Nations Charter And The Use Of Force Against Iraq " www lawyersagainstthewar org/legalarticles/ratner.html

Ratner, M , J Green, and B Olshansky (2003) *Against War with Iraq* New York Seven Stories Press

Red Cross (2002) www redcross org/services/intl/ihl html

Ritter, S (2003) *Frontier Justice: Weapons of Mass destruction And The Bushwhacking Of America.* New York Context Books

Roberts, L , Riyadh Lafta, Richard Garfield, Jamal Khudhairi, and Gilbert Burnham (2004) "Mortality before and after the 2003 invasion of Iraq cluster sample survey " *Lancet* 364 1857-64

Ross J I (1995) *Controlling State Crime: An Introduction* New York. Garland

——— (1998) "Situating the Academic Study of Controlling State Crime " *Crime, Law & Social Change* 29 331-340

——— (2000) *Varieties of State Crime and its Control.* Mosney, NY· Criminal Justice Press

——— (2000) *Controlling State Crime: An Introduction.* Transaction Publishers

——— (2002) "Stumbling Into State Crime " *ACJS Today* (May/June) 8-10

——— (2003) *The Dynamics of Political Crime.* Thousand Oaks, CA Sage

Ross, J I , G Barak, J Ferrell, D Kauzlarich, M Hamm, D Friedrichs, R Matthews, S Pickering, M Presdee, P Kraska, and V Kappeler (1999) "The State of State Crime Research A Commentary " *Humanity & Society* 23 (3) 273-281

Roth, K (2004) *War in Iraq: Not a Humanitarian Intervention* New York Human Rights Watch

Rothe, D (2006) "War Profiteering and the Pernicious Beltway Bandits Halliburton and the War on Terror " In *State-Corporate Crime: Wrongdoing At The Intersection Of Business And Government* Ron Kramer and Raymond J Michalowski (Eds) Piscataway, NJ Rutgers University Press

——— (2004) "The International Criminal Court A Socio/Historical Case Study " Master Thesis Western Michigan University

Rothe, D and Christopher W Mullins (2005) "The International Criminal Court U S Opposition and the Future of the Court." Presented at Midwest Sociological Society, Minneapolis, MN Forthcoming· *Crime, Law, and Social Change.*

Rothe, D and David Friedrichs (2005) "The State of the Criminology of Crimes of the State " Presented at the 14th World Congress of Criminology, Philadelphia Also in *Social Justice* 33 1

Rothe, D , Stephen Muzzatti, and Christopher W Mullins (2005) "Crime on the High Seas Crimes of Globalization and the Sinking of the Senegalese Ferry *Le Joola.*" Presented at Midwest Sociological Society 2004, Kansas, MO Also 2006 *Critical Criminology* 14 3

Rueter, Paul (1957). International Institutions Praeger University Series New York Praeger Publisher

Sadat, L (2002) *The International Criminal Court and the Transformation of International Law: Justice For the New Millennium.* Ardsley, NY Transnational Publishers

Sadat, Leila and S Richard Carden (2000) "The New International Criminal Court An Uneasy Revolution " *Georgetown Law Review* 88 381-474

Sands, Philippe (2005) *Lawless World: America and the Making and Breaking of Global Rules* London Allen Lane

Savoy, Paul (2004) "The Moral Case Against the Iraq War " *The Nation* (May 31) 16-20

Scheer, C , R Scheer, and L Chaudhry (2003) *The Five Biggest Lies Bush Told Us About Iraq* New York Seven Stories Press and Akashic Books

Scheffer, D (1999) "The United States and the International Criminal Court " 93 *American Journal of International Law.* V12 19

Scott, J (1908) "The Work of the Second Hague Peace Conference " *American Journal of International Law.* Vol 2. 1-28 (772) Washington, D C American Society of International Law

Shalom, Stephen (2004) "Where Do We Go From Here?" *Znet.* www znet org/content/print_article cfm/itemID=5398&sectionID=1 Accessed April 26, 2004

Sharkansky, I (1995) "A State Action May Be Nasty but Is Not Likely to be a Crime." Pp 35-52 In Jeff Ross (Ed) *Controlling State Crime: An Introduction.* New York Garland

Shelton, D (2000) *International Crimes, Peace, and Human Rights: The Role of the International Criminal Court.* Ardsley, NY Transnational Publishers, Inc

Sherman, Lawrence W and Richard A Berk (1984) "The Specific Deterrent Effects of Arrest for Domestic Assault " *American Sociological Review* 49 261-272

Simpson, S S , R Paternoster, and N L Piquero (1997) "Exploring the Micro-Macro Link in Corporate Crime Research " *Research in the Sociology of Organizations,* 15 35

Slomanson, W (2003) *Fundamental Perspectives on International Law* Fourth Edition Belmont, CA Thomson/West

Solomon, N and R Erlich (2003) *Target Iraq: What The News Media Didn't Tell You.* New York Context Books

Stafford, M and M Warr (1993) "A Reconceptualization of General and Specific Deterrence " *Journal of Research in Crime and Delinquency* 30 123-35

Suskind, R. (2004). *The Price of Loyalty: George W. Bush, the White House, and the Education of Paul O'Neill.* New York: Simon & Schuster

Sutherland, E (1939) "White Collar Criminality" Presidential Address to the American Society of Sociology Reprinted 1940. *American Sociological Review.* 5: 1-12

——— (1948) "Crime of Corporations" In A Cohen, Alfred Lindsmith, and Karl Schuessler (Eds). *The Sutherland Papers* (1956). The Indiana University Press

——— (1949) *White Collar Crime.* New York Holt, Rinehart, and Winston.

Tunnell, K D (1993) *Political Crime in Contemporary America.* New York: Garland

Turk, A. (1982) *Political Criminality.* Beverly Hills Sage

United Nations Library http://www un.org/Depts/dhl

United Nations. (2002). http.//www hrweb.org/legal/undocs.html

Waldheim, Security General of the United Nations (1987) *Annual Report of the Progress of the UN to General Assembly.* New York United Nations

Weber, M. (1946). *The Theory of Social and Economic Organization.* T Parsons (Ed) Free Press of Glencoe New York Oxford University Press Inc

Weeramantry, C G (2003) *Armageddon or Brave New World? Reflections On The Hostilities In Iraq* Ratmalana, Sri Lanka Sarvodaya Vishva Lekha

Wilkinson, T and A Rubin (2004) "Pervasive Abuse Alleged by Freed Detainees" Los Angeles Times, May 19 1

Zatz, S (1993). "Preface" In Chambliss and Zatz (1993). *Making Law: The State, The Law, and Structural Contradictions* Bloomington Indiana University Press.

Zachar, M (1995) "Liberal International Theory Common Threads, Divergent Strands" In C Kegley (1995) *Controversies in Realism and International Neoliberal Theory* New York St Martins Press

Zernike, K (2004a) "Only a Few Spoke Up on Abuse as Many Soldiers Stayed Silent" *New York Times*, May 22, 2004a 1

——— (2004b) "The Accused Prison Guard Calls Abuse Routine and Sometimes Amusing" *The New York Times*, May 16 3

Zigler, David (1977) *War, Peace, and International Politics* Boston, Toronto Little, Brown and Company

Zunes, S (2003) *Tinderbox: U.S. Middle East Policy And The Roots Of Terrorism.* Monroe, Maine Common Courage Press

Documents:

American Branch International Law Association American Branch Proceedings and Committee Reports (1977-1978)

American Servicemembers' Protection Act (August 2002) HR 4775

Association for the Reform and Codification of the Law of Nations (August 1882) Report of the Tenth Annual Conference Liverpool William Clowes and Sons, Limited, London 1883

Committee for the Repression of International Terrorism (1935). C 184 M 102 1935 V Geneva

Committee for the Repression of International Terrorism (1936) A 7 1936 V C 36x 1936 v

Economic Security Council Res 7(1), 1 UN ESCOR, 1st Session, Resolution 127 (1946)

Fifth Assembly Resolution (1926) *American Journal of International Law* V 20 2, Supp (1926)

The Hague (1920) *Advisory Committee of Jurists. Procès-Verbaux of Proceedings of the Committee with Annexes* Van Langenhuysen Brothers

Hearing Before the Subcommittee on Foreign Relations United States Senate· One Hundred Fifth Congress, 2nd Session, July 23, 1998 *Is A UN International Criminal Court In The U.S. National Interest?* U S Government Printing Office, Washington S HRG 105-724

Hearing Before the Committee on Foreign Relations United States Senate One Hundred Sixth Congress, 2nd Session, June 14, 2000 *The International Criminal Court: Protecting American Servicemen And Officials From The Threat Of International Prosecution.* U S Government Printing Office, Washington 67-980 CC S HRG 106-769

Hearings Before the Committee On International Relations House of Representatives One Hundred Sixth Congress, 2nd Session July 25, 2000 *The International Criminal Court.* U S Government Printing Office, Washington 68-483 CC Serial No 106-176/

International Law Association (1873) *Report of the First Conference*, Brussels

International Law Association (1882) *Report of the Tenth Conference*, Liverpool, William Clowes and Sons

International Law Association (1920) *Report of the Twenty-ninth Conference*, Portsmouth, England London, Sweet & Maxwell Ltd

International Law Association (1921) *Report of the Thirtieth Conference*, Holland. London, Sweet & Maxwell Ltd

International Law Association Report (1926) *Report of the Thirty-fourth Conference* Vienna London, Sweet and Maxwell, Ltd

International Law Association Report (1938) *Report of the Fortieth Conference Amsterdam.* 1939, England

International Law Association, *Report of the 34th Conference* Vienna August 5 to November 1927 In B Ferencz (1980) *An International Criminal Court, a Step Toward Peace· a Documentary Analysis. Vol. I Half Century of Hope.* New York Oceana Publications, Inc

International Criminal Court Documents (2002) http //www ICCNOW org/html/new html

League of Nations (1937) *Proceedings of the International Conference on the Repression of Terrorism* C 94 M 47 1938 V Geneva, June 1938

League of Nations Document Archived C 547 m 384 1937

Rome Statute (1998)

Subcommittee On International Operations of the Committee On Foreign Relations United States Senate One Hundred Fifth Congress, 2nd Session, July 23, 1998 U S Government Printing Office, Washington 50-976 CC S HRG 105-724

Taguba Report Investigation of the 800th Military Police Brigade Joint Interrogation and Debriefing Center [JIDC],U S Military Occupation Facilities, Abu Ghurayb Prison, Iraq www globalsecurity org/intell/world/iraq/abu-ghurayb-prison-abuse htm

UN A /CN 4/15 –1950 Yearbook of the International Law Commission UN A/CN 4/15/1950 II

UN Doc, A/332, 1947

UN Doc A/362, 1947

UN Doc, A/CN 4/7/Rev 1, 1949

UN Doc A/2136, A/2136, A/2186/Add 1, November 1952

UN Doc A/2693, 1954 Supp 9

UN Doc A/CN 4/7/ Rev 1 UN No.1949 V 8

UN DOC A/26645, 1954 Supplement No 12 at 21
UN Doc A/CONF 20/13 (April 16, 1961), United Nations
UN DOC A/2645 Supplement No 12 at 21
UN Doc A/810 @ 71 (archived 1948) United Nations
UN Doc A/CONF 20/13 1961
UN Doc A/33/45 Supp No 45, 1978/79
UN Doc A/RES/47/33 1992 GA Res 47/33 UN GOAR 47th Session, Supp 49, at 287
UN GOAR, 7th Session, Supplement, No 11 (21-25)
UN GOAR UN DOC A/2186 Add 1
UN Resolution 678
UN Resolution 687
UN Resolution 898 (IX)
UN Resolution 1441
UN Resolution 1479
Union Interparliemetaire, Compte Rendu de la October (1925) Librairie Payot Co
United Nations Conference on International Organization (1945) Vol 3 670-671
United Nations General Assembly (1949) *Historical Survey of the Question of International Criminal Jurisdiction. Submitted by Secretary General* New York International Law Commission
United Nations War Crimes Commission (UNWCC) (1942) Doc C 56 (a) Record Group 238 United States National Archives
Universal Declaration of Human Rights (1948) GA Res 217A III0, UN Doc A/810 at 71
U S UN Press Release # 85 (03) June 12, 2003
Utilaianism, Chapter IV, 24th Conf ILA, 1907
War Crimes Act (18 U S C § 2441)
Expanded War Crimes Act of 1997, 18 U S C & 2401 (SEC 583)
1948 Universal Declaration of Human Rights General Assembly Resolution 217a.
1951 Report Committee for an International Criminal Court, 7th Session, Supplement 11 UN DOC A/2136 at 21
1961 Vienna Convention on Diplomatic Relations
(2001) Open Documents-May 1996, 1998 archives, 1999 Annual Report, council-meeting www amnesty org/ai nsf/COUNTRIES%2FU S A?OpenView&Start=1 151&Count=30&
(2002) Security Council Resolution 1422 12 July
2003 Norms on the Responsibilities of Transnational Corporations and Other Business Enterprises with regard to Human Rights Agreement

Index

accountability command responsibility, 100, immunity, 42, 57, 59, 73, 82–85, 95, 114, impunity, 11, 17, 26–27, 56–57, 75, 78, 82, 84–86, 107, 113, 115

Cold War, 29, 57, 59–60
collective consciousness, 28
complimentary and ICC, 34, 35, 41, 54, 56–60, 73, 76, 85–86, 89, 101, 107, 113
contradictions of international law, x, 4, 9–10, 33–35, 61, 70–86
Conventions torture against, 100, 122
criminology relevance to ICC, 1–8, 211
customary international law, 50, 65, 86, 108

Darfur, xi, 114
Democratic Republic of Congo, x, 20–25, 27, 69, 110, 114

enhancing the International Criminal Court, 105–15, empowerment, enhancement of, 112–13, enforcement, expansion of, 112–13, expanded crimes, 110–12
erga omnes, 35, 43, 50, 58, 60–61, 73–74, 82, 106

Geneva Conventions 1949, xiii, 21, 34, 44, 68, 72, 74, 77, 81, 97, 121, 122, Additional Protocol I, 77, 97; Additional Protocol II, 78

Human Rights Law, 6–8, 21–22, 68, 74

International Court of Justice, 39, 41, 44–45, 47, 65, 74, 90, 106
International Criminal Court chambers of, 63, judge of, 63–65, prosecutor of, 65–66, registrar of, 63
International Criminal Courts establishment of, xiii–xv, 29–51, Prepatory Committees, xv, 53, 57, 62, 83, 109, 123, United States stance towards, x, 54–61
international law aggression, 35, 42–46, 54–55, 65, 68, 74, 78–79, 87, 95, 101, 102, 106, 111–12, 113, 115, 122, crimes against humanity, xiv, xv, 1, 4, 5, 7, 9, 20, 23–24, 26–28, 44, 54–55, 61, 68–69, 75–76, 83–84, 87, 89, 102, 105, 110–13, 115, genocide, xi, xv, 1, 6, 16, 17, 21, 37–40, 42, 46, 54–55, 68, 76, 83–84, 105, 111, 113, 122, history of, 71–73, international humanitarian law, 6, 43, 46, 64, 97–98, 100, war crimes, x, xv, 1, 6, 9, 16, 20–21, 23–24, 26, 32, 38–39, 44, 46, 54–55, 60, 68, 75–78, 80–81, 83–87, 97–101, 105, 111, 113, 122
International Law Commission, 40–42, 45–48, 107, 112, 122, 123

International Military Tribunals, xiv, 59, principles of Nuremberg, xiii, xiv, 43, 44, 74, 107, for Rwanda, 46, 55, for Yugloslavia, 46, 55
International Red Cross, 30, Moynier, xiv, 30, 121
investigations· process of ICC, 66–68

Jurisdiction possibility of ICC becoming universal, 74–76, 101–2, 106–7, principle of universal, 43, 49, 50, 54, 57–58, 71–73, 106–7
jus cogens, 35, 43, 50, 58, 60, 73–74, 82

League of Nations, xiii, xiv, 5, 32, 33–39, 72, 76
Like-Minded States, 49, 54, 60, 70n2

militias, 18, 21–22, 25–27

nongovernmental organizations Amnesty International, 20, 50, 84, 98, 122, Human Rights Watch, 20, 22, 23, 96, 97, 122

organizational crime, xv, 3, 5, 11–12

political crimes, 3–4
public international law, 2

sanctions, 12, 14, 15, 17, 26, 29–30, 96, 99, 108–10
social control mechanism, ICC as, xi, 11, 24, 27–28
sovereignty, x, 2, 31–34, 37, 40–49, 53–54, 57–59, 61, 70, 73, 76–80, 82, 85–86, 89, 112, 119
state-corporate crime, 3, 6–8, 113
state crime, x, xv, xvii, 1–3, 5–6; integrated theory of, 9–28
Status of Force Agreements (SOFA), 57, 84, United States Bilateral, 98(2), 83–85

terrorism, xiv, 4–5, 6, 35–37, 45, 50, 82, 91, 105, 106, 110–11, 113, 115, prevention and repression of, xiv, 36–37, 122
transnational organizations, 106, 109–10

Uganda, 20–24, 69, 114
United Nations, ix, xiii, xiv, 14, 20, 46, 47, 48, 54, 64, 73, 75, 79, 82, 87, 90, 111, 114, establishment of, 35–43, 90, Security Council, 65, 66, 72, 113, 114
United States invasion of Iraq, ix, xv, 7, 10, 87–103
Universal Declaration of Human Rights, 68, 122

white collar crime· concept of, 3

About the Authors

Dawn Rothe holds the doctoral degree from Western Michigan University and is an Assistant Professor of Criminology at the University of Northern Iowa. Her work focuses on state crime, transnational and international organizational crime, international organizations of social control and international law. Her work has appeared in *Social Justice* and *Critical Criminology*, as well as several edited volumes. Her latest work includes, "The Masquerade of Abu Ghraib: State Crime, International Law, and Torture."

Christopher W. Mullins is an Assistant Professor of Criminology at the University of Northern Iowa. His work focuses on violence and its control. His work has appeared in *Criminology*, *Critical Criminology*, and *Contemporary Justice Review*, as well as in several edited volumes. He is also the author of *Holding Your Square: Masculinities, Streetlife, and Violence* (2006). He lives in Northeastern Iowa with his wife Robin, and his children, Jerry and Arwen.

www.ingramcontent.com/pod-product-compliance
Ingram Content Group UK Ltd.
Pitfield, Milton Keynes, MK11 3LW, UK
UKHW040909190926
475560UK00008B/65